SICK!

*Diseases and
Disorders,
Injuries and
Infections*

SICK!

*Diseases and
Disorders,
Injuries and
Infections*

volume

4

R to **Z**

**David Newton,
Donna Olendorf,
Christine Jeryan,
Karen Boyden,
Editors**

AN IMPRINT OF THE GALE GROUP

DETROIT · SAN FRANCISCO · LONDON
BOSTON · WOODBRIDGE, CT

Sick!
Diseases and Disorders, Injuries and Infections

David Newton, Donna Olendorf, Christine Jeryan, Karen Boyden, Editors

STAFF

Christine Slovey, *U·X·L Editor*
Carol DeKane Nagel, *U·X·L Managing Editor*
Meggin Condino, *Senior Analyst, New Product Development*
Thomas L. Romig, *U·X·L Publisher*

Shalice Shah-Caldwell, *Permissions Specialist (Pictures)*

Rita Wimberley, *Senior Buyer*
Evi Seoud, *Assistant Production Manager*
Dorothy Maki, *Manufacturing Manager*
Mary Beth Trimper, *Production Director*

Robert Duncan, *Imaging Specialist*
Michelle Di Mercurio, *Senior Art Director*

GGS Information Services, Inc., *Typesetting*
Michelle Cadoree, *Indexer*
Cover illustration by Kevin Ewing Illustrations.

Library of Congress Cataloging-in-Publication Data

Sick! diseases and disorders, injuries and infections/ David E. Newton…[et al.].
    p. cm.
Includes bibliographical references and indexes.
Summary: Presents articles describing the causes and symptoms, diagnosis, treatment (both traditional and alternative), prognosis, and prevention of various diseases, disorders, injuries, and infections.
    ISBN 0-7876-3922-2 (set)
    1. Diseases—Encyclopedias, Juvenile. [1. Health—Encyclopedias. 2.Diseases—Encyclopedias.] I.Newton, David E.
R130.5 .S53 1999
616'.003–dc21   Gale 3/00   115.00 Set   99-044739

ISBN 0-7876-3922-2 (set)
ISBN 0-7876-3923-0 (vol. 1)
ISBN 0-7876-3924-9 (vol. 2)
ISBN 0-7876-3925-7 (vol. 3)
ISBN 0-7876-3926-5 (vol. 4)

Printed in United States of America
10 9 8 7 6 5 4 3 2 1

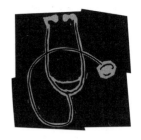

Contents

Reader's Guide .... **xi**

Words to Know .... **xv**

Research and Activity Ideas .... **xlv**

VOLUME 1: A–C

Acne **1**

Addiction **7**

AIDS **14**

Alcoholism **25**

Allergies **32**

Alzheimer's disease **40**

Amyotrophic lateral sclerosis **48**

Anemias **53**

Anorexia nervosa **61**

Appendicitis **67**

Arthritis **71**

Asthma **78**

Atherosclerosis **87**

Athlete's foot **94**

Attention-deficit/hyperactivity disorder **97**

Autism **103**

Autoimmune disorders **110**

Bipolar disorder **117**

Breast cancer **123**

Bronchitis **128**

Bulimia nervosa **135**

Burns and scalds **140**

Cancer **147**

Carpal tunnel syndrome **158**

Cateracts **162**

Cerebral aneurysm **165**

Cerebral palsy **170**

Chickenpox **180**

Chronic fatigue syndrome **185**

Color blindness **191**

Colorectal cancer **194**

Common cold **199**

Concussion **206**

Conjunctivitis **211**

Creutzfeldt-Jakob disease **215**

Crohn's disease **222**

Cystic fibrosis **226**

Cystitis **233**

VOLUME 2: D–H

Decompression sickness **239**

Depressive disorders **244**

Diabetes mellitus **251**

Down's syndrome **259**

Dyslexia **266**

Earache **271**

Emphysema **276**

Encephalitis **283**

Epilepsy **287**

Flesh-eating disease **295**

Food poisoning **298**

Fractures, sprains, strains **309**

Frostbite **317**

Glaucoma **323**

Hantavirus infections **329**

Hay Fever **333**

Head injury **340**

Headache **346**

Hearing loss **351**

Heart attack **355**

Heart murmur **363**

Heat disorders **367**

Hemophilia **371**

Hemorrhagic fevers **378**

Hepatitis **384**

Hernia **391**

Herpes infections **395**

Hodgkin's disease **401**

Hypertension **406**

Hypoglycemia **413**

Hypothermia **419**

VOLUME 3: I–P

Infectious mononucleosis **423**

Influenza **427**

Insomnia **434**

Irritable bowel syndrome **439**

Juvenile arthritis **445**

Kaposi's sarcoma **451**

Laryngitis **457**

Lead poisoning **460**

Learning disorders **467**

Leukemia **471**

Lice **478**

Lung cancer **482**

Lupus **487**

Lyme disease **492**

Malaria **499**

Measles **505**

Meningitis **509**

Mental retardation **515**

Multiple sclerosis **520**

Mumps **529**

Muscular dystrophy **534**

Obesity **543**

Obsessive-compulsive disorder **551**

Osteoporosis **558**

Panic disorder **565**

Parkinson's disease **571**

Periodontal disease **579**

Pneumonia **582**

Pneumothorax **587**

Polio **591**

Posttraumatic stress disorder **596**

Prostate cancer **601**

VOLUME 4: R–Z

Rabies **607**

Radiation injuries **612**

Reye's syndrome **620**

Rheumatic fever **623**

Ringworm **628**

Rubella **633**

Scarlet fever **639**

Schizophrenia **642**

Scoliosis **649**

Seasonal affective disorder **654**

Sexually transmitted diseases **659**

Shaken baby syndrome **667**

Sickle cell anemia **670**

Skin cancer **677**

Skin disorders **683**

Sleep disorders **690**

Smallpox **697**

Smoke inhalation **701**

Sore throat **706**

Spina bifida **711**

Spinal cord injury **716**

Strep throat **723**

Stroke **727**

Sudden infant death syndrome **734**

Tay-Sachs disease **741**

Temporomandibular joint disorder **745**

Tendinitis **748**

Tetanus **752**

Tonsillitis **756**

Tooth decay **760**

Tourette syndrome **765**

Toxic shock syndrome **769**

Tuberculosis **773**

Ulcerative colitis **781**

Ulcers (digestive) **786**

Vision disorders **793**

Warts **801**

Whiplash **807**

Whooping cough **809**

Bibliography .... **xlix**

Index .... **li**

contents

Reader's Guide

Sick! Diseases and Disorders, Injuries and Infections presents the latest information on 140 wide-ranging illnesses, disorders, and injuries. Included are entries on familiar medical problems readers might encounter in daily life, such as acne, asthma, chickenpox, cancer, and learning disorders. Some rare and fascinating illnesses are covered as well, such as smallpox, hantaviruses, and Creutzfeld Jakob disease (also known as mad cow disease).

Entries are arranged alphabetically across the four-volume set and generally range from three to eight pages in length. Each entry provides the details students need for reports and other health-related assignments under the following standard subheads: definition, description, causes, symptoms, diagnosis, treatment, prognosis, and prevention.

A "Words to Know" box included at the beginning of each entry provides definitions of words and terms used in that entry. Sidebars highlight interesting facts and individuals associated with the medical condition discussed. At the end of each entry, under the heading "For More Information," appears a list of sources for further information about the disease. The set has approximately 240 black-and-white photos. More than 80 images appear in color in an insert in each volume.

Each volume of *Sick!* begins with a comprehensive glossary collected from all the "Words to Know" boxes in the entries and a selection of research and activity ideas. Each volume ends with a general bibliography section listing comprehensive sources for studying medical conditions and a cumulative index providing access to all major terms and topics covered throughout *Sick!*

Related Reference Sources

Sick! is only one component of the three-part U•X•L Complete Health Resource. Other titles in this library include:

- *Body by Design:* This two-volume set presents the anatomy (structure) and physiology (function) of the human body in twelve chapters spread over two volumes. Each chapter is devoted to one of the eleven organ systems that make up the body. The last chapter focuses on the special senses, which allow humans to connect with the real world. Sidebar boxes present historical discoveries, recent medical advances, short biographies of scientists, and other interesting facts. More than 100 photos, many of them in color, illustrate the text.
- *Healthy Living:* This three-volume set examines fitness, nutrition, and other lifestyle issues across fifteen subject chapters. Topics covered include hygiene, mental health, preventive care, alternative medicine, and careers in health care. Sidebar boxes within entries provide information on related issues, while over 150 black-and-white illustrations help illuminate the text.

Acknowledgments

A note of appreciation is extended to U•X•L's Complete Health Resource advisors, who provided invaluable suggestions when this work was in its formative stages:

Carole Branson
Seminar Science Teacher
Wilson Middle School
San Diego, California

Bonnie L. Raasch
Media Specialist
Vernon Middle School
Marion, Iowa

Doris J. Ranke
Science Teacher
West Bloomfield High School
West Bloomfield, Michigan

Comments and Suggestions

We welcome your comments on *Sick! Diseases and Disorders, Injuries and Infections.* Please write: Editors, *Sick!,* U•X•L, 27500 Drake Rd., Farmington Hills, Michigan 48331–3535; call toll free: 1–800–877–4253; fax: 248–414–5043; or send e-mail via http://www.galegroup.com.

Please Read: Important Information

Sick! Diseases and Disorders, Injuries and Infections is a medical reference product designed to inform and educate readers about medical conditions. U•X•L believes this product to be comprehensive, but not necessarily definitive. While U•X•L has made substantial efforts to provide information that is accurate and up to date, U•X•L makes no representations or warranties of any kind, including without limitation, warranties of merchantability or fitness for a particular purpose, nor does it guarantee the accuracy, comprehensiveness, or timeliness of the information contained in this product.

Readers should be aware that the universe of medical knowledge is constantly growing and changing, and that differences of medical opinion exist among authorities. They are also advised to seek professional diagnosis and treatment for any medical condition, and to discuss information obtained from this book with their health care provider.

Words to Know

Diseases that are featured as main entries in *Sick!* are not covered in Words to Know.

A

Abortive: Describes an action that cuts something short or stops it.

Abscess: A pocket of infection within tissue.

Accommodation: The ability of the lens of the eye to change its shape in order to focus light waves from distant or near objects.

Acetylsalicylic acid: The chemical name for the primary compound from which aspirin is made. Shorthand terms for acetylsalicylic acid include acetylsalicylate, salicylic acid, and salicylate.

Acute: A disorder that comes on suddenly and usually does not last very long.

Acute retroviral syndrome: A group of symptoms resembling mononucleosis that are the first sign of HIV infection in 50 to 70 percent of all patients and in 45 to 90 percent of women.

Adenoid: A mass of lymph tissue located near the pharynx.

Adenoviruses: A group of viruses that usually cause infections of the lungs and ears.

African endemic Kaposi's sarcoma: A form of Kaposi's sarcoma that affects boys and men, has symptoms like those of classic Kaposi's sarcoma, and can spread rapidly and cause death.

Agoraphobia: A fear of open spaces.

AIDS dementia complex: A type of brain dysfunction caused by HIV infection that causes confusion, difficulty thinking, and loss of muscular coordination.

AIDS-related Kaposi's sarcoma: A form of Kaposi's sarcoma that occurs primarily in gay and bisexual men; it is much more dangerous than classic Kaposi's sarcoma.

Allergen: A substance that provokes an allergic response.

Allergic reaction: A series of events initiated by the immune system against substances that are normally harmless to the body.

Alveoli: Small air sacs at the ends of bronchioles through which oxygen passes from the lungs into blood.

Amalgam: A mixture of mercury, silver, and other metals used to make fillings for dental cavities.

Amenorrhea: Absence of menstrual periods.

Amnesia: Loss of memory sometimes caused by a brain injury, such as a concussion.

Amniocentesis: A medical procedure in which a sample of the fluid surrounding the fetus in a woman's womb is withdrawn and examined.

Amputation: A surgical procedure in which an arm, leg, hand, or foot is removed.

Anaphylaxis: An increased sensitivity to an allergen causing dilation (expansion) of blood vessels and tightening of muscles. Anaphylaxis can result in sharp drops in blood pressure, difficulty in breathing, and death if left untreated.

Androgen: A male sex hormone found in both males and females.

Anemia: A medical condition caused by a reduced number of red blood cells and characterized by general weakness, pale skin color, irregular heartbeat, shortness of breath, and fatigue.

Aneurysm: A weak spot in a blood vessel that may break open and lead to a stroke.

Angiography: A method for studying the structure of blood vessels by inserting a catheter into a vein or artery, injecting a dye in the blood vessel, and taking X-ray photographs of the structure.

Anti-androgen: A drug that slows down the production of androgens.

Antibiotic: A substance derived from bacteria or other organisms that fights the growth of other bacteria or organisms.

Antibody: Specific protein produced by the immune system to destroy specific invading organisms.

Anticoagulant: Describes a substance that prevents the blood from clotting.

Anticonvulsant medication: A drug used to prevent convulsions or seizures that is sometimes also effective in the treatment of bipolar disorder.

Antidepressant: A drug used to prevent or relieve depression.

Antigen: Any substance that stimulates the body to produce antibodies.

Antioxidant: A substance that prevents oxidation from taking place. Oxidation is a chemical reaction that can create heat, pain, and inflammation in the body.

Anxiety: Feeling troubled, uneasy, or worried.

Anxiety disorder: An experience of prolonged, excessive worry about the circumstances of one's life.

Aplastic: Having incomplete or faulty development.

Apnea: A temporary pause in one's breathing pattern. Sleep apnea consists of repeated episodes of temporary pauses in breathing during sleep.

Appendectomy: Surgical removal of the appendix.

Appendix: The worm-shaped pouch near the beginning of the large intestine.

Appetite suppressant: Drugs that decrease feelings of hunger and control appetite.

Aqueous humor: A watery fluid that fills the inside of the eyeball, providing nourishment to the eye and maintaining internal pressure in the eyeball.

Arteries: Blood vessels that carry blood from the heart to organs and tissues of the body.

Arteriosclerosis: Hardening of the arteries that can be caused by a variety of factors. Atherosclerosis is just one form of arteriosclerosis, but the two terms are often used interchangeably.

Artery: A blood vessel that carries blood from the heart to other parts of the body.

Arthrography: An imaging technique in which a dye is injected into a joint to make X-ray pictures of the inside of the joint easier to study.

Asperger syndrome: A type of autism that involves no problems with language.

Aspiration: Inhalation of food or saliva.

Astigmatism: A condition in which light from a single point fails to focus on a single point of the retina. The condition causes the patient to see a blurred image.

Ataxia: A condition in which balance and coordination are impaired.

Athetonia: A condition marked by slow, twisting, involuntary muscle movements.

Atopy: A condition in which people are more likely to develop allergic reactions, often because of the inflammation and airway narrowing typical of asthma.

Atrium: (plural: atria) One of the two upper chambers of the heart.

Audiometer: An instrument for testing a person's hearing.

Auditory nerve: A bunch of nerve fibers that carries sound from the inner ear to the brain.

Auditory canal: A tube that leads from the outside of the ear to the tympanic membrane.

Auricle: The external structure of the ear.

Autoimmunity: A condition in which the body's immune system produces antibodies in response to its own tissues or blood components instead of foreign particles or microorganisms.

Autonomic responses: Bodily responses that occur automatically, without the need for a person to think about it.

Autopsy: A medical examination of a dead body.

B

Bacillus Calmette-Guérin (BCG): A vaccine made from a weakened mycobacterium that infects cattle. It is used to protect humans against pulmonary tuberculosis and its complications.

Barium enema: A procedure in which a white liquid is injected into a patient's rectum in order to coat the lining of the colon so that X-ray photographs of the colon can be taken.

Becker muscular dystrophy (BMD): A type of muscular dystrophy that affects older boys and men and usually follows a milder course than Duchenne muscular dystrophy (DMD).

Benign: A growth that does not spread to other parts of the body, making recovery likely with treatment. Often used to describe noncancerous growths.

Binge: To consume large amounts of food without control in a short period of time.

Biofeedback: A technique in which a person learns to consciously control the body's response to a stimulus. Biofeedback enables a person to gain some control over involuntary body functions.

Biopsy: A procedure in which a small sample of tissue is removed and then studied under a microscope.

Blind spot: An area on the retina that is unable to respond to light rays.

Blood-brain barrier: A network of blood vessels between the neck and the brain that prevents many chemicals from passing into the brain.

Bone marrow: Soft, spongy material found in the center of bones from which blood cells are produced.

Bone marrow biopsy: A procedure by which a sample of bone marrow is removed and studied under a microscope.

Bone marrow transplantation: A process by which marrow is removed from the bones of a healthy donor and transferred to the bones of a person with some kind of blood disorder.

Bortadella pertussis: The bacterium that causes whooping cough.

Brain stem: A mass of nervous tissue that connects the forebrain and the cerebrum to the spinal cord.

Bronchi: Two large tubes that branch off the trachea and lead to the lungs; each tube is called a bronchus when referred to singularly. Also called bronchial tubes.

Bronchial tubes: Another name for bronchi. The major airways that lead to the lungs.

Bronchioles: Smaller extensions of the bronchi.

Bronchodilator: A substance that causes muscles in the respiratory system to relax, making breathing easier.

Bronchoscope: A device consisting of a long thin tube with a light and camera on the end for looking into a patient's airways and lungs.

BSA: Refers to "body surface area," a unit used in the treatment of burns to express the amount of the total body surface area covered by the burn.

C

C. botulinum: A very deadly bacteria that causes a disease known as botulism.

Calcium: An essential mineral with many important functions in the body, one of which is in the formation of bone.

Campylobacter jejuni (*C. jejuni*): A bacteria that is the leading cause of bacterial diarrhea in the United States. It occurs in healthy cattle, chickens, birds, and flies.

Carcinogen: Any substance capable of causing cancer.

Cardiovascular: A term that refers to the heart and blood system.

Carditis: Inflammation of the heart.

Caries: The medical term for tooth decay.

Carpal tunnel: A passageway in the wrist, created by bones and ligaments, through which the median nerve passes.

Carrier: A person whose body contains the organisms that cause a disease but who does not show symptoms of that disease.

Cartilage: Tough, elastic tissue that covers and protects the ends of bones.

Cataplexy: A sudden loss of muscular control that may cause a person to collapse.

Catatonic behavior: Behavior characterized by muscular tightness or rigidity and lack of response to the environment.

Catheter: A thin tube inserted into the patient's body, often into a vein or artery, to allow fluids to be sent into or taken out of the body.

Cavity: In dentistry, a hole or weak spot in tooth enamel caused by decay.

CD4: A type of protein molecule in human blood that is present on the surface of 65 percent of immune cells. The HIV virus infects cells that have CD4 surface proteins, and as a result, depletes the number of T cells, B cells, natural killer cells, and monocytes in the patient's blood. Most of the damage to an AIDS patient's immune system is done by the virus's destruction of CD4 lymphocytes.

Central nervous system: A system of nerve cells in the brain and the spinal cord.

Cephalosporin: A specific type of antibiotic used to treat many types of infections.

Cerebral thrombosis: Blockage of a blood vessel in the brain by a blood clot that formed in the brain itself.

Cerebral edema: Swelling of the brain caused by an accumulation of fluid.

Cerebral embolism: Blockage of a blood vessel in the brain by a blood clot that originally formed elsewhere in the body and then traveled to the brain.

Cerebrospinal fluid (CSF): Fluid made in chambers of the brain that flows over the surface of the brain and the spinal cord. CSF provides nutrients to cells of the nervous system and provides a cushion for the structures of the nervous system. It is often used to diagnose infections of the central nervous system (the brain and spinal cord).

Cerumen: Earwax.

Cervical traction: The process of using a mechanism to create a steady pull on the neck in order to keep it in the correct position while it heals.

CFTR: An abbreviation for cystic fibrosis transmembrane conductance regulator, a chemical that controls the amount of water in mucus.

Chelation therapy: Treatment with chemicals that bind to a poisonous metal and help the body quickly eliminate it.

Chemotherapy: A method of treating cancer using certain chemicals that can kill cancer cells.

Child abuse: Intentional harm done to infants and children, usually by parents or care givers.

Chlamydia: A family of microorganisms that causes several types of sexually transmitted diseases in humans.

Chloroquine: An antimalarial drug first used in the 1940s as a substitute for quinine, and still widely used in Africa because of its relatively low cost.

Cholesterol: A waxy substance produced by the body and used in a variety of ways.

Chorea: Involuntary movements that may cause the arms or legs to jerk about uncontrollably.

Chromosome: A structure located inside the nucleus (center) of a cell that carries genetic information.

Chronic: Recurring frequently or lasting a long time.

Cilia: Fine, hair-like projections that line the trachea and bronchi. Cilia wave back and forth, carrying mucus through the airways and clearing the airways of foreign materials.

Circadian rhythm: Any body pattern that follows a twenty-four-hour cycle, such as waking and sleeping.

Circumcision: The procedure in which the foreskin is removed from the penis.

Cirrhosis: A liver disorder caused by scarring of liver tissue.

Classic Kaposi's sarcoma: A form of Kaposi's sarcoma that usually affects older men of Mediterranean or eastern European background.

Clostridium tetani: The bacterium that causes tetanus.

Clonic phase: The stage of a grand mal seizure in which muscles alternately contract and relax.

Clotting factor: One of the chemicals necessary for blood clotting.

Cobb angle: A measure of the curvature of the spine, determined from measurements made on X-ray photographs.

Cognitive-behavioral therapy: A form of psychological counseling in which patients are helped to understand the nature of their disorder and reshape their environment to help them function better.

Colonoscopy: A procedure in which a long, thin tube is inserted through a patient's rectum into the colon to permit examination of the inner walls of the colon.

Colostomy: An opening created surgically that runs from the colon to the outside of the body to provide an alternative route for the evacuation of body wastes.

Comedo: A hard plug composed of sebum and dead skin cells that develops in the pores of the skin. The mildest form of acne.

Comedolytic: Drugs that break up comedos and open clogged pores.

Compulsion: A very strong urge to do or say something that usually cannot be resisted and is repeated again and again.

Computed tomography (CT) scan: A technique in which X-ray photographs of a particular part of the body are taken from different angles. The pictures are then fed into a computer that creates a single composite image of the internal (inside) part of the body. CT scans provide an important tool in the diagnosis of brain and spinal disorders, cancer, and other conditions.

Computerized axial tomography (CAT) scan: Another name for a computed tomography (CT) scan.

Condom: A thin sheath (covering) worn over the penis during sexual activity to prevent pregnancy and the spread of sexually transmitted diseases.

Conduct disorder: A behavioral and emotional disorder of childhood and adolescence. Children with a conduct disorder act inappropriately, infringe on the rights of others, and violate social rules.

Conductive hearing loss: Hearing loss that occurs in the external or middle ear.

Cone cells: Special cells in the retina responsible for color vision.

Congenital disorder: A medical condition that is present at birth.

Contact dermatitis: Inflammation of the skin caused by exposure to an allergen.

Contracture: A permanent shortening and tightening of a muscle or tendon causing a deformity.

Contrast hydrotherapy: A procedure in which a series of hot- and cold-water applications is applied to an injured area.

Contusion: A bruise.

Cornea: The transparent outer coating on the front of the eyeball.

Coronary: Referring to the heart.

Coronavirus: A type of virus that can cause the common cold.

Coxsackie virus: A virus that causes a disease known as herpangina.

Crabs: A slang term for pubic lice.

Crib death: Another name for sudden infant death syndrome.

Cryosurgery: The use of liquid nitrogen for the purpose of removing diseased tissue.

Cyanosis: A condition that develops when the body does not get enough oxygen, causing the skin to turn blue.

D

Debridement: The surgical removal of dead skin.

Decompression stops: Stops divers should make when returning to the surface to let the nitrogen in their blood dissolve safely out of their bodies. Charts developed by the U.S. Navy and other groups list the number of stops and the time to be spent at each stop.

Delusion: A fixed, false belief that is resistant to reason or factual disproof.

Dementia: Impaired intellectual function that interferes with normal social and work activities.

Densitometry: A technique for measuring the density of bone by taking photographs with low-energy X rays from a variety of angles around the bone.

Dentin: The middle layer of a tooth.

Dependence: A state in which a person requires a steady amount of a particular drug in order to avoid experiencing the symptoms of withdrawal.

Depot dosage: A form of medication that can be stored in the patient's body for several days or weeks.

Depression: A psychological condition with feelings of sadness, sleep disturbance, fatigue, and inability to concentrate.

Detoxification: The phase of treatment during which a patient gives up a substance and harmful chemicals are removed from his or her system.

Diaphragm: As a form of birth control, a thin rubber cap inserted into the vagina.

Diastolic blood pressure: Blood pressure exerted by the heart when it is resting between beats.

Digital rectal examination: A medical procedure in which a doctor inserts a lubricated gloved finger into the rectum to look for abnormal structures.

Dimercaprol (BAL): A chemical agent used in chelation therapy.

Diopter: The unit of measure used for the refractive (light bending) power of a lens.

Diplegia: Paralysis of the arm and leg on one side of the body.

Disease reservoir: A population of animals in which a virus lives without causing serious illness among the animals.

Distal muscular dystrophy (DD): A form of muscular dystrophy that usually begins in middle age or later, causing weakness in the muscles of the feet and hands.

Dominant gene: A form of a gene that predominates over a second form of the same gene.

Dopamine: A neurotransmitter that helps send signals that control movement.

DSM-IV: The *Diagnostic and Statistical Manual of Mental Disorders*, Fourth Edition, the standard reference book used for diagnosing and treating mental disorders.

Duchenne muscular dystrophy (DMD): The most severe form of muscular dystrophy, usually affecting young boys, beginning in the legs, and resulting in progressive muscle weakness.

Duodenum: The upper part of the small intestine, joined to the lower part of the stomach.

Dyslexia: Difficulty in reading, spelling, and/or writing words.

Dysthymic disorder: An ongoing, chronic depression that lasts two or more years.

Dystonia: Loss of the ability to control detailed muscle movement.

E

Echocardiogram: A test that uses sound waves to produce an image of the structure of the heart.

ECT: Electroconvulsive shock therapy, a method for using electric shocks to treat patients with mental disorders, such as bipolar disorder.

Edetate calcium disodium (EDTA calcium): A chemical agent used in chelation therapy.

Electrocardiogram: A test that measures the electrical activity of the heart to determine whether it is functioning normally.

Electroencephalogram (EEG): A test used to measure electrical activity of the brain to see if the brain is functioning normally.

Electrolytes: Salts and minerals present in the body that produce electrically charged particles (ions) in body fluids. Electrolytes control the fluid balance in the body and are important in muscle contraction, energy generation, and almost all major biochemical reactions in the body.

Electromagnetic radiation (ER): Radiation that travels as waves at the speed of light.

Electromyography: A test used to measure how well a nerve is functioning.

Enamel: The hard, outermost layer of a tooth.

Encephalopathy: A brain disorder characterized by loss of memory and other mental problems.

Endemic: The widespread occurrence of a disease over a given area that lasts for an extended period of time.

Endoscope: An instrument consisting of a long, narrow tube that can be inserted down a patient's throat to study the health of a patient's digestive system.

Enema: The injection of liquid into the intestine through the anus. This procedure is used either to induce a bowel movement or to coat the lining of the colon so that X-ray photographs can be taken of the colon.

Enzymes: Chemicals present in all cells that make possible the biological reactions needed to keep a cell alive.

Epidemic: An outbreak of a disease that spreads over a wide area in a relatively short period of time.

Epidermis: The outer layer of skin.

Epithelium: The layer of cells covering the body's outer and inner surfaces.

Epstein-Barr virus (EBV): A virus that causes mononucleosis and other diseases.

***Escherichia coli* (*E. coli*):** A bacteria that commonly causes food poisoning, most often from food products derived from cows, especially ground beef.

Estrogen: A female hormone with many functions in the body, one of which is to keep bones strong.

Eustachian tube: A passageway that connects the middle ear with the back of the throat.

Evoked potential test (EPT): A test that measures the brain's electrical response to certain kinds of stimulation, such as light in the eyes, sound in the ears, or touch on the skin.

Extrapulmonary: Outside of the lungs.

F

Facioscapulohumeral muscular dystrophy (FSH): A form of muscular dystrophy that begins in late childhood to early adulthood; affects both men and women; and causes weakness in the muscles of the face, shoulders, and upper arms.

Fecal occult blood test: A laboratory test designed to find blood in feces.

Fibrin: A thick material formed over an injured section of a blood vessel by the process of blood clotting.

Fibromyalgia: Pain, tenderness, and stiffness in muscles.

Fistula: An abnormal tubelike passage in tissue.

Flashback: A sudden memory of an event that occurred months or years earlier.

Fluoride: A chemical compound that is effective in preventing tooth decay.

Fragile X syndrome: A genetic condition involving the X chromosome that results in mental, physical, and sensory problems.

Frequency: The rate at which a wave vibrates in space.

Frostbite: A medical condition in which some part of the body has become frozen.

Fungus: A large group of organisms that includes mold, mildew, rust fungi, yeast, and mushrooms, some of which may cause disease in humans and other animals.

G

Ganglioside: A fatty substance found in brain and nerve cells.

Gangrene: Death and decay of body tissue.

Gastrointestinal system: The digestive system, consisting of the stomach and intestines.

Gel electrophoresis: A laboratory test that separates different types of molecules from each other.

Gene: A chemical unit found in all cells that carries information telling cells what functions they are to perform.

General autoimmune disorder: An autoimmune disorder that involves a number of tissues throughout the body.

Genetic disorder: A medical problem caused by one or more defective genes.

Genital: Having to do with the organs of the reproductive system.

Gingiva: The outer layer of the gums.

Ginkgo: An herb obtained from the ginkgo tree, thought by some alternative practitioners to be helpful in treating patients with Alzheimer's disease.

Glucose: A type of sugar present in the blood and in cells that is used by cells to make energy.

Gonorrhea: A sexually transmitted disease caused by the *Gonococcus* bacterium that affects the mucous membranes, particularly in the urinary tract and genital area. It can make urination painful and cause puslike discharges through the urinary tract.

Grand mal: An alternate term used for tonic-clonic epilepsy.

Granules: Small packets of reactive chemicals stored within cells.

Gray (Gy): A unit used to measure damage done to tissue by ionizing radiation.

H

Hairy leukoplakia of the tongue: A white area of diseased tissue on the tongue that may be flat or slightly raised. It is caused by the Epstein-Barr virus and is an important diagnostic sign of AIDS.

Hallucination: A perception of objects (or sounds) that have no reality. Seeing or hearing something that does not actually exist.

Helicobacter pylori: A bacterium that lives in mucous membranes and is responsible for the development of ulcers.

Hemiplegia: Paralysis of one side of the body.

Hemodialysis: A mechanical method for cleansing blood outside the body.

Hemoglobin: A molecule found in blood that gives blood its red color. Hemoglobin is responsible for transporting oxygen through the blood stream.

Hemorrhage: Heavy or uncontrollable bleeding.

Herpes virus: A group of viruses that cause many different infections in the human body, including cold sores and infections of the genital area.

Histamine: A chemical released by mast cells that activates pain receptors and causes cells to leak fluids.

Hormone replacement therapy (HRT): A method of treating osteoporosis by giving supplementary doses of estrogen and/or other female hormones.

Hormone therapy: Treatment of cancer by slowing down the production of certain hormones.

Hormones: Chemicals that occur naturally in the body and control certain body functions.

Human immunodeficiency virus (HIV): A transmissible virus that causes AIDS in humans. Two forms of HIV are now recognized: HIV-1, which causes most cases of AIDS in Europe, North and South America, and most parts of Africa; and HIV-2, which is chiefly found in West African patients. HIV-2, discovered in 1986, appears to be less virulent than HIV-1 and may also have a longer latency period.

Human papilloma virus (HPV): A family of viruses that cause hand, foot, flat, and genital warts.

Hydrocephalus: An abnormal accumulation of cerebrospinal fluid (CSF) in the brain.

Hyperbaric chamber: A sealed compartment used to treat decompression sickness, in which air pressure is first increased and then gradually decreased.

Hyperopia: Farsightedness. A condition in which vision is better for distant objects than for near ones.

Hypersomnia: The need to sleep excessively; a symptom of dysthymic and major depressive disorder.

Hyperthermia: The general name for any form of heat disorder.

Hyperventilation: Deep, heavy breathing.

Hypotonia: A condition in which muscles lack strength.

I

Iatrogenic: Caused by a medical procedure.

Iatrogenic Kaposi's sarcoma: A form of Kaposi's sarcoma that develops in people who have had organ transplants and are taking immunosuppressant drugs.

Ideal weight: Weight corresponding to the appropriate, healthy rate for individuals of a specific height, gender, and age.

Idiopathic epilepsy: A form of epilepsy for which no cause is known.

Immune system: A system of organs, tissues, cells, and chemicals that work together to fight off foreign invaders, such as bacteria and viruses.

Immunization: The process of injecting a material into a person's body that protects that person from catching a particular infectious disease.

Immunodeficient: A condition in which the body's immune response is damaged, weakened, or is not functioning properly.

Immunotherapy: Treatment of cancer by stimulating the body's immune system.

Incubation period: The time it takes for symptoms of a disease to appear after a person has been infected.

Infestation: A situation in which large numbers of organisms come together in a single area.

Inflammation: The body's response to tissue damage that includes heat, swelling, redness, and pain.

Inflammatory bowel disease: A group of disorders that affect the gastrointestinal (digestive) system.

Insomnia: Difficulty in falling asleep or in remaining asleep.

Insulin: A hormone (type of protein) produced by the pancreas that makes it possible for cells to use glucose in the production of energy.

Intestinal perforation: A hole in the lining of the intestine that allows partially digested foods to leak into the abdominal cavity.

Intracerebral hemorrhage: Bleeding that occurs within the brain.

Intraocular pressure (IOP): The pressure exerted by aqueous humor (clear liquid) inside the eyeball.

Ionizing radiation (IR): Any form of radiation that can break apart atoms and molecules and cause damage to materials.

J

Jaundice: A yellowing of the skin, often caused by a disorder of the liver.

Jet lag: A temporary disruption of the body's sleep/wake rhythm caused by high-speed air travel through different time zones.

Joint: A structure that holds two or more bones together.

K

Karyotype: The specific chromosomal makeup of a particular organism.

Ketoacidosis: A condition that results from the build-up of toxic chemicals known as ketones in the blood.

Koplik's spots: Tiny white spots on a reddish bump found inside of the mouth that are a characteristic marker for measles.

L

Lactobacillus acidophilus: A bacterium found in yogurt that changes the balance of bacteria in the intestine in a beneficial way.

Laparoscopy: A procedure in which a tube with a small light and viewing device is inserted through a small incision near the navel, allowing a surgeon to look directly into the patient's abdomen.

Laparotomy: A surgical procedure that allows a surgeon to view the inside of the abdominal cavity.

Larva: An immature form of an organism.

Larynx: The part of the airway between the pharynx and trachea, often called the voice box.

Laser: A device for producing very intense beams of light of a single color. Used in surgery to cut and/or dissolve tissues.

Latency: A period during which a disease-causing organism is inactive but not dead.

Lens: In the eye, a transparent, elastic, curved structure that helps focus light on the retina.

Lesion: Any change in the structure or appearance of a part of the body as the result of an injury or infection.

Ligament: Tough, fiber-like tissue that holds bones together at joints.

Limb-girdle muscular dystrophy (LGMD): A form of muscular dystrophy that begins in late childhood to early adulthood, affects both men and women, and causes weakness in the muscles around the hips and shoulders.

Lumbar puncture: A procedure in which a thin needle is inserted into the space between vertebrae in the spine and a sample of cerebrospinal fluid is withdrawn for study under a microscope.

Lumpectomy: A procedure in which a cancerous lump is removed from the breast.

Lymph nodes: Small round or oval bodies within the immune system. Lymph nodes provide materials that fight disease and help remove bacteria and other foreign material from the body.

Lymphocyte: A type of white blood cell that is important in the formation of antibodies and that can be measured to monitor the health of AIDS patients.

Lymphoma: A cancerous tumor in the lymphatic system that is associated with a poor prognosis in AIDS patients.

M

Macrophage: A large white blood cell, found primarily in the bloodstream and connective tissue, that helps the body fight off infections by ingesting the disease-causing organism. HIV can infect and kill macrophages.

Magnetic resonance imaging (MRI): A procedure that uses electromagnets and radio waves to produce images of a patient's internal tissue and organs. These images are not blocked by bones, and can be useful in diagnosing brain and spinal disorders and other diseases.

Malignant: Describes a tumor that can spread to other parts of the body and that poses a serious threat to a person's life.

Malnutrition: A condition in which a person is not eating enough of the right kinds of foods.

Mammogram: An X-ray photograph of the breast.

Mandible: The scientific term for the lower jaw.

Mania: A mental condition in which a person feels unusually excited, irritated, or happy.

Mantoux test: Another name for the purified protein derivative (PPD) test, which is used to determine whether a person has been infected with the tuberculosis bacterium.

Mast cells: A type of immune system cell that is found in the lining of the nasal passages and eyelids. It displays a type of antibody called immunoglobulin type E (IgE) on its cell surface and participates in the allergic response by releasing histamine from intracellular granules.

Mastectomy: Surgical removal of a breast.

Meconium ileus: A condition that appears in newborn babies with cystic fibrosis, in which the baby's first bowel movement is abnormally dark, thick, and sticky.

Median nerve: A nerve that runs through the wrist and into the hand, providing feeling and movement to the hand, thumb, and fingers.

Melanocyte: A specialized skin cell that produces melanin, a dark pigment (color) found in skin.

Melatonin: A hormone thought to control the body's natural sleep rhythms.

Meninges: The three-layer membranous covering of the brain and spinal cord.

Menopause: The end of menstruation.

Menstruation: The discharge of menses (a bloody fluid) from the uterus of women who are not pregnant that occurs approximately every four weeks from puberty to menopause.

Metabolism: A series of chemical reactions by which cells convert glucose to energy.

Metastasis: The process by which cancer cells travel from one area of the body to another.

Methadone: A chemical given to heroin addicts to help them overcome their addiction.

Miliary tuberculosis: A form of tuberculosis in which the bacillus spreads throughout the body producing many thousands of tubercular lesions.

Miscarriage: When a human fetus is expelled from the mother before it can survive outside of the womb.

MMR vaccine: A vaccine that contains separate vaccines against three diseases: measles, mumps, and rubella.

Monocyte: A large white blood cell that is formed in the bone marrow and spleen. About 4 percent of the white blood cells in normal adults are monocytes.

Mosaic: Medically, a condition in which an individual cell may contain more than one type of chromosomal composition, with forty-six chromosomes in one cell, for example, and forty-seven chromosomes in another cell, which causes relatively mild symptoms of Down's syndrome.

Motor function: A body function controlled by muscles.

Motor neuron: A nerve cell that controls a muscle.

Mucolytic: Any type of medication that breaks up mucus and makes it flow more easily.

Mucus: A mixture of water, salts, sugars, and proteins, which has the job of cleansing, lubricating, and protecting passageways in the body.

Myalgia: Muscle pain.

Myalgic encephalomyelitis: An inflammation of the brain and spinal cord.

Myelin: A layer of tissue that surrounds nerves and acts as an insulator.

Myelograph: A test in which a dye is injected into the spinal column to allow examination of the spine with X rays or a computed tomography (CT) scan.

Myocardial infarction: The technical term for heart attack.

Myopia: Nearsightedness. A condition in which far away objects appear fuzzy because light from a distance doesn't focus properly on the retina.

Myotonic dystrophy: A form of muscular dystrophy that affects both men and women and causes generalized weakness in the face, feet, and hands.

N

Narcolepsy: A sleep disorder characterized by sudden sleep attacks during the day and often accompanied by other symptoms, such as cataplexy, temporary paralysis, and hallucinations.

Narcotic: A drug that relieves pain and induces sleep.

Natural killer cells: Cells in the immune system that help fight off infections.

Necrosis: Abnormal death of body tissues.

Nervous tic: An involuntary action, continually repeated, such as the twitching of a muscle or repeated blinking.

Neural tube: A structure that forms very early in the life of a fetus and eventually develops into the central nervous system of the body.

Neurasthenia: Nervous exhaustion.

Neurofibrillary tangle: Twisted masses of peptides (fragments of protein fibers) that develop inside brain cells of people with Alzheimer's disease.

Neuron: A nerve cell.

Neurotransmitter: A chemical found in the brain that carries electrical signals from one nerve cell to another nerve cell.

Nitrogen: A tasteless, odorless gas that makes up four-fifths of Earth's atmosphere.

Nits: The eggs produced by head or pubic lice.

Nonsteroidal anti-inflammatory drugs (NSAIDs): A group of drugs, including aspirin, ibuprofen, and acetaminophen, used to treat pain and fever.

Nucleoside analogues: A medication that interferes when HIV tries reproduce by making copies of itself inside cells.

O

Obsession: A troubling thought that occurs again and again and causes severe distress in a person.

Oculopharyngeal muscular dystrophy (OPMD): A form of muscular dystrophy that affects adults of both sexes and causes weakness in the muscles of the eyes and throat.

Opiate blockers: Drugs that interfere with the action of natural opiates, substances that cause sleepiness and numbness.

Opportunistic infection: An infection by organisms that usually don't cause infection in people whose immune systems are working normally.

Optic nerve: A nerve at the back of the eyeball that carries messages from the retina to the brain.

Organ specific disorder: An autoimmune disorder in which only one type of organ is affected.

Ossicles: Tiny bones located within the middle ear responsible for transmitting sound vibrations from the outer ear to the inner ear.

Osteoarthritis: A type of arthritis that weakens the joint cartilage. It is most common among the elderly.

Otosclerosis: A disorder in which the bones of the middle ear become joined to each other.

P

Pancreas: A gland located behind the stomach that produces insulin.

Paralysis: The inability to move one's muscles.

Paranoia: Excessive or irrational suspicion or distrust of others.

Penicillin: A specific type of antibiotic used to treat many types of infections.

Peptic ulcer: A general name referring to ulcers in any part of the digestive system.

Pericardium: The membrane surrounding the heart.

Peristalsis: Periodic waves of muscular contractions that move food through the digestive system.

Peritonitis: Inflammation of the membranes that line the abdominal wall.

Persistent generalized lymphadenopathy (PGL): A condition in which HIV continues to produce chronic painless swellings in the lymph nodes during the latency period.

Petit mal: An alternative term for absence epilepsy.

Pharynx: The part of the throat that lies between the mouth and the larynx, or voice box. It connects the nose and mouth with the upper part of the digestive system.

Phenylketonuria (PKU): A genetic disorder in which a person's body is unable to break down the amino acid phenylalanine, causing damage to the brain.

Physiological dependence: A condition in which a person's body requires the intake of some substance, without which it will become ill.

Plaque: Generally refers to a build-up of some substance. The fatty material and other substances that form on the lining of blood vessels are called plaque. Patches of scar tissue that form in areas where myelin tissue has been destroyed are also called plaque. Dental plaque is a thin, sticky film composed of sugars, food, and bacteria that cover teeth.

Platelet: A type of blood cell involved in the clotting of blood.

Pleural: Having to do with the membrane that surrounds the lungs.

Polyps: Small, abnormal masses of tissue that can form on the lining of an organ.

Polysomnograph: An instrument used to measure a patient's body processes during sleep.

Positron emission tomography (PET): A diagnostic technique that uses radioactive materials to study the structure and function of organs and tissues within the body.

Primary progressive: A form of multiple sclerosis in which the disease continually becomes worse.

Prion: A form of protein that can cause an infectious disease.

Process addiction: A condition in which a person is dependent on some type of behavior, such as gambling, shopping, or sexual activity.

Prodrome: A period of time during which certain symptoms signal the beginning of a disease.

Prophylactic: Referring to a treatment that prevents the symptoms of a condition from developing.

Protease inhibitors: The second major category of drug used to treat AIDS. They work by suppressing the replication of the HIV virus.

Protein: A type of chemical compound with many essential functions in the body, one of which is to build bones.

Psychological dependence: A condition in which a person requires the intake of some substance in order to maintain mental stability.

Psychosis: Extremely disordered thinking accompanied by a poor sense of reality.

Psychosocial therapy: Any means by which a trained professional holds interviews with a patient and tries to help that patient better understand himself or herself and the reasons for his or her thoughts and actions.

Psychotic disorder: A mental disorder characterized by delusions, hallucinations, and other symptoms indicating a loss of contact with the real world.

Pulmonary: Relating to the lungs.

Pulmonary function test: A test that measures the amount of air a patient can breath in and out.

Pulmonary hypertension: High blood pressure in the arteries and veins associated with the lungs.

Pulp: The soft, innermost layer of a tooth.

Purge: To rid the body of food by vomiting, the use of laxatives, or some other method.

Purified protein derivative (PPD): A substance injected beneath the skin to see whether a person presently has or has ever had the tubercle bacillus.

Q

Quadriplegia: Paralysis of both arms and both legs.

Quinine: One of the first successful treatments for malaria, derived from the bark of the cinchona tree.

R

Rad: A unit once used to measure the amount of damage done to tissue by ionizing radiation, now replaced by the gray.

Radial keratotomy (RK): A surgical procedure in which the shape of the cornea is changed in order to correct myopia.

Radiation: Energy transmitted in the form of electromagnetic waves or subatomic particles.

Radiation therapy: Treatment that uses high-energy radiation, like X rays, to treat cancer.

Radical mastectomy: Surgical removal of an entire breast along with the chest muscles around the breast and all the lymph nodes under the arm.

Radioactive isotope: A substance that gives off some form of radiation.

Radiotherapy: Treatment of a disease using some form of radiation, such as X rays.

Radon: A radioactive gas that occurs naturally and is often found in the lower levels of buildings.

Rash: A spotted pink or red skin condition that may be accompanied by itching.

Recessive gene: A form of a gene that does not operate in the presence of a dominant form of the same gene.

Reconstructive surgery: A medical procedure in which an artificial breast is created to replace the breast removed during a mastectomy.

Rectum: The lower part of the digestive system from which solid wastes are excreted.

Red blood cells: Blood cells that carry oxygen from the lungs to the rest of the body.

Reduction: The restoration of a body part to its original position after it has been displaced, such as during a fracture.

Refraction: The bending of light waves as they pass through a dense substance, such as water, glass, or plastic.

Relapse: A reoccurrence of a disease.

Relapsing-remitting: A form of multiple sclerosis in which symptoms appear for at least twenty-four hours and then disappear for a period of time.

Rem: An older unit used to measure the amount of damage done to tissue by ionizing radiation, now replaced by the sievert.

Renal: Relating to the kidneys.

Resorption: The process by which the elements of bone are removed from bone and returned to the body.

Respiratory system: The nose, tonsils, larynx, pharynx, lungs, and other structures used in the process of breathing.

Restless leg syndrome: A condition in which a patient experiences aching or other unpleasant sensations in the calves of the legs.

Retina: A thin membrane at the back of the eyeball that receives light rays that pass through the eyeball and transmits them to the optic nerve.

Rhabdovirus: The virus that causes rabies.

Rhinovirus: A type of virus that can cause the common cold.

RICE: The term stands for the program of rest, ice, compression, and elevation that is recommended for treating tendinitis.

Rickets: A condition caused by the deficiency of certain minerals, including vitamin D and calcium, causing abnormal bone growth.

S

Salmonella: A bacteria that commonly causes food poisoning, most often from poultry, eggs, meat, and milk.

Scald: A burn caused by a hot liquid or steam.

Scoliometer: A tool for measuring the amount of curvature in a person's spine.

Screening: Using a test or group of tests to look for some specific medical disorder.

Sebum: An oily material produced by sebaceous glands that keeps the skin moist.

Secondary progressive: A form of multiple sclerosis in which a period of relapses and remissions is followed by another period in which the disease becomes progressively worse without improvement.

Secondhand smoke: Smoke that someone inhales after it is exhaled by another person.

Sedative: A substance that calms a person. Sedatives can also cause a person to feel drowsy.

Seizure: A convulsion; a series of involuntary muscular movements that alternate between contraction and relaxation.

Selective serotonin reuptake inhibitors (SSRIs): A class of drugs used to reduce depression.

Semen: A white fluid produced by the male reproductive system that carries sperm.

Seminal vesicles: The organs that produce semen.

Senile plaque: Deposits that collect inside the brain cells of people with Alzheimer's disease.

Sensory hearing loss: Hearing loss that occurs in the inner ear, auditory nerve, or brain.

Serotonin: An important neurotransmitter in the brain.

Shigella: A bacterium that grows well in contaminated food and water, in crowded living conditions, and in areas with poor sanitation. It is transmitted by direct contact with an infected person or with food that has been contaminated by an infected person.

Shingles: A disease that causes a rash and a very painful nerve inflammation. An attack of chickenpox eventually gives rise to shingles in about 20 percent of the population.

Shock: A life-threatening condition that results from low blood volume due to loss of blood or other fluids.

Sickle cell: A red blood cell with an abnormal shape due to the presence of an abnormal form of hemoglobin.

Sievert (Sv): A unit used to measure the amount of damage done to tissue by ionizing radiation.

Sigmoidoscopy: A medical procedure in which a doctor looks at the rectum and lower colon through a flexible lighted instrument called a sigmoidoscope.

Silicosis: A disease of the lungs caused by inhaling fine particles of sand.

Skin graft: A surgical procedure in which dead skin is removed and replaced by healthy skin, usually taken from elsewhere on the patient's own body.

Sleep disorder: Any condition that interferes with sleep. The American Sleep Disorders Association has identified eighty-four different sleep disorders.

Somnambulism: Also called sleepwalking, it refers to a range of activities a patient performs while sleeping, from walking to carrying on a conversation.

Spasm: A contraction of the muscles that can cause paralysis and/or shaking.

Spastic: A condition in which muscles are rigid, posture may be abnormal, and control of muscles may be impaired.

Sphygmomanometer: An instrument used to measure blood pressure.

Spinal cord: A long rope-like piece of nervous tissue that runs from the brain down the back.

Spinal transection: A complete break in the spinal column.

Spirometer: An instrument that shows how much air a patient is able to exhale and hold in his or her lungs as a test to see how serious a person's asthma is and how well he or she is responding to treatment.

Spondylosis: Arthritis of the spine.

Sputum: Secretions produced inside an infected lung. When the sputum is coughed up it can be studied to determine what kinds of infection are present in the lung.

Staphylococcus aureas: A bacteria that causes food poisoning, commonly found on foods that are kept at room temperature.

Staphylococcus: A class of bacteria found on human skin and mucous membranes that can cause a variety of infectious diseases.

Streptococcus: A class of bacteria that causes a wide variety of infections.

Stem cells: Immature blood cells formed in bone marrow.

Steroids: A category of naturally occurring chemicals that are very effective in reducing inflammation and swelling.

Stimulant: A substance that makes a person feel more energetic or awake. A stimulant may increase organ activity in the body.

Stress test: An electrocardiogram taken while a patient is exercising vigorously, such as riding a stationary bicycle.

Subarachnoid hemorrhage (SAH): Loss of blood into the subarachnoid space, the fluid-filled area that surrounds brain tissue.

Subdural hematoma: An accumulation of blood in the outer part of the brain.

Substance addiction: A condition in which a person is dependent on some chemical substance, such as cocaine or heroin.

Substantia nigra: A region of the brain that controls movement.

Succimer (Chemet): A chemical agent used to remove excess lead from the body.

Symptomatic epilepsy: A form of epilepsy for which some specific cause is known.

Synovial fluid: A fluid produced by the synovial membranes in a joint that lubricates the movement of the bones in the joint.

Synovial membrane: A membrane that covers the articular capsule in a joint and produces synovial fluid.

Syphilis: A sexually transmitted disease that can cause sores and eventually lead to brain disease, paralysis, and death.

Systemic treatment: A form of treatment that affects the whole body.

Systolic blood pressure: Blood pressure exerted by the heart when it contracts (beats).

T

T-cells: Lymphocytes that originate in the thymus gland. T-cells regulate the immune system's response to infections, including HIV.

Tartar: Plaque that has become hardened and attached to the tooth surface.

Temporal bones: The bones that form the right and left sides of the skull.

Tendon: A tough, rope-like tissue that connects muscle to bone.

Tennis elbow: A form of tendinitis that occurs among tennis players and other people who engage in the same movement of the elbow over and over again.

Testosterone: A male sex hormone.

Thermal burns: Burns caused by hot objects or by fire.

Thoracentesis: A procedure for removing fluids from the pleural space by inserting a long, thin needle between the ribs.

Throat culture: A sample of tissue taken from a person's throat for analysis. The culture is often taken by swiping a cotton swab across the back of the throat.

Thrombolytic: Capable of dissolving a blood clot.

Thrombosis: The formation of a blood clot.

Thyroid: An organ that controls a number of important bodily functions.

Tic: A muscular contraction or vocal sound over which a patient has very little control.

Tinea capitis: Scalp ringworm; a fungal infection of the scalp.

Tinea corporis: Scientific name for body ringworm, a fungal infection of the skin that can affect any part of the body except the scalp, feet, and facial area.

Tinea cruris: An fungal infection that affects the groin and can spread to the buttocks, inner thighs, and external genitalia; also called "jock itch."

Tinea unguium: Ringworm of the nails; a fungal infection that usually begins at the tip of a toenail.

Tissue plasminogen activator (tPA): A substance that dissolves blood clots in the brain.

Tolerance: The ability of a body to endure a certain amount of a substance that had previously been too much for it to tolerate.

Tonic phase: The stage of a grand mal seizure in which muscles become rigid and fixed.

Tonometer: A device used to measure intraocular pressure in the eyeball.

Tonsillectomy: A surgical procedure to remove the tonsils.

Tonsils: Oval-shaped masses of lymph gland tissue located on both sides of the back of the throat.

Toxic dilation of the colon: An expansion of the colon that may be caused by inflammation due to ulcerative colitis.

Toxin: A poison.

Trachea: The windpipe, extending from the larynx (the voice box) to the lungs.

Traction: The process of placing an arm or leg bone, or group of muscles under tension by applying weights to them in order to keep them in alignment while they heal.

Tranquilizers: Drugs that help a person to calm down.

Transcutaneous electrical nerve stimulation: A procedure in which mild electrical currents are used to stimulate nerves in order to prevent the transmission of pain messages in the body.

Translocation: A condition in which a piece of one chromosome breaks off and becomes attached to another chromosome.

Tretinoin: A drug that increases the rate at which skin cells are formed and die.

Triglyceride: A type of fat.

Trimester: Three months. Often used to refer to one third of a woman's pregnancy.

Trisomy: A condition in which three identical chromosomes, rather than two, are matched with each other.

Tumor: A mass or lump of tissue made of abnormal cells.

Twelve-step program: A plan for overcoming an addiction by going through twelve stages of personal development.

Tympanic membrane: A thin piece of tissue between the external ear and the middle ear.

U

Ulcer: An open wound in the skin or mucous membrane that is usually sore and painful.

Ultrasound test: A medical procedure in which a sound wave is transmitted into a pregnant woman's womb. The reflections produced from the sound wave can be studied for the presence of abnormalities in a fetus.

Ultraviolet (UV) light: A naturally occurring part of ordinary sunlight that may, under some circumstances, have beneficial effects in curing certain medical disorders.

Urethra: The tube through which the bladder empties to the exterior of the body.

V

Vaccine: A substance that causes the body's immune system to build up resistance to a particular disease.

Varicella-zoster immune globulin (VZIG): A substance that can reduce the severity of chickenpox symptoms.

Varicella-zoster virus: The virus that causes chickenpox and shingles.

Variola: The virus that causes smallpox. The only two small samples of variola that remain on Earth are being stored in two separate research laboratories.

Varivax: A vaccine for the prevention of chickenpox.

Vasodilator: Any drug that causes a blood vessel to relax.

Vector: An animal that transmits an infectious agent, such as a virus, from one animal to another animal.

Vector-borne disease: A disease transferred from one organism to another by means of a third organism, such as an insect or tick.

Ventricle: One of the two lower chambers of the heart.

Vertebrae: Bones that make up the spinal column.

Virus: A very small organism that can live only within a cell and that can cause some form of disease.

Volume reduction surgery: A surgical procedure in which damaged portions of a patient's lung are removed to make it easier for the patient to use healthy parts of the lung to get the oxygen needed for ordinary functioning.

Voluntary muscle: A muscle under a person's conscious control.

W

Wasting Syndrome: A progressive loss of weight and muscle tissue caused by AIDS.

White blood cells: Blood cells that fight invading organisms, such as bacteria and viruses.

Withdrawal: The process by which a person adjusts to the absence of some substance or activity to which he or she has become addicted.

X

X rays: A kind of high-energy radiation that can be used to take pictures of the inside of the body, to diagnose cancer, or to kill cancer cells.

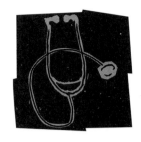

Research and Activity Ideas

The following research and activity ideas are intended to offer suggestions for complementing science and health curricula, to trigger additional ideas for enhancing learning, and to suggest cross-disciplinary projects for library and classroom use.

Disease graph: Different environments create different opportunities for diseases to spread. Obtain current data for your city or county on occurrences of a disease such as rabies or lyme disease or a condition such as asthma. Create a graph that compares the number of outbreaks in urban areas with the number in rural areas. If there are differences, brainstorm some of the environmental factors that may be causing such differences.

Public service announcement: Choose a disease or disorder and write a public service announcement that would appear on television to inform people about the condition. Your ad should include information about symptoms, warn of risk factors, mention current treatments, and dispel any myths that are associated with the disease. Record the public service announcement using a video camera or present it in class.

Geographic study: Different parts of the world often face unique challenges in controlling diseases. Choose two different countries with different cultures and environments. Find out what the top five health concerns are in each country. For each one, determine the major risk factors. Discuss what aspects of the culture or the environment may be increasing the incidences of these diseases in each country.

Disease transmission: With a group of five to eight people choose one daily activity that you will act out. This could be going to the grocery store, going through the lunch line at school, playing a game, or going out to dinner. Assign each person a role in the activity. Choose one player who will be infected with a contagious disease, such as influenza. Coat that person's hands with flour. Act out the scene as realistically as possible. At the end of the scene, note how many other players have flour on themselves and how many places the ill person left his or her germs.

Diabetic diet: Research the dietary requirements of a person with diabetes. Keep a food diary for two days, recording everything you eat. Examine how your eating habits would have to change if you had diabetes. What foods couldn't you have eaten? What might you have to eat more of?

AIDS risk factors: What are some of the myths about the transmission of AIDS? Choose five activities sometimes incorrectly thought to be risk factors for contracting AIDS. For each myth give the scientific reasons that the activity does not put one at risk of contracting AIDS.

The following Web sites offer many more research and activity ideas as well as interactive activities for students:

The American Museum of Natural History: Infection, Detection, Protection. http://www.amnh.org/explore/infection/smp_index.html

Cool Science for Curious Kids. http://www.hhmi.org/coolscience/

The Gateway to Educational Materials. http://thegateway.org/index1/SubjectIndex.html#health

Newton's Apple®. http://ericir.syr.edu/Projects/Newton/index.html

The University of Arizona. The Biology Project: An Online Interactive Resource for Learning Biology. http://www.biology.arizona.edu/

WNET School. http://www.wnet.rog/wnetschool

SICK!

*Diseases and
Disorders,
Injuries and
Infections*

RABIES

DEFINITION

Rabies is a rare but serious disease caused by a virus. The virus that causes rabies is carried in saliva. It is transmitted when an infected animal bites another animal. Rabies affects humans and other mammals.

Another name for rabies is hydrophobia (pronounced HI-dro-fo-bee-uh). Hydrophobia means "fear of water." About half the people infected with rabies develop this symptom. Other symptoms include fever; depression; confusion; painful muscle spasms; sensitivity to touch, loud noise, and light; extreme thirst; painful swallowing; excessive salivation; and loss of muscle quality. Rabies can be prevented and treated by immunization (a protective treatment that causes the body's immune system to build up resistance to a particular disease; usually given as a shot). Without treatment, however, a person who is infected with rabies will almost certainly die.

DESCRIPTION

Worldwide, approximately fifteen thousand cases of human rabies occur each year. Remarkably, although more than one million persons in the United States are bitten each year by animals, only one or two die of rabies each year. Nonetheless, rabies is likely to remain a public-health problem in the future. Humans are continually moving into lands occupied by wild animals. As they do, they run the risk of being bitten by an animal with rabies.

Both domestic and wild animals can transmit rabies. At one time, domestic animals, such as cats and dogs, were the main source of rabies bites in the United States. In 1955, 47 percent of all reported rabies cases were caused by dog bites.

That situation has changed. Most cities, towns, and counties now require that dogs be vaccinated for rabies. The number of dogs infected with the virus has dropped dramatically. In 1994, fewer than 2 percent of all dogs tested positive for the rabies virus. Today, the vast majority of rabies cases in humans are caused by bites from wild animals, such as bats, raccoons, skunks, foxes, wolves, and coyotes.

Anyone who has been bitten by an animal can contract rabies. Age and sex make no difference in people's chances of getting the disease. However, people who work in certain occupations are at higher risk for rabies than the general public. These populations include farm and ranch workers, animal trainers and caretakers, forest rangers, animal exterminators, and veterinarians. People in these occupations often handle wild animals or domestic animals that may not have been vaccinated.

CAUSES

Rabies is caused by a virus that belongs to the family Rhabdoviridae. The virus is usually transmitted by way of an animal bite. The virus is present in the saliva of an infected animal. When an infected animal bites another animal, the virus in its saliva may flow into the second animal's bloodstream. The second animal becomes infected with the virus.

On rare occasions, the rabies virus can be transmitted in other ways. It can enter an animal's body through moist tissues around the eyes or lips or through a scratch in the skin. Some scientists believe the virus can even be inhaled. For example, the air in a cave occupied by bats may contain high levels of the rabies virus. A person who walks through the cave may breathe in some of the virus.

Once it enters the body, the rabies virus travels to the nerves branching from the spinal cord and brain. It also travels to the salivary glands. The virus may lie dormant for several weeks or months. In its dormant stage, the virus is still alive, but it does not attack the body or produce any symptoms. It may continue to reproduce and spread through the body in its dormant stage. The only sign of a rabies infection at first may be a burning or painful sensation around the bite wound.

WORDS TO KNOW

Antibody: A protein produced by the immune system in response to a specific foreign substance that enters the body.

Biopsy: A procedure by which a small sample of tissue is removed and studied for the purpose of diagnosis.

Lumbar puncture: A procedure in which a long, thin needle is inserted between the vertebrae in a person's spine in order to remove a sample of cerebrospinal fluid.

Rhabdovirus: The virus that causes rabies.

SYMPTOMS

Eventually, early symptoms of rabies begin to appear. These symptoms include a sore throat, low-grade fever (above normal, but in the lower ranges), headache, loss of appetite, nausea and vomiting, and diarrhea. Painful spasms (contractions) may develop in the muscles that control breathing and swallowing. The infected person may begin to drool thick saliva. Other symptoms include dilated (enlarged) pupils, increased flow of tears and perspiration, and low blood pressure.

As the disease progresses the patient may begin to feel excited, confused, and sensitive to bright lights, loud noises, and touch. He or she becomes very thirsty but is unable to drink because swallowing is so painful. Just looking at water can cause painful spasms. It is this reaction that accounts for the name hydrophobia. Other severe symptoms include excessive salivation, dehydration, and loss of muscle tone (quality). Death usually occurs three to twenty days after symptoms first appear. Once a person or animal has developed rabies, recovery is very rare.

DIAGNOSIS

A doctor who sees these symptoms will order tests to confirm the diagnosis. One test is called a lumbar puncture or spinal tap. A lumbar puncture is a procedure in which a long, thin needle is inserted between the vertebrae in a person's spinal cord. A sample of the fluid surrounding the vertebrae is removed. This fluid is called cerebrospinal fluid (CSF). A lumbar puncture is important because it rules out other possible causes of the patient's symptoms.

Tests can also be performed to detect the virus or antibodies produced by the body against the virus. Antibodies are chemicals produced by the immune system. They are manufactured when some kind of foreign substance enters the body. A different kind of antibody is produced for each different foreign substance. If the rabies virus is present, the immune system will have produced a very specific kind of antibody.

Some tests can detect the virus itself. For example, a small amount of liquid material in the cornea of the eye can be collected on a slide. The liquid can then be examined under a microscope. If the rabies virus is present in the body, it can be seen under a microscope.

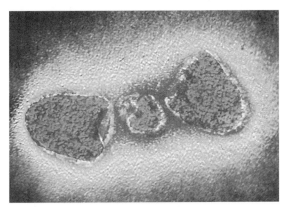

Rabies virus as seen through a microscope. (Reproduced by permission of Custom Medical Stock Photo)

TREATMENT

Any animal bite should be treated first with standard cleansing procedures. The wound should be washed thoroughly with medical soap and water. Antibiotics and tetanus injections (see tetanus entry) are usually given as well. These injections protect against bacterial infections.

The most important aspect of treatment is deciding whether a rabies immunization should be given. In some cases, the bite may have come from a domestic animal, such as a dog or a cat. If the animal is caught, it is placed in seclusion and observed. If the animal shows no signs of rabies in four to seven days, it is probably not rabid (not infected with rabies). The person who was bitten does not need a rabies immunization. If there is doubt as to whether the animal is rabid, it is killed. Its brain can then be examined to see if the rabies virus is present.

Sometimes the animal is not caught. In that case, a doctor has to decide whether to give the person who was bitten an immunization. That decision is usually based on how common rabies is in the area. If the disease is very rare, an immunization may not be necessary. If rabies is fairly common, an immunization will probably be given.

A rabies immunization usually consists of two parts. One part consists of injecting the patient with rabies antibodies taken from a person who has already been immunized. These antibodies will be of some help in destroying the rabies virus in the infected person's body. This part of the immunization process is given once, at the beginning of the treatment.

The second part of the immunization consists of injecting the patient with dead rabies viruses. These viruses will cause the patient's body to start manufacturing antibodies of its own without causing infection because they are dead. This part of the rabies immunization is given in a series of five injections, usually given one, three, seven, fourteen, and twenty-eight days after the animal bite. If successful, the antibodies from these two different sources will fight off the rabies infection.

Until the 1970s the rabies vaccination was a painful and frightening procedure that consisted of between fourteen and twenty-one shots that had to be given in the abdomen. Today the vaccine is given in the arm muscle, like a flu or tetanus shot.

UNTIL THE 1970S THE RABIES VACCINATION WAS A PAINFUL AND FRIGHTENING PROCEDURE THAT CONSISTED OF BETWEEN FOURTEEN AND TWENTY-ONE SHOTS GIVEN IN THE ABDOMEN.

Sometimes it may be too late to start immunizations. In that case, the main goal of treatment is to relieve the symptoms of the disease. For example, pain relievers can be given for painful muscle spasms. Other forms of medication can prevent seizures and relieve a person's anxiety. In the late stages of the disease, a patient may need mechanical devices to aid with breathing and heart function. Survival in such cases is rare but not unheard of.

PROGNOSIS

The key to successful treatment of rabies is timing. An infected person must begin a series of immunizations as soon as possible after being bitten. If immunizations begin within two days of the bite, chances of survival are very good. Even if the immunizations do not begin until later, there is a chance that the patient can survive. The longer the delay in starting immunizations, however, the less hopeful the prognosis for recovery is. Without immunizations, a patient will almost certainly die of the disease.

PREVENTION

Rabies can be prevented to a large extent by following some simple rules. These rules govern the way people interact with domestic and wild animals. They include:

- Domesticated animals, including household pets, should be vaccinated against rabies on a regular basis.
- Wild animals should not be touched or petted. Even if they seem friendly, they should be avoided. Special care should be taken with animals that behave strangely. For example, an animal may seem to have no fear of humans. Or animals that are normally out only at night may show up during the day. Such behaviors may be symptoms of rabies.
- Do not interfere in fights between animals.
- Use extra caution in handling a pet that has come into contact with a wild animal. Wear rubber gloves with the pet until you are sure that it has not been infected with rabies.
- Windows and doors should be covered with screens. Animals sometimes enter a building through unprotected openings. People have been bitten by rabid animals that got into their houses by this route.
- Citizens can become informed about the frequency of rabies in an area by calling the local health department.
- People who work with domestic or wild animals should be vaccinated against rabies.
- Bites from mice, rats, and squirrels rarely transmit rabies. Small animals like these that are bitten by a larger rabid animal usually die. Therefore, they are not likely to carry the disease.
- Ask about the prevalence of rabies in new areas to which you might be traveling.

FOR MORE INFORMATION

Books

Cockrum, E. Lendell. *Rabies, Lyme Disease, Hanta Virus, and Other Animal-Borne Human Diseases in the United States and Canada.* Tucson, AZ: Fisher Books, 1997.

Finley, Don. *Mad Dogs: The New Rabies Plague.* Texas Station: Texas A&M University Press, 1998.

Silverstein, Alvin, Virginia Silverstein, and Robert Silverstein. *Rabies.* Hillside, NJ: Enslow Publishers, Inc., 1994.

Web sites

Rabies.com. [Online] http://www.rabies.com (accessed on October 31, 1999).

"Rabies—What You Need To Know." [Online] http://www.cfainc.org/articles/rabies.html (accessed on October 31, 1999).

"Rabies." *Who Information Fact Sheets.* [Online] http://www.who.int/inffs/en/fact099.html (accessed on October 31, 1999).

RADIATION INJURIES

DEFINITION

Radiation injuries are damage to the body caused by ionizing radiation. Ionizing radiation (IR) is given off by the sun, X-ray machines, and radioactive elements.

DESCRIPTION

The word radiation comes from a Latin term that means "ray of light." It is used in a general sense to cover all forms of energy that travel through space from one place to another as "rays." Some forms of radiation are relatively harmless, like radio waves. Some forms of radiation carry a tremendous amount of energy and cause damage when they come into contact with other materials.

These high energy forms of radiation cause damage to substances by tearing apart the atoms and molecules that make up the substances. This may cause materials to undergo harmful changes. For example, an X ray that passes through water can tear the molecules of water apart. An X ray that passes through a living cell can also damage the cell by tearing apart the chemicals that make up the cell. The cell may be badly injured or killed.

Any form of radiation that can tear atoms and molecules apart is called ionizing radiation (IR). Damage to the body caused by IR is known as radiation injury. Ionizing radiation can come in the form electromagnetic waves or subatomic particles.

Electromagnetic Waves

Radio and television signals, radar, heat, infrared and ultraviolet radiation, sunlight, starlight, gamma rays, cosmic rays, and X rays are all forms of electromagnetic radiation (ER). All forms of electromagnetic radiation travel in the form of waves at the speed of light (182,282 miles per second, 299,727 kilometers per second). Because ER travels in waves, its energy can be expressed in terms of wavelengths. Types of ER differ with regard to wavelength. The higher the energy wave, the shorter its wavelength. Types of ER also differ from one another with regard to their frequency. The frequency of a wave is the rate at which it vibrates in space.

X rays, gamma rays, and cosmic rays all have very high frequencies and short wavelengths. They vibrate very rapidly—many billions of times per second—in space. Radio and television signals and radar all have very low frequencies and long wavelengths. They vibrate quite slowly in space.

Waves that vibrate rapidly (have high frequencies) are carry more energy and can cause damage to substances by tearing apart the atoms and molecules that make up the substances.

Particulate Radiation

Radioactive elements also give off forms of radiation similar to electromagnetic radiation, but it is given off in sprays of subatomic particles. These

WORDS TO KNOW

Bone marrow: Tissue found in the center of bones from which all types of blood cells are formed.

Electromagnetic radiation (ER): Radiation that travels as waves at the speed of light.

Frequency: The rate at which a wave vibrates in space.

Gray (Gy): A unit used to measure the amount of damage done to tissue by ionizing radiation.

Ionizing radiation (IR): Any form of radiation that can break apart atoms and molecules and cause damage to materials.

Rad: An older unit used to measure the amount of damage done to tissue by ionizing radiation, now replaced by the gray.

Radiation: Energy transmitted in the form of electromagnetic waves or subatomic particles.

Radioactive element: An element that gives off some form of radiation and breaks down into a different element or a different form of the same element.

Rem: An older unit used to measure the amount of damage done to tissue by ionizing radiation, now replaced by the sievert.

Sievert (Sv): A unit used to measure the amount of damage done to tissue by ionizing radiation.

particles may be produced intentionally in machines know as particle accelerators (atom-smashers) or they may be given off spontaneously by naturally occurring radioactive materials such as uranium 235 and radium 226. These forms of radiation can also cause damage to atoms and molecules.

Measuring Damage

There are two units used to measure the damage done to tissue by ionizing radiation. Those units were once called the rad and the rem. They have now been given new names, the gray (Gy) and the sievert (Sv). These units are very similar to, but not exactly the same as, each other.`

The damage IR causes to a body can range from very mild to very severe. The damage depends on a number of factors, including the kind of radiation, how close the person is to the source of radiation, and how long the person was exposed to the radiation. In mild cases, a radiation injury may be no more serious than a mild sunburn. In the most serious cases, radiation injury can cause death within a matter of hours.

Humans are exposed to ionizing radiation from a variety of sources. These sources fall into four general categories: natural, intentional, accidental, and therapeutic. Natural sources include sunlight and cosmic radiation. Sunlight includes not only visible light, which has relatively few health effects, and radiation of higher frequency, such as ultraviolet radiation. Just stepping outdoors exposes a person to IR in sunlight.

Cosmic rays are similar to sunlight in that they are always present around us. They are not visible, but they do contain ionizing radiation. Exposure to natural sources of IR account for a very small fraction of radiation injuries.

Intentional exposure to IR is rare. It occurs when nuclear weapons (hydrogen and atomic bombs) are used as weapons of war. This has occurred only twice in history, when the United States dropped atomic bombs on Hiroshima and Nagasaki, Japan, at the end of World War II. Many thousands of people were killed or injured by these attacks. They are the only people ever to have been injured by intentional exposure to IR.

Accidental exposure occurs when a person is exposed to IR by mistake. For example, radioactive elements are sometimes spilled in a research laboratory. Workers in the lab may be exposed to the IR from those elements.

Accidental exposure to IR has caused a number of radiation injuries and deaths. Between 1945 and 1987, there were 285 nuclear reactor accidents worldwide. More than fifteen hundred people were injured and sixty-four were killed in these accidents.

Therapeutic exposure to IR occurs during various medical procedures. Radioactive elements and ionizing radiation have many valuable applications in diagnosing and treating disorders. But those treatments can have harmful as well as beneficial effects on patients. The rate of radiation injuries due to this cause probably cannot be measured. Many people who may have been injured by a radiation treatment probably died of the condition for which they were being treated.

CAUSES

Radiation causes damage because it destroys chemicals in a cell. The cell loses its ability to function normally and dies.

Cells in tissues that are growing rapidly are more sensitive to radiation. For example, bone marrow cells in the center part of a bone are the fastest-

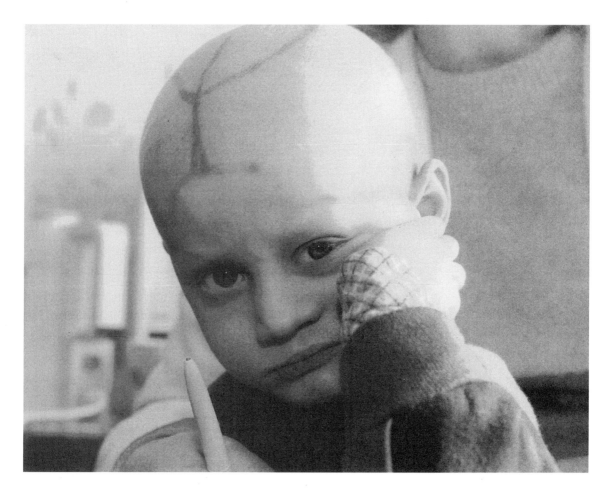

Five-year-old Alec Zhloba from a town in Belarus is suffering from leukemia. Some 70 percent of the fallout from the 1986 Chernobyl disaster fell on Belarus. (Reproduced by permission of AP/Wide World Photos)

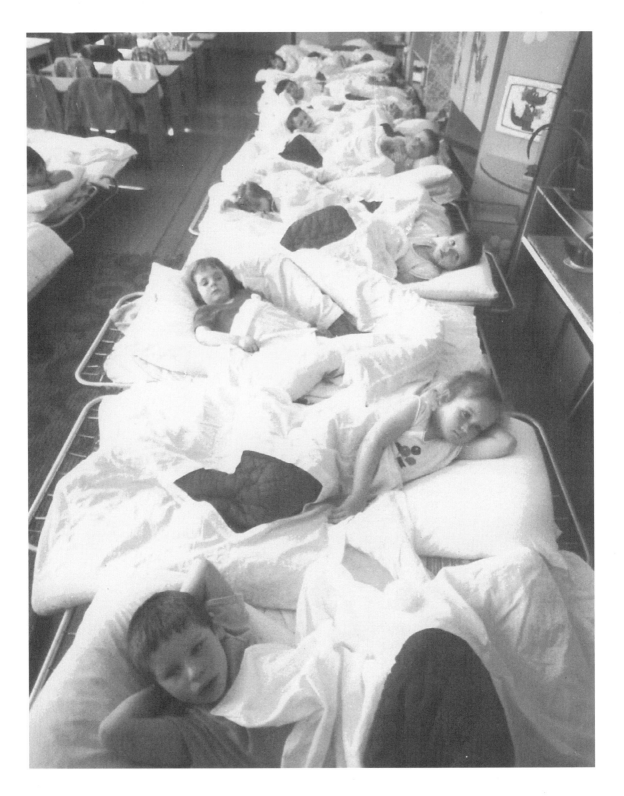

growing cells in the body. They are the most sensitive of all body cells to IR. The cells of a fetus are also growing very rapidly. They are also at high risk for damage from IR.

The sensitivity of various types of cells is shown below. The dose given in each case is the lowest amount of radiation that cells in the tissue can absorb without being damaged:

- Fetus: 2 Gy
- Bone marrow: 2 Gy
- Ovaries: 2–3 Gy
- Lens of the eye: 5 Gy
- A child's bone: 20 Gy
- An adult's bone: 60 Gy
- A child's muscle: 20–30 Gy
- An adult's muscle: 100 or more Gy

SYMPTOMS

A great deal of research was conducted on people who survived the atomic bomb explosions in Japan in 1945. From that research, we know what effect large doses of IR have on people. Those effects include:

- 1–2 Sv: Vomiting, loss of appetite, and generalized discomfort. These symptoms usually disappear in a short time.
- 2–6 Sv: Good chance for survival, provided the patient is given blood transfusions and antibiotics.
- 6–10 Sv: Massive destruction of bone marrow. If bone marrow is destroyed, the body cannot produce new blood cells. The patient usually dies in less than two months from infection or uncontrolled bleeding.
- 10–20 Sv: Destruction of intestinal tissue, causing serious digestive problems. The patient usually dies within three months from vomiting, diarrhea, infection, and starvation.
- More than 20 Sv: Massive damage to the nervous system and the circulatory (heart and blood vessels) system. The patient usually dies within a few days.

The most severe symptoms are very rare. They have been seen only in atomic bomb blasts and the most serious nuclear power plant accidents.

Far more commonly, doctors see symptoms of exposure to much lower levels of radiation. These symptoms most often appear in the form of cancer.

Opposite: These children live in a village not far from the Chernobyl nuclear plant. Four years after the 1986 Chernobyl accident, these children are suffering intestinal problems from exposure to radiation. (Reproduced by permission of AP/Wide World Photos)

Cancers (see cancer entry) develop when the number of cells damaged by IR gradually increases over time. Cells begin to grow out of control and spread throughout the body. Ionizing radiation is believed to be responsible for about 3 percent of all human cancers. The most common forms of cancer caused by IR are leukemia and cancers of the thyroid, brain, bone, breast, skin, stomach, and lungs (see breast cancer, leukemia, lung cancer, and skin cancer entries).

TREATMENT

Patients who have received more than about 10 Sv of radiation are unlikely to survive. No treatment is available for people in this group.

Patients who receive very low doses of IR are most likely to develop some form of cancer. When the cancer has developed, it is treated by the techniques usually used for cancers, such as chemotherapy, radiation, and surgery.

Patients who are exposed to about 1 to 6 Sv can benefit from medical treatment. One step usually involves the use of antibiotics to protect the patient against infection. The patient may also require a blood transfusion. In some cases, superficial damage to the skin can be treated with surgery. The damaged portion of skin is removed and replaced with a skin graft.

Alternative Treatment

There is much current interest in helpful chemicals called "free radical scavengers." It is not yet known how they work, but studies strongly suggest that diets full of free radical scavengers are beneficial. Free radical scavengers are also called antioxidants and include beta-carotene, vitamins E and C, and selenium. Beta-carotene is present in yellow and orange fruits and vegetables. Vitamin C is found in citrus fruits such as oranges.

Traditional Chinese medicine, acupuncture, and herbal medicines may help in recovery from radiation injuries.

CHERNOBYL

Nuclear power plants are normally constructed with very high levels of safety in mind and there is little or no evidence that humans are at risk as the result of the normal operation of a nuclear power plant. When damage occurs at the plant, however, the situation changes dramatically.

One such accident occurred in April 26, 1986, at the Chernobyl Plant outside Kiev in Ukraine in 1986. This was the most serious accident at a nuclear plant that the world has seen so far. The accident occured when an improperly conducted experiment in one of the reactors caused an explosion. The explosion blew off the top of the reactor, releasing 100 million curies of radionuclides into the atmosphere. More than thirty people who were at the site of the reactor when it exploded died immediately or shortly after the accident.

An area around the site with a 30-mile radius was evacuated. Since the accident doctors have found a striking increase of thyroid cancer among people, especially children, living in contaminated regions in Ukraine and Belarus.

PROGNOSIS

The prognosis for radiation injuries depends strongly on the amount of IR received by the patient. People who have been exposed to more than 10 Sv stand little or no chance of survival. People who have received a dose of 1 to 10 Sv may survive, provided they receive prompt treatment with antibiotics and blood transfusions, where needed. People who develop cancers as the result of low exposure to radiation have the same prognosis as those who develop the same cancers for other reasons.

PREVENTION

There is no way to protect against radiation injuries caused by natural radiation. Some natural radiation reaches us even if we never leave our homes. Injuries caused by intentional exposure can be prevented, of course, by avoiding the use of nuclear weapons, such as atomic and hydrogen bombs.

Accidental exposure to radiation is difficult to avoid. Facilities where radiation is present, as in nuclear power plants, have developed safety measures to protect workers against exposure to IR. In most cases, these measures are very effective. However, it is impossible to prevent all accidents. When those accidents occur, some workers are likely to be exposed to IR and develop radiation injuries.

Exposure to IR during therapeutic procedures can always be avoided. A person can choose not to have the procedure, thereby avoiding exposure to the radiation. But in the vast majority of cases, the potential benefits of the procedure are greater than the potential risks. People choose to be treated with radiation because it is likely to help them get better or live longer. The careful use of equipment to protect healthy parts of the body is probably the best guarantee against radiation injuries due to therapeutic procedures.

FOR MORE INFORMATION

Books

Lebaron, Wayne. *Preparation for Nuclear Disaster.* Commack, NY: Nova Science Publishers, Inc., 1998.

Murphy, Jack, et al. *Nuclear Medicine.* New York: Chelsea House Publishers, 1993.

Web sites

"Radiation Injuries." [Online] http://www.ohsu.edu/cliniweb/C21C21.866 .733.html (accessed on October 31, 1999).

REYE'S SYNDROME

DEFINITION

Reye's syndrome is a disorder that primarily affects the liver and brain. It attacks the nervous system very quickly and can cause death.

DESCRIPTION

Reye's syndrome primarily affects children and teenagers. In almost all cases, it follows a viral illness, such as a cold (see common cold entry), the flu (see influenza entry), or chickenpox (see chickenpox entry). The disorder can affect any organ in the body, but its most serious effects occur in the brain and the liver. As the disorder develops, it attacks the body's nervous system. It produces symptoms such as listlessness, confusion, seizures, and coma. In extreme cases, it can lead to death.

Reye's syndrome is a rare disorder. It was first discovered in the early 1970s. The number of cases of Reye's syndrome rose slowly until 1980. In that year, 555 cases of the disorder were diagnosed. Researchers had learned at that point that children who are given aspirin are at risk for Reye's syndrome. Doctors began to warn parents against the use of aspirin with sick children. As a result of those warnings, the number of cases of Reye's syndrome began to fall. By the late 1990s the condition was very rare in the United States.

Reye's syndrome is sometimes confused with other nervous-system disorders. The reason for this confusion is that many doctors have never seen a case of Reye's syndrome. They may diagnose a patient with encephalitis, diabetes, poisoning, or some other condition by mistake. The actual number of cases of Reye's syndrome may therefore be somewhat higher than the official total.

WORDS TO KNOW

Acetylsalicylic acid: The chemical name for the primary compound from which aspirin is made. Shorthand terms for acetylsalicylic acid include acetylsalicylate, salicylic acid, and salicylate.

Encephalitis: An infection of the brain, also known as "brain fever."

Enzymes: Chemicals present in all cells that make possible the biological reactions needed to keep a cell alive.

Hyperventilation: Deep, heavy breathing.

CAUSES

The cause of Reye's syndrome is not known. What researchers do know is that the disorder usually appears after a viral infection in the upper respiratory (breathing) system.

One important fact researchers have discovered is the role of aspirin in Reye's syndrome. They have learned that people who take aspirin to treat the viral infection are at greater risk for Reye's syndrome. For that reason, aspirin is no longer recommended for children under the age of nineteen who have a fever.

SYMPTOMS

Whatever the cause, Reye's syndrome is accompanied by two kinds of effects on the body. First, there is a buildup of fats in body organs, especially the liver. These fats interfere with the normal operation of the organ. They may cause it to shut down.

Second, fluids begin to accumulate in the brain. These fluids push on blood vessels in the brain. The pressure may become so great that blood can no longer flow into the brain. If the brain can no longer function death will result.

The symptoms of Reye's syndrome appear after a viral infection—after the original viral infection has gotten better. The patient may think that the original disease is over. But new symptoms then appear quite suddenly. The first of these symptoms is violent vomiting. This may be followed by a state of quietness, lethargy, agitation, seizures, and coma. In infants, diarrhea may be more common than vomiting. Fever is usually absent at this point.

DIAGNOSIS

Diagnosis of Reye's syndrome is often based on the patient's pattern of illness. The patient may have been ill with a viral disease and then gotten better. If the symptoms described above then suddenly appear, Reye's syndrome may be suspected.

Confirmation of this diagnosis can be made with a blood test. The test is designed to look for certain liver enzymes. Enzymes are chemicals in the body that change the rate at which reactions take place in cells. When an organ is diseased, the number of enzymes present may increase dramatically. The blood test for Reye's syndrome involves measuring changes in liver enzymes.

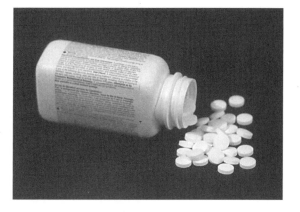

TREATMENT

Reye's syndrome is a life-threatening emergency. It requires immediate medical attention.

Children under the age of nineteen who take aspirin to treat a viral infection have an increased risk of contracting Reye's syndrome. (Photograph by Robert Huffman. Reproduced by permission of Field Mark Publications.)

The likelihood of recovery is best if the condition is recognized and treated promptly.

The first two steps in treatment are usually an intravenous (into the bloodstream) feeding of sugar and a blood transfusion. These steps help the body recover some of its normal functions. Pressure in the brain is carefully monitored. If it becomes too high, hyperventilation may be needed. Hyperventilation is any process by which the patient is made to breathe more rapidly. The process helps tighten blood vessels in the brain, releasing pressure on the brain.

PROGNOSIS

The death rate for Reye's syndrome is between 30 percent and 50 percent. The chance of recovery can be as high as 90 percent if the disorder is recognized and treated early. Almost all children who survive Reye's syndrome recover fully. However, recovery may take a long time. Some patients who recover experience permanent damage to the nervous system. These patients may require special physical and/or educational services and equipment.

PREVENTION

Since the cause of Reye's syndrome is not known, there is no certain way to prevent the condition. The best advice seems to be to avoid giving aspirin to children. Aspirin appears to be associated with many cases of Reye's syndrome. Many products contain aspirin even if that name is not used. Other names that indicate the presence of aspirin in a product include:

- Acetylsalicylate
- Acetylsalicylic acid
- Salicylic acid
- Salicylate

Children who require medication for fever or pain should take other, non-aspirin products, such as acetaminophen (pronounced uh-SEE-tuh-MIN-uh-fin, trade name Tylenol) or ibuprofen (pronounced I-byoo-pro-fen, trade names Motrin, Advil).

FOR MORE INFORMATION

Organizations

National Reye's Syndrome Foundation. PO Box 829, Bryan, OH 43506–0829. (800) 233–7393. reyessyn@mail.bright.net.

Web sites

"Childhood Infections—Reye's Syndrome." *Kidshealth.org.* [Online] http://kidshealth.org/parent/common/reye.html.

"Reye's Syndrome." [Online] http://www.ama-assn.org/insight/h_focus/nemours/infectio/childhd/reyes.htm.

"Reye's Syndrome." [Online] http://gi.ucsf.edu/alf/info/inforeyes.html.

RHEUMATIC FEVER

DEFINITION

Rheumatic fever (RF; pronounced roo-MAT-ic FEE-ver) is a disease caused by a group of bacteria known as Group A streptococcus (pronounced STREP-tuh-cac-us). The exact conditions that lead to rheumatic fever are not well understood. However, the condition often follows a case of strep throat that was not treated or not treated correctly. Rheumatic fever can seriously damage the valves of the heart.

DESCRIPTION

Streptococcal infections of the throat and ear are common in young children. These infections can be treated efficiently with antibiotics. When so treated, the infections clear up in about a week. Patients seldom experience complications.

Some streptococcal infections are very mild, however. Children may experience no symptoms, so their parents do not seek medical advice. Also, patients sometimes do not take their full course of medication. They stop taking pills when their symptoms are gone. But streptococcal bacteria may still be present. In either of these cases, complications may develop. One of the most serious complications is rheumatic fever.

Children between the ages of five and fifteen are at greatest risk for RF. The rate of RF in the United States has dropped dramatically. Today, it is rarely seen in this country. It continues to be widespread in developing nations, however. Poverty, overcrowding, and lack of access to proper medical care contribute to the high rate of RF in these areas.

CAUSES

There is still some debate as to how rheumatic fever develops. The most popular theory is that the condition is caused by the body's own immune system. The immune system consists of organs, tissues, cells, and chemicals designed to attack foreign invaders, such as bacteria or viruses. One way the immune system protects the body is with antibodies. Antibodies are chemicals produced to fight off specific foreign agents. There is a specific type of antibody, for example, for every bacterium and virus that can invade the human body.

But the immune system sometimes makes mistakes and produces antibodies that attack the body's own cells. The antibodies kill cells and cause a type of disease known as an autoimmune ("against itself") disorder. Rheumatic fever is thought to be an autoimmune disorder (see autoimmune disorder entry).

SYMPTOMS

In addition to fever, there are five main symptoms of RF. One symptom is arthritis (see arthritis entry). Arthritis is an inflammation of the joints that causes severe pain and swelling. In the case of RF, arthritis produces red, hot, swollen, shiny, and very painful joints of the ankles, knees, elbows, and wrists. The joints may become so sore that even the touch of bed sheets or clothing is too painful to endure.

A second symptom of RF is chorea (pronounced co-REE-uh). Chorea is a disorder of the nervous system. It causes a patient to lose coordination and develop jerky movements of the arms and legs. The patient may also develop emotional problems. He or she may become angry or sad for no reason at all. The chorea that occurs as a result of RF is called Syndenham's chorea. At one time, the condition was known as St. Vitus's Dance.

A third symptom of RF is a rash. The rash consists of pink splotches on the body that are not itchy. The medical term for this rash is erythema marginatum (pronounced air-uh-THEE-muh MAR-gin-ay-tum). Along with the rash there may be small bumps just under the skin. The bumps are hard to the touch but not painful. They occur most commonly over the knee and elbow joints. The bumps constitute the fourth symptom of RF. They are also known as subcutaneous nodules (pronounced sub-CYOO-tayn-ee-us NOD-yools).

The fifth and most serious symptom of rheumatic fever is called carditis (pronounced

WORDS TO KNOW

Antibodies: Chemicals produced by the body's immune system to fight off very specific foreign invaders, such as bacteria and viruses.

Arthritis: Inflammation of the joints.

Autoimmune disorder: A medical condition in which the body's immune system mistakes the body's own tissues for foreign invaders and attempts to destroy those tissues.

Carditis: Inflammation of the heart.

Chorea: Involuntary movements that may cause the arms or legs to jerk about uncontrollably.

Immune system: A system of organs, tissues, cells, and chemicals that work together to fight off foreign invaders, such as bacteria and viruses.

Inflammation: The body's response to tissue damage that includes heat, swelling, redness, and pain.

car-DIE-tis). The term "carditis" means an inflammation of the heart. About 40 percent to 80 percent of all patients with rheumatic fever develop carditis. It is the most serious complication associated with RF.

One common effect of carditis is damage to the heart valves. The heart valves are flaps of tissue that control the flow of blood in the heart. They ensure that blood always flows in the right direction as it passes through the heart.

If heart valves are damaged, one of two things can happen. First, the flow of blood reverses direction. Second, the valves become so stiff that it is difficult for blood to get through them. Either way, the heart has to work unusually hard to keep blood moving properly. In some cases, the heart has to work so hard that it becomes weakened or fails. The patient develops chronic (long-term) heart disease or dies of a heart attack.

DIAGNOSIS

Diagnosis of rheumatic fever can be difficult because patients may have one, two, or more of the five symptoms listed above. The five symptoms for which a doctor looks include arthritis, chorea, carditis, erythema marginatum, and subcutaneous nodules. Fever is also present. However, fever by itself is not of much use in making a diagnosis. Many kinds of medical disorders have fever as a symptom.

A number of laboratory tests are also used to diagnose RF. For example, a throat smear can be taken to look for the presence of streptococcal bacteria. In a throat smear, a cotton swab is rubbed across the back of the patient's

GERHARD DOMAGK

Gerhard Domagk was a German biochemist who was born on October 30, 1895. He earned his medical degree in 1921 and then took a job with a large company, *Farbenindustrie*. Farbenindustrie manufactured industrial dyes.

Domagk was interested in finding out whether any of the dyes produced by Farbenindustrie had biological effects on animals. In one study, he injected a dye called Prontosil Red into a group of experimental mice. The mice had been given a streptococcus infection. Domagk was amazed to discover that the mice were cured of their disease by the dye.

That discovery might have lead nowhere except for a terrible event in Domagk's life. His daughter Hildegarde pricked herself with a knitting needle and developed a streptococcal infection herself. In desperation, Domagk injected Prontosil Red into his daughter. Again, the dye seemed to work miracles. Hildegarde quickly recovered from the disease.

Shortly after these events, the French chemist Daniele Bovet explained how Prontosil Red works. He showed that only one part of the compound was involved in killing bacteria. That part was a molecule called *sulfanilamide*. Sulfanilamide was the first of a large group of related compounds, called sulfanamides (or "sulfa drugs") to be used against bacterial infections.

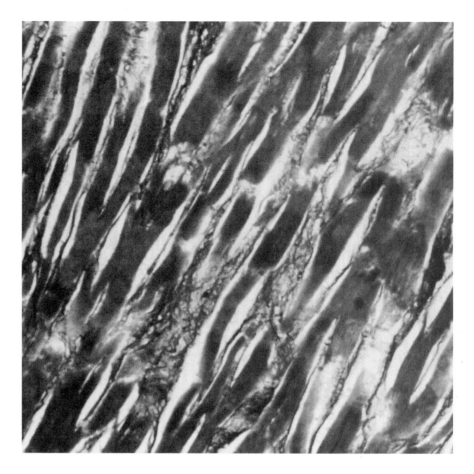

A magnified image of human cardiac muscle with chronic myocarditis. (© 1995 Astrid & Hanns-Frieder Michler/Science Photo Library. Reproduced by permission of Custom Medical Stock Photo.)

throat. The material collected on the swab is then placed in a warm, moist environment for twenty-four to seventy-two hours. Any bacteria present in the material begin to grow during that period. If streptococcal bacteria are present, they can be seen with a microscope.

Laboratory tests can also be used to look for antibodies to the streptococcal bacteria. Blood taken from the patient's arm can be treated with chemicals that make these antibodies show up. The presence of the antibodies means that the patient has been infected with the streptococcal bacteria.

An electrocardiogram (ECG; pronounced ih-LEK-tro-KAR-dee-o-gram) can also be used to diagnose RF. An electrocardiogram is a test that measures the electrical activity of the heart. If the heart has been damaged by carditis, its electrical rhythms will be different from those of a healthy heart.

All of these symptoms and tests taken together can provide a diagnosis of rheumatic fever.

TREATMENT

Rheumatic fever is usually treated with penicillin. The patient usually receives a single injection or a ten-day course of pills. Doctors often prescribe a regular dose of penicillin after the symptoms of RF disappear. This program helps prevent the return of RF. Other patients who continue to receive regular doses of penicillin are those individuals who may come into contact with the streptococcal bacterium. This group includes teachers and medical workers, as well as patients with known RF heart disease.

The symptoms of arthritis can be treated with aspirin, acetaminophen (Tylenol), or ibuprofen (Motrin, Advil). These same drugs can be used to treat mild cases of carditis. Aspirin should not be given to children with a fever because it may cause the serious illness Reye's syndrome (see Reye's syndrome entry). More severe cases of carditis are treated with steroid medications. Chorea is treated with a variety of sedatives and tranquilizers that help relax the patient.

PROGNOSIS

RF patients who do not develop carditis have an excellent prognosis. Other symptoms of the disease eventually disappear without complications. Even patients who have mild cases of carditis are likely to experience a full recovery. Severe cases of carditis are another matter. In this case, patients are likely to develop a variety of heart problems that may lead to heart failure. Serious heart problems can often be treated by surgery.

PREVENTION

Rheumatic fever can be prevented with early and proper diagnosis of streptococcal infections of the throat and ears. If antibiotics are given within ten days, the risk of the infection's developing into rheumatic fever is very low.

People who have had rheumatic fever are at risk for contracting the disease again. To prevent the condition from returning, a patient may have to stay on antibiotics for a long time—perhaps for life. People who already have heart damage resulting from RF can prevent further complications. The usual procedure is for the patient to take antibiotics any time he or she might be exposed to the streptococcal bacterium.

FOR MORE INFORMATION

Books

Stoffman, Phyllis. *The Family Guide to Preventing and Treating 100 Infectious Diseases.* New York: John Wiley and Sons, Inc. 1995.

Web sites

"Rheumatic Fever." *Yahoo! Health.* [Online] http://dir.yahoo.com/Health/Diseases_and_Conditions/Rheumatic_Fever (accessed on November 5, 1999).

"Rheumatic fever." *HealthAnswers Medical Reference Library.* [Online] http://www.healthanswers.com/adam/top/view.asp?filename=003940.htm&rdir (accessed on November 5, 1999).

RINGWORM

DEFINITION

Ringworm is a common infection with a misleading name. The disease is actually caused by a fungus, not a worm. There are many types of ringworm and each is caused by a different type of fungus.

DESCRIPTION

Ringworm gets its name from its appearance, not from the agent that causes it. The characteristic feature of ringworm is patches of rough, reddened skin. The patches often contain circular lesions (pronounced LEE-zhuns), open wounds, that look as if they were caused by tiny worms under the skin.

> RINGWORM GETS ITS NAME FROM ITS APPEARANCE, NOT FROM THE AGENT THAT CAUSES IT.

Over time, the lesions grow outward from their center. The center heals up and becomes hard and crusty. But the outer edges of the lesions become inflamed and spread outwards.

Types of Ringworm

The most common types of ringworm are often named for the part of the body on which they occur.

Body ringworm is also known as tinea corporis (pronounced tin-EE-uh KORE-pur-iss). It can affect any part of the body except the scalp, feet, and facial area where a man's beard grows. These areas are infected with other types of ringworm. Tinea corporis causes well-defined flaky sores. The sores can be dry and scaly or moist and crusty.

Scalp ringworm is called tinea capitis (pronounced tin-EE-uh KAP-ih-tiss). This type of ringworm is seen most commonly in children. It causes scaly, swollen blisters or a rash that looks like black dots. Scalp ringworm sometimes becomes inflamed and filled with pus. These areas can cause crusty, flaky, round bald patches. Scalp ringworm can cause scarring and permanent hair loss.

Ringworm of the groin is also called tinea cruris (pronounced tin-EE-uh KROOR-iss) or "jock itch." It causes raised red sores with well-marked edges. This type of ringworm can spread to the buttocks, inner thighs, and external genitalia.

Ringworm of the nails is also known as tinea unguium (pronounced tin-EE-uh UN-gwee-um). It usually starts at the tip of a toenail. The nail gradually becomes thicker and discolored. It may begin to die off and pull away from the nail bed. Infections of the fingernails are much less common.

Tinea pedis is ringworm of the feet and is more commonly known as athlete's foot (see athlete's foot entry).

CAUSES

The fungus that causes ringworm is spread from one person to another. Sometimes this happens through direct contact. An infected person may touch someone who does not have the disease and directly transfer the fungus to the second person.

At other times, the fungus is transferred indirectly. For example, people with ringworm may leave the fungus on towels, hairbrushes, or other objects. A second person may then pick up the fungus while handling these objects.

Certain conditions increase the risk of spreading the fungi (more than one fungus) that cause ringworm. These include dampness, humidity, and dirty, crowded living conditions.

SYMPTOMS

Symptoms of ringworm include inflammation and scaling of the infected area, along with itching.

WORDS TO KNOW

Fungus: A large group of organisms that includes mold, mildew, rust fungi, yeast, and mushrooms, some of which may cause disease in humans and other animals.

Lesion: A change in the structure or appearance of a part of the body as the result of an injury or infection.

Tinea corporis: Scientific name for body ringworm, a fungal infection of the skin that it can affect any part of the body except the scalp, feet, and facial area.

Tinea capitis: Scalp ringworm, a fungal infection of the scalp.

Tinea cruris; An fungal infection that affects the groin and can spread to the buttocks, inner thighs, and external genitalia; also called "jock itch."

Tinea unguium: Ringworm of the nails; a fungal infection that usually begins at the tip of a toenail.

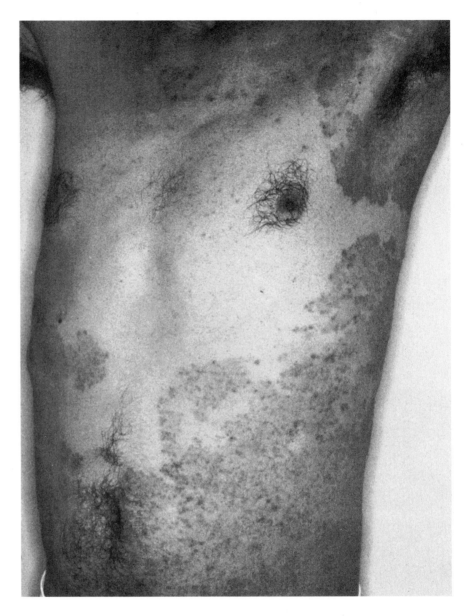

Body ringworm is also known as tinea corporis. The sores from the infection can be dry and scaly or moist and crusty. (Reproduced by permission of Custom Medical Stock

DIAGNOSIS

The various types of ringworm have distinctive appearances. A doctor or nurse will often suspect the disease simply from looking at a patient's skin. This preliminary diagnosis can be confirmed by taking scrapings of the infected skin. A small knife is used to scrape off a small amount of the infected material. The material can then be examined under a microscope where any fungi that may be present can be seen.

TREATMENT

Some cases of ringworm disappear without treatment. Other cases can be treated with various forms of medication. Some medications are applied directly to the infected skin in the form of powder or cream. Others must be taken orally (by mouth). Doctors recommend that medications be continued for two weeks after symptoms disappear. This precaution guarantees that all fungi are killed.

There are also specific treatments for each type of ringworm. These include:

- Body ringworm: Wear loose clothing and check daily for open sores. Apply wet dressings to those sores two to three times a day.
- Ringworm of the nails: Cut infected nails short and clear dead cells with an emery board.

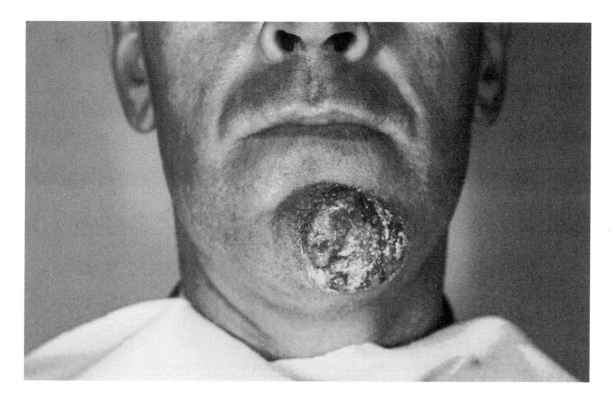

Ringworm on a man's chin. Ringworm infections are most common on the feet, scalp, on the body, or in toenails, but they can infect any part of the skin. (© 1989. Reproduced by Custom Medical Stock Photo.)

- Ringworm of the groin: Wear cotton underwear and change it more than once a day. Keep the infected area dry. Use antifungal powder and/or lotion.
- Scalp ringworm: Use antifungal shampoo containing selenium sulfide or a prescription shampoo.

Alternative Treatment

Both homeopathic and herbal remedies are recommended for the treatment of ringworm. Some homeopathic products suggested include sepia, tellurium, graphite, and sulfur.

Herbs recommended for the treatment of ringworm include tea tree oil, thuja, and lavender. Practitioners may recommend other herbs to improve the body's immune system in general. Echinacea and astragalus are the two herbs most commonly recommended for this purpose. Alternative practitioners also suggest a well-balanced diet that includes protein, complex carbohydrates, fresh fruits and vegetables, and good quality fats to strengthen the immune system.

PROGNOSIS

Ringworm infections usually clear up with treatment. However, they tend to reoccur. About one in five patients experience a chronic infection that reappears time and time again.

Once scalp ringworm has cleared up, new hair starts to grow back. It usually takes six to twelve months for new hair to cover bald patches. New fingernails also grow out to replace those lost to ringworm of the nails. Complete recovery usually takes three to twelve months. Infections of the toenail are among the most difficult of all ringworm infections to cure.

PREVENTION

The best way to avoid getting ringworm is to avoid coming into contact with the fungi that cause the disease. That means staying away from people who have ringworm. It also means not handling objects that may have been used by an infected patient.

See also: Athlete's foot.

FOR MORE INFORMATION

Books

Cummings, Stephen, and Dana Ullman. *Everyone's Guide to Homeopathic Medicine.* Los Angeles: Jeremy P. Tarcher, 1984.

Shaw, Michael. *Everything You Need to Know about Diseases.* Springhouse, PA: Springhouse Corporation, 1996.

Web sites

Athlete's Foot, Jock Itch and Ringworm. [Online] http://www.2.ccf.org/ed/ pated/kiosk/hinfo/docs/0039.htm (accessed on April 7, 1998).

"Ringworm." *Thriveonline.* [Online] http://www.thriveonline.com/health/ Library/pedillsymp/pedillsymp361.html (accessed on April 5, 1998).

Ringworm. [Online] http://www.yourhealth.com/ohl/1282/html (accessed April 7, 1998).

RUBELLA

DEFINITION

Rubella (pronounced roo-BELL-uh) is a highly contagious (catching) viral disease also known as German measles. It is spread through contact with discharges from the nose and throat of an infected person. The symptoms of the disease include swollen glands, joint pain, low fever, and a fine red rash. While relatively mild in most instances, Rubella can have serious complications for pregnant women and may cause a miscarriage (prematurely ended pregnancy) or severe birth defects in the infected woman's child.

DESCRIPTION

Rubella was once a common childhood disease. However, an effective vaccine (pronounced vak-SEEN) against the disease was invented in 1969. A vaccine is a material that causes the body's immune system to build up resistance to a particular disease. Over the next three decades the number of rubella cases dropped more than 99.6 percent. In 1996 only 229 cases of the disease were reported in the United States and public health officials hoped to eliminate the disease completely within a few years.

The virus that causes rubella is spread when an infected person coughs or sneezes, sending droplets of water containing the virus into the air. If these droplets come to rest on another person, the virus may enter the healthy person's body, causing that person to develop the disease.

Rubella has an incubation period of about twelve to twenty-three days. The incubation period is the time after a person is infected before the symptoms of the disease first appear. An infected person is contagious (can spread the disease) during a period of about seven days before the symptoms appear until four days after they appear.

Rubella is usually considered a childhood disease but people of any age can catch it if they have not been vaccinated. People who have been vaccinated are protected against the disease forever.

Rubella poses the greatest danger to pregnant women and their fetuses. Women who develop the disease during the first trimester (three months) of their pregnancy face a serious risk. The virus passes from an infected woman's body into the body of the fetus. The virus may cause a serious infection that can cause birth defects or even kill the fetus.

This risk is considered very low in the United States because most women in this country were vaccinated against rubella when they were children. However, in some parts of the world countries do not have the money or the medical facilities to vaccinate all children. Many girls still grow up unprotected against the disease and the risk it poses if they become pregnant.

CAUSES

Rubella is caused by a virus called *Rubivirus*.

WORDS TO KNOW

Antibody: A chemical produced by the body's immune system to fight off infections.

Incubation period: The time it takes for symptoms of a disease to appear after a person has been infected.

Miscarriage: When a human fetus is expelled from the mother before it can survive outside of the womb.

MMR vaccine: A vaccine that contains separate vaccines against three diseases: measles, mumps, and rubella.

Trimester: Three months. Often used to refer to one third of a woman's pregnancy.

Vaccine: a substance that causes the body's immune system to build up resistance to a particular disease.

SYMPTOMS

The first sign of rubella is a fine red rash on the face. The rash spreads across the whole body within twenty-four hours and lasts about three days. Because of this fact, rubella is sometimes called the three-day measles (see measles entry).

Other symptoms include swollen glands and a low fever. There may also be pain or swelling in the joints. Interestingly, some patients show no symptoms of the disease at all. Symptoms usually disappear after about three days. Some joint pain may remain for a week or two. Most people recover with no complications.

The one exception is pregnant women. If these women get rubella during the first three months of pregnancy, the health of their fetus is threatened. Birth defects occur in about half of all women who get rubella in the first month of pregnancy. The rate of birth defects drops to 20 percent in the second month and 10 percent in the third month.

Some birth defects caused by rubella include:

- Eye defects, such as cataracts (see cataract entry), glaucoma (see glaucoma entry), and blindness
- Deafness
- Heart defects
- Mental retardation (see mental retardation entry)

The risk of birth defects drops dramatically after the first trimester. After the twentieth week of pregnancy, there are rarely any complications caused by rubella.

DIAGNOSIS

The symptoms of rubella are similar to those of other diseases. A positive diagnosis can be made only with a blood test. The blood test is designed to look for antibodies to the rubella virus. An antibody is a chemical produced by the body's immune system to fight off infections. Each antibody is designed to attack a specific virus or bacterium. If antibodies to the *Rubivirus* are present, the person has been infected with the virus.

TREATMENT

There is no treatment for rubella. The disease runs its course in a short time. Bed rest and fluids may help the body heal itself. Painkillers, such as aspirin or acetaminophen, can be used to reduce any discomfort and fever. Aspirin should not be given to children because of the risk of Reye's syndrome (see Reye's syndrome entry).

Alternative Treatment

A number of alternative treatments have been suggested in order to make patients comfortable during the period they have rubella. These treatments include ginger tea or clove tea, which some people believe make the disease run its course faster. Other herbs suggested for the treatment of rubella symptoms include peppermint, cicada, witch hazel, and eyebright. Homeopathic practitioners may recommend *Belladonna, Pulsatilla,* or *Phytolacca.*

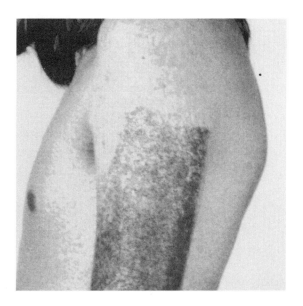

Rubella rash. (Reproduced by permission of Custom Medical Stock Photo)

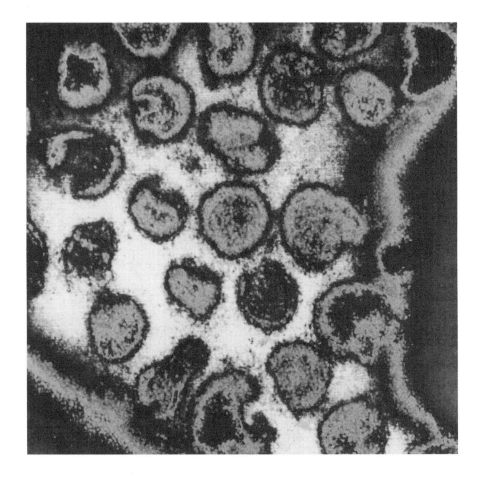

Rubella virus particles, magnified 300,000 times. (© 1994. Reproduced by permission of Custom Medical Stock Photo.)

PROGNOSIS

The vast majority of patients recover completely from rubella with no further complications. The greatest threat is to pregnant women in their first trimester (roughly the first three months of pregnancy). Fetuses carried by these women are at risk of being miscarried, stillborn, delivered with a low birth weight, or of developing birth defects.

PREVENTION

Vaccination is a safe and certain way to prevent rubella. Most school systems today require that children be vaccinated for rubella before entering school. The rubella vaccine is given in conjunction with vaccines for measles and mumps. The combined vaccine is known as the MMR vaccine. Children receive their first dose of MMR vaccine at the age of twelve to fifteen months and receive a second dose at between the ages of four and six years.

Women who intend to have children should be tested for the *Rubivirus* antibody. If they lack the antibody, they should be vaccinated against the disease. However, they should not be vaccinated after they have become pregnant.

FOR MORE INFORMATION

Books

Silverstein, Alvin, Virginia Silverstein, and Robert Silverstein. *Measles and Rubella*. Hillside, NJ: Enslow Publishers, Inc., 1997.

Organizations

March of Dimes Resource Center. 1275 Mamaroneck Ave., White Plains, NY 10605. (888) 663–4637. http://www.modimes.org.

National Organization of Rare Disorders. PO Box 8923, New Fairfield, CT 01812. (800) 999–6673. http://www.rarediseases.org.

SCARLET FEVER

DEFINITION

Scarlet fever is an infection caused by a bacterium called *Streptococcus* (pronounced strep-tuh-KOK-us). The disease is characterized by a sore throat (see sore throat entry), fever, and a sandpaper-like rash on reddened skin. It is primarily a childhood disease. If scarlet fever is not treated, serious complications, including rheumatic fever (a heart disease; see rheumatic fever entry) and inflammation of the kidney, can result.

DESCRIPTION

Scarlet fever gets its name from the appearance of the patient's skin, especially around the cheeks, which becomes red and flushed. Scarlet fever is accompanied by a sore throat, fever, sluggishness, and a raised rash over much of the body.

The fever that accompanies scarlet fever usually lasts only a few days. By the end of two weeks, the disease has usually run its course. At that point, skin begins to peel off. The most dramatic peeling occurs on the palms of the hands and the soles of the feet.

Scarlet fever primarily affects children ages two to ten. It is highly contagious and is spread by sneezing, coughing, or direct contact. The incubation period is three to five days. The incu-

WORDS TO KNOW

Antibiotic: A substance derived from bacteria or other organisms that fights the growth of other bacteria or organisms.

Streptococcus: A class of bacteria that causes a wide variety of infections including scarlet fever.

bation period is the time between infection and the first appearance of symptoms. The symptoms of scarlet fever usually last four to ten days.

At one time, scarlet fever was a very common disease, but it has since become quite rare. This is due in part to the availability of antibiotics that are able to kill off the infection. Some scientists believe another reason for the decline is that the organism that causes scarlet fever became weaker.

CAUSES

Scarlet fever is caused by an organism known as Group A streptococcal bacterium. Other organisms of this kind also cause sore throats, skin infections, pneumonia (see pneumonia entry), and serious kidney infections. The bacteria that cause scarlet fever produce a toxin (poison) that causes skin to turn red.

SYMPTOMS

The main symptoms of scarlet fever are fever, lethargy (sluggishness), sore throat, and a bumpy rash that turns white under pressure. The rash first appears on the upper chest then spreads to the neck, abdomen, legs, arms, armpits, and groin. The patient's cheeks become flushed, but the skin around the mouth tends to be pale. The patient usually has a "strawberry tongue." This name comes from the fact that there are inflamed bumps on the tongue on top of a bright red coating.

DIAGNOSIS

Diagnosis of scarlet fever also depends on eliminating other possible diseases with similar symptoms. For example, measles (see measles entry) has many of the same symptoms as scarlet fever. However, a scarlet fever rash looks quite different from a measles rash. Also, scarlet fever is usually accompanied by a sore throat, and measles is not.

Some symptoms of strep throat (see strep throat entry), such as a sore throat and fever, are also similar to those of scarlet fever. But the two diseases are easily distinguished from each other by the appearance of the sandpaper-like rash that is associated with scarlet fever.

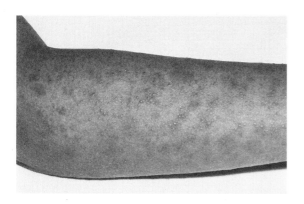

Scarlet fever rash is caused by a streptococcal infection. (Reproduced by permission of Custom Medical Stock Photo)

A doctor looks for the characteristic rash as well as the "strawberry tongue" (which only appears in children). If questions remain, laboratory tests can be used to make a final determination. Blood tests, for example, can distinguish between a bacterial infection (like scarlet fever) and a viral infection (like strep throat). A throat culture can also be used to do this.

A throat culture consists of a small amount of material taken from the patient's throat. with a cotton swab. The material is then allowed to grow in a warm place overnight before the culture is examined to determine whether the infection is caused by bacteria or a virus.

TREATMENT

Scarlet fever usually clears up on its own within a few days. However, treatment with antibiotics, such as penicillin, may be helpful. Antibiotics are substances derived from bacteria or other organisms that fight the growth of other bacteria or organisms. Antibiotics can reduce the severity of the symptoms, prevent complications, and prevent spreading the disease to others.

Penicillin is the drug of choice for treating scarlet fever. It can be injected or swallowed. For people allergic to penicillin, antibiotics such as erythromycin (pronounced ih-rith-ruh-MIS-in) or clindamycin (pronounced klin-duh-MI-sun) can be used as an alternative. As with all medications, the full course of treatment should be completed even if the patient seems well. Stopping a treatment too soon can result in complications such as rheumatic fever or kidney inflammation.

Bed rest is not necessary with scarlet fever, nor is isolation of the patient. Acetaminophen may be given for fever or relief of pain. Aspirin should not be given to children with fever due to the possibility of developing Reye's syndrome (see Reye's syndrome entry).

PROGNOSIS

Full recovery is expected if the disease is treated promptly with antibiotics. A person who has had scarlet fever can not get the disease again.

PREVENTION

The best method of prevention is to avoid others who have the disease.

FOR MORE INFORMATION

Periodicals

Pellman, Harry. "The Sick Child that Has a Rash." *Pediatrics for Parents* (July 1995): p. 4–6.

Web sites

"Scarlet Fever." *KidsHealth.org.* [Online] http://kidshealth.org/parent/common/scarlet_fever.html (accessed on November 2, 1999).

SCHIZOPHRENIA

DEFINITION

Schizophrenia (pronounced skit-suh-FREH-nee-uh) is a psychotic disorder or group of psychotic disorders that cause a patient to lose touch with reality. It is marked by severely impaired reasoning and emotional instability and can cause violent behavior.

Schizophrenic patients are often unable to make sense of the signals they receive from the world around them. They imagine objects and events to be very different from what they really are. If untreated, most people with schizophrenia gradually withdraw from the outside world.

Exactly what schizophrenia is has been the source of considerable disagreement among psychiatrists (doctors who deal with mental disorders). There is some thought that the disease psychiatrists call schizophrenia is actually a number of different conditions classified under a single heading.

DESCRIPTION

Schizophrenia is a serious mental disorder that affects millions of people worldwide. By some estimates, 1 percent of the world's population may be schizophrenic. People diagnosed with schizophrenia make up about half of all patients in psychiatric hospitals and may occupy as many as one quarter of the world's hospital beds.

Schizophrenia can affect people of any age, race, sex, social class, level of education, or ethnic background. Slightly more men than women develop the condition. Most patients are diagnosed in their late teens or early twenties, but the disorder can appear at any time in a person's life. Schizophrenia is rarely diagnosed in children, though it has been reported in children as young as five years of age.

Psychiatrists today recognize five subtypes of schizophrenia.

Paranoid Schizophrenia

Patients diagnosed with paranoid schizophrenia tend to suffer from delusions and hallucinations. A delusion is a belief about the world that is not consistent with the facts. For instance, a patient may believe he or she is someone other than who he or she really is. A patient suffering from a paranoid delusion may believe, unrealistically, that someone intends to do the patient harm.

Hallucinations often take the form of hearing imaginary voices and a patient may believe that he or she is receiving messages from a supernatural or unknown source.

Although people with paranoid schizophrenia have relatively normal emotions and cognitive (thinking) functions, compared to those who suffer other forms of schizophrenia, their delusions and hallucinations, put them at high risk for violent or suicidal behavior.

Disorganized Schizophrenia

Patients with disorganized schizophrenia have confused, disorganized patterns of speech, thought, and behavior. They may act silly or withdraw from the world around them. At one time, disorganized schizophrenia was called hebephrenia (pronounced HEE-buh-FREN-ee-uh).

Catatonic Schizophrenia

Catatonic schizophrenia is characterized by abnormal types of posture and movement. A patient may stand or walk in peculiar patterns, may re-

WORDS TO KNOW

Catatonic behavior: Behavior characterized by muscular tightness or rigidity and lack of response to the environment.

Computed tomography (CT) scan: A technique in which X-ray photographs of a particular part of the body are taken from different angles. The pictures are then fed into a computer that creates a single composite image of the internal (inside) part of the body. CT scans provide an important tool in the diagnosis of brain and spinal disorders, cancer and other conditions.

Computerized axial tomography (CAT) scan: Another name for a computed tomography (CT) scan.

Delusion: A fixed, false belief that is resistant to reason or factual disproof.

Depot dosage: A form of medication that can be stored in the patient's body for several days or weeks.

Hallucination: A perception of objects (or sounds) that have no reality. Seeing or hearing something that does not actually exist.

Neurotransmitters: Chemicals that carry electrical messages between nerve cells.

Paranoia: Excessive or irrational suspicion or distrust of others.

Psychotic disorder: A mental disorder characterized by delusions, hallucinations, and other symptoms indicating a loss of contact with the real world.

peat certain motions over and over again, or become rigid and unmoving for long periods of time.

Undifferentiated Schizophrenia

This category is reserved for patients who show some symptoms of schizophrenia but do not fit into any of the three categories described above.

Residual Schizophrenia

Patients in this category have had at least one schizophrenic episode but no longer display the most severe symptoms of the first three types of schizophrenia.

CAUSES

People have argued for centuries about the causes of mental illnesses such as schizophrenia. Historically, people with these afflictions have been defined as "mad" or "insane" or were believed to be possessed by evil spirits. Those suffering from mental illness were often beaten, tortured, or locked up in special facilities.

For much of the twentieth century, scientists thought that stressful or traumatic conditions in a person's life could cause mental disorders. Psychiatrists believed that a neglected or abused child, for example, ran a higher risk of developing some mental disorders.

PEOPLE HAVE ARGUED FOR CENTURIES ABOUT THE CAUSES OF MENTAL ILLNESSES SUCH AS SCHIZOPHRENIA.

This theory is now less popular with scientists, who generally agree that the disease is biological and not caused by life experiences. There are, however, several competing theories as to what does cause the illness.

Heredity

Research shows that the condition tends to run in families. A person with schizophrenic relatives is ten times as likely to develop schizophrenia as someone who has no history of the disease in the family.

Viral Infection

Some researchers have argued that schizophrenia is caused by a virus that attacks the brain. The virus is thought to attack the part of the brain that interprets messages from the senses. Damage to this part of the brain may account for a person's delusions and hallucinations.

Chemical Imbalance

A popular theory is that schizophrenia is caused by an imbalance of neurotransmitters in the brain. Neurotransmitters (pronounced NOOR-oh-

TRANZ-mit-urz) are chemicals that carry electrical messages between nerve cells. Too much of a neurotransmitter, or too little, may account for various mental disorders, including schizophrenia.

There is still no consensus (agreement) as to which, if any, of these theories is correct, or whether the disease is caused by a combination of factors.

SYMPTOMS

Because schizophrenia's cause is unknown, the disease is defined by a set of symptoms. Most patients have some, but not all, of these symptoms. The most common symptoms are delusions and hallucinations, which may include hearing imaginary voices.

Another common symptom is called insertion or withdrawal of thought. This term refers to the patient's belief that someone or something can put thoughts in the patient's head or take them out. For example, some patients believe that God, the FBI, or alien beings talk to them and tell them how to behave.

Disorganized thinking and behavior are also characteristic of schizophrenia. A patient may have trouble completing a sentence, thinking through an idea, or answering a question clearly. He or she may also have trouble carrying out routine tasks such as tying shoe laces, washing, or getting dressed.

Those suffering from schizophrenia may exhibit other abnormal behavior. For example a patient may show no emotions, or be unable to speak, or may avoid taking any action at all.

DIAGNOSIS

There are currently no laboratory tests by which schizophrenia can be diagnosed. Some imaging techniques, such as computed tomography (CT) scans, which use X rays to create a picture of internal organs, can be helpful in showing abnormal structures in the brain. CT scans are also sometimes called computerized axial tomography (CAT) scans. For the most part, however, doctors must observe a patient's behavior to decide if he or she is schizophrenic.

The first step in this process is to rule out other physical and mental disorders. Some diseases and disorders of the brain cause symptoms similar to those of schizophrenia. Encephalitis (see encephalitis entry), or brain fever, is one such disease. Encephalitis is caused by a virus and must be treated very differently from schizophrenia.

Psychiatrists also try to distinguish various types of mental disorders from each other. While many disorders have symptoms similar to those of schizophrenia, they may require quite different treatments.

Psychiatrists usually rely on the *Diagnostic and Statistical Manual of Mental Disorders, Fourth Edition (DSM-IV)* in diagnosing a mental disorder. *DSM-IV* is a standard reference book that lists all recognized mental disorders. It also lists the basis on which each disorder is diagnosed. The standards used for diagnosing schizophrenia are as follows:

- A patient must have two or more of the following symptoms during a one-month period: delusions, hallucinations, disorganized speech, disorganized behavior, or lack of normal behaviors (such as the ability to speak).
- The patient shows a decline in social, personal, or occupational functions, including the ability to care for him or herself.
- The disturbed behavior must last for at least six months.
- Other physical and mental problems must be ruled out as causes of the abnormal behavior.

TREATMENT

The treatment for schizophrenia depends in part on the stage of the patient's condition.

Hospitalization

In the early stages, hospitalization may be necessary. Hospitalization prevents patients from doing harm to themselves or others. Hospitalization often lasts until treatment with medications begins.

Medication

The primary form of treatment for schizophrenia is medication. Drugs are now available to control many of the symptoms of the disorder. Between 60 to 70 percent of patients with schizophrenia respond to drug treatment.

In the early stages of the disorder, patients may be given regular doses of medicine. The drugs may be swallowed or given by injections. As the patient improves, drugs may be given in depot doses, a form of medication that works in the system for two to four weeks. Depot doses are used because patients often forget to take their medication. Most people with schizophrenia will need to stay on medication throughout their lives.

The most successful medications used in the treatment of schizophrenia are neurotransmitter antagonists. An antagonist is a chemical that acts against some substance in the body.

Researchers now believe that schizophrenia may be caused when the brain produces too much neurotransmitter. Neurotransmitters are chemicals that carry electrical messages between nerve cells. Too much neurotransmitter can cause brain cells to remain active far longer than they would normally. Neurotransmitter antagonists fight off the excess neurotransmitters, helping the brain cells relax and behave more normally.

Psychotherapy

At one time doctors thought that counseling could help cure schizophrenia, by helping patients understand the events in their history that led to the disorder. That view is no longer as popular because most researchers think schizophrenia is a biological problem rather than a problem caused by early upbringing or life events.

Still, some forms of psychotherapy can help schizophrenic patients. Behavior therapy, example, can teach patients to cope with daily activities and may improve the way they interact with other people.

The primary form of treatment for schizophrenia is medication. Drugs are now available to control many of the symptoms of the disorder. (Reproduced by permission of AP/Wide World Photos)

Family therapy

Family members can also benefit from some forms of therapy. For instance, parents may feel that they are somehow responsible for a child's schizophrenia. Professional therapists can help all family members better understand the mental disorder. They can also outline ways in which family members can provide support for the patient. Family therapy may also focus on improving the family's ability to communicate with each other and solve mutual problems brought about by the disease.

PROGNOSIS

The prognosis for schizophrenia is related to the age at which a patient first develops symptoms. The earlier the condition appears, the more permanent the damage is likely to be. Patients who develop the condition later in life have a better chance for leading relatively symptom-free lives.

PREVENTION

There is currently no way to prevent the development of schizophrenia.

FOR MORE INFORMATION

Books

Mueser, Kim Tornval. *Coping With Schizophrenia: A Guide for Families.* Oakland, CA: New Harbinger Publications, 1994.

Torrey, E. Fuller. *Surviving Schizophrenia: A Manual for Families Consumers and Providers,* 3rd edition. New York: Harperperennial Library, 1995.

Tsuang, Ming T., et al. *Schizophrenia: The Facts,* 2nd edition. New York: Oxford University Press, 1997.

Periodicals

Winerip, Michael. "Schizophrenia's Most Zealous Foe." *New York Times Magazine* (February 22, 1998): 26–29.

Web sites

"Ask NOAH About: Mental Health." *NOAH: New York Online Access to Health.* [Online] http://www.noah.cuny.edu/mentalhealth/mental.html#Schizophrenia (accessed on October 31, 1999).

SCOLIOSIS

DEFINITION

Scoliosis (pronounced SKO-lee-OH-siss) is a side-to-side curvature of the spine (backbone).

DESCRIPTION

When viewed from the back, the spine usually appears perfectly straight. In some cases, however, the spine is curved rather than straight. In addition, the vertebrae (the bones that make up the spinal column) are twisted. This condition is known as scoliosis.

A small degree of curving in the spine does not usually cause any medical problems. But larger curves can lead to certain disorders, such as posture imbalance, muscle fatigue, and back pain. Severe scoliosis can interfere with breathing and lead to spondylosis (arthritis of the spine; pronounced spon-dl-OH-siss).

About 10 percent of all adolescents have some degree of scoliosis. Less than 1 percent, however, require medical attention other than careful observation of the problem. Scoliosis occurs in both sexes, but appears in girls about five times more often than in boys. Scoliosis appears most often in adolescents between the age of ten and thirteen.

CAUSES

Scoliosis is not caused by poor posture, diet, or carrying heavy objects. The cause of scoliosis is known in only about 20 percent of all cases. These cases are classified as follows:

- Congenital scoliosis is caused by defects in the spine present at birth. This form of scoliosis is also accompanied by other disorders of various organs.
- Neuromuscular scoliosis is caused by problems with the nerves or muscles. They are unable to support the spine in its normal position. The most common causes of this type of scoliosis are cerebral palsy (see cerebral palsy entry) and muscular dystrophy (see muscular dystrophy entry).

WORDS TO KNOW

Cobb angle: A measure of the curvature of the spine, determined from measurements made on X-ray photographs.

Magnetic Resonance Imaging (MRI): A procedure that uses electromagnets and radio waves to produce images of a patient's internal tissue and organs. These images are not blocked by bones, and can be useful in diagnosing brain and spinal disorders and other diseases.

Scoliometer: A tool for measuring the amount of curvature in a person's spine.

Spondylosis: Arthritis of the spine.

• Degenerative scoliosis is caused by deterioration of the bony material (discs) that separate the vertebrae. Arthritis in the spinal cord can also lead to degenerative scoliosis.

In four out of five scoliosis cases, however, the cause is unknown. Such cases are known as idiopathic scoliosis. Children with idiopathic scoliosis have not suffered from related disorders such as bone or joint disease early in life. Some researchers believe that the condition may be inherited, but scientists have yet to find a gene responsible for the disease.

SYMPTOMS

Scoliosis causes a curvature in the upper body that is easy to notice from the front or back. The curvature may be noticed when a child is wearing a bathing suit or underwear. The child may appear to be standing with one shoulder higher than the other, or one shoulder blade may be pushed forward because the body has been rotated by scoliosis.

The amount of curvature increases during the adolescent years. During this period, a person's bones are growing and developing. Any curvature present before adolescence is likely to become more pronounced. As a result, cases of scoliosis that begin early in life tend to get worse than those that develop later in life.

More than thirty states have set up screening programs for scoliosis. A screening program is a plan for the detection of some specific medical problem.

DIAGNOSIS

Diagnosis for scoliosis is usually done by an orthopedist. An orthopedist is a doctor who specializes in bones and joints. The orthopedist normally takes a complete medical history and conducts a physical examination. In the medical history, the orthopedist attempts to find out whether scoliosis has been present in other family members.

One purpose of the medical examination is to look for specific physical causes for the scoliosis. For example, the doctor might look for nerve or muscle disorders that might cause the problem.

A major part of the examination involves a careful observation of the patient's upper body. The patient may be asked to stand, bend over, and lie down. The doctor is able to study the patient's spine in all of these positions. A simple device called a scoliometer can be used to determine the extent to which the spine is curved.

The most conclusive diagnosis of scoliosis is based on X rays. An X ray of the back shows exactly where and how much the spine is curved. The doctor can make very precise calculations from the X-ray photograph to determine a measurement known as the Cobb angle. The Cobb angle combines all of the data provided by an X-ray photograph to determine the extent of a person's scoliosis.

Occasionally, magnetic resonance imaging (MRI), which uses electromagnets and radio waves to produce images of a patient's internal tissue and organs, can be used in the diagnosis of scoliosis. MRI shows the condition of the spinal cord and the nerves extending from it. It can be used to tell if problems with the nervous system are responsible for the scoliosis.

TREATMENT

A number of factors determine the kind of treatment for scoliosis. These factors include the amount of curvature, the likelihood of improvement, and the amount of pain that may be involved, if any.

Observation

A perfectly straight spine is said to have a curvature of 0 degrees. Children who have curvature of less than 20 degrees usually do not receive any form of treatment.

In many cases, the only medical attention required for scoliosis is careful observation over time. This observation allows doctors to decide whether some form of treatment may be necessary or not. Observation is usually used with adolescents whose spine has a curvature of 20 to 30 degrees. It is also used with adults with a curvature as high as 40 degrees, as long as there is no pain.

Bracing

In more serious cases of curvature, a procedure known as bracing may be used. Bracing is a method of treatment in which the upper body is held in position by metal rods. Three types of bracing are used for scoliosis:

- The Milwaukee brace consists of metal rods attached to pads at the hips, rib cage, and neck.
- The underarm brace uses rigid plastic to surround the lower rib cage, abdomen, and hips.
- The Charleston bending brace is used at night to bend the spine in the opposite direction.

Braces are usually worn for twenty-two to twenty-four hours each day. Bracing is used with children or adolescents whose curvature is greater than 30 degrees and who are expected to grow for at least another year.

The procedure cannot correct curvature that has already occurred. But it can help to prevent the problem from getting worse. Bracing is seldom used with adults. Two situations in which it may be used are with people who suffer great pain and those who cannot undergo surgery.

Surgery

Scoliosis can also be treated with surgery. Surgery is usually recommended under the following conditions:

- The curvature has progressed despite bracing.
- The curvature is greater than 40 to 50 degrees before growth has stopped in an adolescent.
- The curvature is greater than 50 degrees and continues to increase in an adult.
- The patient is in significant pain.

Surgery for neuromuscular surgery is often done earlier. The three goals of surgery are to correct the curvature as much as possible, to prevent further curvature, and to relieve pain. Surgery can usually correct 40 to 50 percent of the curvature, and sometimes as much as 80 percent. It is not always successful in completely removing pain.

The surgical procedure for scoliosis is called spinal fusion. The goal of this procedure is first to straighten the spine as much as possible. Then, the vertebrae are joined together to prevent further curvature.

The first step in spinal fusion is to uncover the vertebrae in the region of curvature. These vertebrae are then scraped clean to produce smooth surfaces. The vertebrae are then joined to each other. When joined in this way, the vertebrae eventually grow together. Metal rods are then inserted along the spine. The vertebrae are attached to the rods with hooks, screws, or wires. The rods hold the spine in position until the vertebrae grow together.

Spinal fusion leaves the involved section of the spine permanently stiff and inflexible. A person no longer has a full range of motion. However, most activities are usually not affected by this change. Normal mobility (movement), exercise, and even contact sports are possible after spinal fusion. Full recovery following spinal fusion takes about six months.

Alternative Treatment

Exercise may help relieve the pain of scoliosis. However, it has no effect on the overall development of the disorder. Good nutrition is also helpful in maintaining a healthy body. But nutrition also has no effect on the progression of scoliosis.

Chiropractic treatment can sometimes relieve the pain of scoliosis. But it does not stop or slow down the progress of the disorder. It also should not be used in place of standard medical treatments. Acupuncture and acupressure may also help reduce and pain and discomfort, but have no effect on the disorder itself.

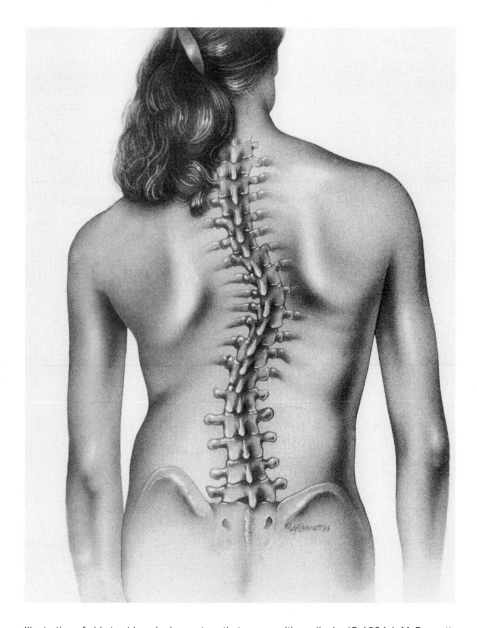

Illustration of side-to-side spinal curvature that occurs with scoliosis. (© 1994 J. McDermott. Reproduced by permission of Custom Medical Stock Photo.)

PROGNOSIS

The prognosis for a person with scoliosis depends on many factors. One of the most important factors is the age at which scoliosis begins. Another factor is the kind of treatment used and the stage at which it was started. Probably the most important factors of all are those beyond the control of medical science, that is, the unknown factors that produce scoliosis in the first place.

Most cases of mild adolescent idiopathic scoliosis need no treatment and do not progress. Untreated severe scoliosis may lead to arthritis of the spine and impair breathing.

PREVENTION

There is no known way to prevent scoliosis. Bracing or surgery, however, can prevent the disorder from progressing.

FOR MORE INFORMATION

Books

Eisenpreis, Bettijane. *Coping With Scoliosis.* New York: Rosen Publishing Group, 1999.

Neuwirth, Michael, and Kevin Osborn. *The Scoliosis Handbook.* New York: Henry Holt & Co., 1996.

Schommer, Nancy. *Stopping Scoliosis: The Complete Guide to Diagnosis and Treatment.* Garden City Park, NY: Avery Publishing Group, 1991.

Organizations

National Scoliosis Foundation, 72 Mount Auburn St., Watertown, MA 02172. (617) 926–0397.

Scoliosis Research Society. 6300 N. River Rd., Suite 727, Rosemont, IL 60018–4226. (708) 698–1627.

The Scoliosis Association. P.O. Box 811705, Boca Raton, FL 33481–0669. (407) 368–8518.

SEASONAL AFFECTIVE DISORDER

DEFINITION

Seasonal affective disorder (SAD) is a form of depression (see depression entry) most often associated with the lack of daylight. The condition usually occurs in the extreme southern and northern latitudes from late fall to early spring.

DESCRIPTION

SAD occurs in parts of the world where days are very short during some seasons of the year. In Alaska and parts of Canada, for example, there may be no more than a few hours of daylight during the winter months. During these periods, some people may become very depressed. That condition is known as seasonal affective disorder, or SAD. When SAD occurs in the spring, when there is more daylight, it is sometimes called reverse SAD.

Though SAD is not officially listed as a mental disorder by psychiatrists, some authorities think as many as ten million Americans may be affected by the condition. Another twenty-five million Americans may have a mild form of SAD, called the "winter blues" or "winter blahs." The farther a person lives from the equator, the more likely he or she is to develop SAD. Women make up the majority of people with the disorder.

CAUSES

Scientists are not sure what causes SAD, but a hormone known as melatonin may be involved. A hormone is a chemical that occurs naturally in the body and controls certain body functions. Melatonin (pronounced mell-uh-TOE-nin) is thought to act as an internal body clock, "reminding" people when to go to bed at night and when to get up in the morning. If the hormone does not function properly, a person's body rhythms may be disturbed, which could lead to depression.

The amount of melatonin produced by the body is partly a function of the amount of daylight the body is exposed to. The more daylight, the less melatonin the body makes. The less daylight, the more melatonin. Scientists know that our bodies produce more melatonin at night and during the winter, when days are short.

One function of melatonin is to make the body feel sleepy. Some researchers think SAD is caused by an excess of melatonin during the winter months. People with too much melatonin may feel tired and depressed.

SYMPTOMS

The symptoms of SAD are similar to those of other forms of depression. People with SAD may feel sad, irritable, or tired. They may find themselves sleeping too much. They may also

PEOPLE WITH SAD MAY FEEL SAD, IRRITABLE, OR TIRED. THEY MAY FIND THEMSELVES SLEEPING TOO MUCH. THEY MAY ALSO LOSE INTEREST IN NORMAL ACTIVITIES AND BECOME WITHDRAWN.

WORDS TO KNOW

Antidepressant: A drug used to prevent or relieve depression.

Hormones: Chemicals that occur naturally in the body and control certain body functions.

Melatonin: A hormone thought to control the body's natural sleep rhythms.

lose interest in normal activities and become withdrawn. A tendency to overeat and gain weight is another common symptom of SAD.

DIAGNOSIS

One step in diagnosing SAD is to eliminate other possible causes of a person's depression. A doctor also relies on the patient's description of his or her own symptoms, including the time of the year in which they occur.

TREATMENT

One obvious way to treat SAD is to expose a patient to a greater amount of light. One device used for this purpose is a light box. A light box contains a set of lights in front of a reflector. The light produced by this device is about fifty times as bright as ordinary indoor light. The patient sits next to the light box for about thirty minutes each session. The light box replaces a portion of the natural light that is absent in the winter months.

Light therapy is generally considered safe for most people. However, it may be harmful to people with eye disorders. The most common side effects of using a light box are vision problems, such as eye strain; headaches; irritability; and insomnia. In addition, a person may experience an excited mood after using the light box.

Another possible treatment for SAD that is being studied is injections of melatonin. Some researchers think that the hormone might help the body adjust to longer periods of darkness without causing depression.

NIELS TYBERG FINSEN

It's easy to take the common things in life for granted. Sunlight is an example. We are so used to seeing sunlight that we may not realize how important it is to health. For example, sunlight helps the production of vitamin D in the skin. Vitamin D prevents bone disease.

One of the first scientists to study the effects of light on health was Niels Tyberg Finsen (1860–1903). Finsen was born in the Faroe Islands in the North Atlantic Ocean. The Faroe Islands are close to the Arctic Circle. They receive relatively little sunshine throughout the year.

When Finsen became a doctor, he decided to study the effects of ultraviolet light on biological tissue. He became convinced that light can be used to treat human disease. He invented a powerful lamp for the treatment of lupus vulgaris, a skin disorder. The lamp was called the Finsen light in his honor.

Some of Finsen's ideas were incorrect. For example, he mistakenly thought that light could be used to cure smallpox. But, overall, his research was very important. It led the way to using many forms of radiation, including X rays and gamma rays, to treat human disorders. For his work in this field, Finsen was awarded the 1903 Nobel Prize in medicine and physiology.

Seasonal affective disorder may also respond to medication. The four classes of drugs used for the disorder are:

- Heterocyclic antidepressants (HCAs), such as amitriptyline (trade name Elavil)
- Selective serotonin reuptake inhibitors (SSRIs), such as fluoxetine (trade name Prozac), paroxetine (trade name Paxil), and sertraline (trade name Zoloft)
- Monoamine oxidase inhibitors (MAO inhibitors), such as phenelzine sulfate (trade name Nardil) and tranylcypromine sulfate (trade name Parnate)
- Lithium salts, such as lithium carbonate (trade name Eskalith), often used by people with bipolar disorder

One obvious way to treat SAD is to expose a patient to a greater amount of light. One device used for this purpose is a full-spectrum light box. (Reproduced by permission of AP/ Wide World Photos)

Counseling

Counseling can sometimes help people with SAD, by helping patients understand the cause of their disorder and how it can affect their interaction with other people.

PROGNOSIS

Most patients with seasonal affective disorder respond to light therapy and/or medications.

PREVENTION

SAD can be prevented by increasing one's exposure to natural light.

FOR MORE INFORMATION

Books

Peters, Celeste A. *Don't Be SAD: Your Guide to Conquering Seasonal Affective Disorder.* Calgary, Alberta: Good Health Books, 1994.

Rosenthal, Norman E. *Winter Blues: Seasonal Affective Disorder: What It Is and How to Overcome It.* New York: Guilford Press, 1998.

Taylor, Clifford A., and Robin Karol Levinson. *If You Think You Have Seasonal Affective Disorder.* New York: Dell Publishing Company, 1998.

Organizations

American Psychiatric Association. 1400 K Street NW, Washington, DC 20005. (202) 682–6000. http://www.psych.org.

National Depressive and Manic Depressive Association. 730 N. Franklin Street, Suite 501, Chicago, IL 60610. (312) 642–0049.

National Institutes of Mental Health. Mental Health Public Inquiries. 5600 Fishers Lane, Room 15C-05, Rockville, MD 20857. (301) 443–4513. (888) 826–9438. http://www.nimh.nih.gov.

Web sites

"Ask NOAH About: Mental Health." *NOAH: New York Online Access to Health.* [Online] http://www.noah.cuny.edu/mentalhealth/mental.html#SAD (accessed on October 31, 1999).

SEXUALLY TRANSMITTED DISEASES

DEFINITION

A sexually transmitted disease (STD) is a disease transmitted through sexual contact between two people. They may be transmitted through the exchange of semen, blood, and other body fluids or by direct body contact. The term sexually transmitted disease applies to more than twenty different infections. At one time, these diseases were more commonly referred to as venereal diseases.

DESCRIPTION

Sexually transmitted diseases are very common medical conditions. In the United States, about 85 percent of the most common infectious diseases can be spread by sexual contact. The rate of STD infection in the United States is more than 50 times as great as that in other developed countries. Experts estimate that 1 in 4 of all sexually active Americans will get an STD at least once in their lives.

About twelve million new STD infections occur in the United States each year with teenagers between the ages of sixteen and nineteen accounting for 1 in 4 cases.

Sexually transmitted diseases are often mild infections that can be cleared up with simple medical treatment. If left untreated, however, serious complications can result. These complications include:

EXPERTS ESTIMATE THAT 1 IN 4 OF ALL SEXUALLY ACTIVE AMERICANS WILL GET AN STD AT LEAST ONCE IN THEIR LIVES.

- Birth defects
- Blindness
- Bone deformities
- Cancer
- Heart disease
- Infertility
- Mental retardation
- Death

The majority of these complications develop only when an STD is not treated properly.

Types of STD

The following are some of the more common STDs in the United States.

- **Chlamydia.** Chlamydial diseases are caused by microscopic organisms that belong to the family *chlamydia* (pronounced kluh-MID-ee-uh). Two common chlamydial infections are nongonococcal (not gonorrhea) urethritis (NGU) and nonspecific urethritis (NSU). Urethritis (pronounced YOOR-ih-THRY-tiss) means an inflammation of the urethra.

- **Gonorrhea.** Gonorrhea (pronounced gahn-uh-REE-uh) is caused by a microorganism called *Neisseria gonorrhoea* (pronounced ny-SEER-ee-uh gahn-UH-ree-uh). It is easily cured when treated properly.

- **Genital warts.** Genital warts are caused by the human papillomavirus (HPV). It is the single most important risk factor for cervical cancer in women (see cancer entry).

- **Syphilis.** Syphilis (SIF-uh-liss) is caused by a microorganism called *Treponema pallidum* (pronounced trep-uh-NEE-muh PAL-ee-um). Like most STDs, syphilis can be cured if treated promptly and correctly. However, when left untreated, it can cause serious damage to the body and even death.

- **Human immunodeficiency virus (HIV) infection.** HIV is the virus responsible for acquired immunodeficiency syndrome or AIDS (see AIDS entry). No cure is presently available for HIV infection. However, major steps have been made in finding ways to control the disease.

WORDS TO KNOW

Antibiotic: A substance derived from bacteria or other organisms that fights the growth of other bacteria or organisms.

Chlamydia: A family of microorganisms that causes several types of sexually transmitted diseases in humans.

Condom: A thin sheath (covering) worn over the penis during sexual activity to prevent pregnancy and the spread of STD.

Diaphragm: A dome-shaped device used to cover the back of a woman's vagina to prevent pregnancy.

Gonorrhea: An STD that affects the mucous membranes, particularly in the urinary tract and genital area. Can make urination painful and cause pus-like discharges through the urinary tract.

Lymph nodes: Small round or oval bodies within the immune system. Lymph nodes provide materials that fight disease and help remove bacteria and other foreign material from the body.

Monogomy: When both people in a relationship have no sexual activities outside of the relationship. The practice of having only one sexual partner.

Nongonococcal urethritis (NGU): An inflammation of the urethra that is not caused by the microorganism that causes gonorrhea.

Nonspecific urethritis (NSU): An inflammation of the urethra caused by a chlamydia microorganism. The term arose because at one time, the cause of the infection was not known.

Syphilis: An STD that can cause sores and eventually lead to brain disease, paralysis, and death.

Semen: A white fluid produced by the male reproductive system that carries sperm.

Vaccine: A substance that causes the body's immune system to build up resistance to a particular disease.

STDs are transmitted during sexual activity. Sexual activity often involves the exchange of bodily fluids between two people. These bodily fluids include semen, blood, and saliva. The risk of contracting an STD is low in any sexual activity in which no bodily fluids are exchanged.

During sexual activity, the organisms that cause STDs are passed from an infected person to an uninfected person. Once those organisms enter the healthy person's body, they begin to grow and reproduce. After a certain period of time, enough organisms are present in the body to begin causing the symptoms of the disease.

The period after infection, during which the organisms are developing, is known as the incubation period. The incubation period varies widely for various STDs. For gonorrhea, NGU and NSU, the incubation may be as short as a few days. For HIV infections, the incubation period may be as long as ten years.

The symptoms of various STDs vary widely. In some cases, there may be no symptoms at all, but in most cases symptoms develop that are characteristic of a specific form of STD. Common symptoms of STDs include:

- In men, a discharge from the tip of the penis accompanied by pain while urinating
- In women, vaginal itching, burning, and odor, sometimes accompanied by bleeding not associated with menstruation

EHRLICH'S "MAGIC BULLET"

Syphilis is one of the most terrible diseases known to humans. When the organism that causes the disease (a *spirochete*) enters the body, it produces relatively mild symptoms. The spirochete then goes into hibernation for many years. Later in the patient's life, the spirochete becomes active again. It then causes horrible symptoms. The patient may lose control of nervous and muscular functions, often accompanied by severe pain. Eventually severe mental disorders may develop, including insanity. The disease may also cause death.

A cure for syphilis was not available until the early twentieth century. It was found quite by accident. The German bacteriologist Paul Ehrlich was searching for a drug that would kill bacteria that cause disease. He called that drug his "magic bullet."

Ehrlich and his students organized their search for a "magic bullet" in a very systematic way. They made a list of all the chemical compounds they wanted to test. Then they tried each chemical on the list, one at a time.

In 1907, Ehrlich's team had reached compound #606. They found it had no effect on bacteria, so they set it aside. Two years later, one of Ehrlich's assistants decided to test compound #606 on spirochetes. He found that it killed them very effectively. A "magic bullet" for syphilis had been found!

The compound Ehrlich's team discovered contains the element arsenic. Arsenic is a powerful poison. The team named the compound salvarsan.

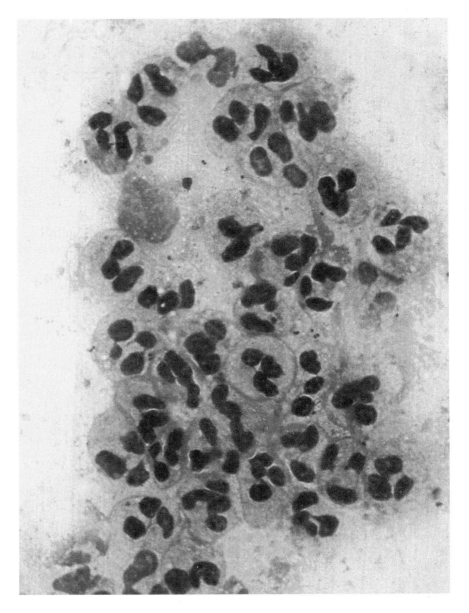

A magnified image of the bacteria that cause gonorrhea. (© 1992 Mike Peres, RBP. Reproduced by permission of Custom Medical Stock.)

- In both men and women, swelling of lymph nodes in the groin
- In both men and women, skin rashes, sores, bumps, or blisters near the mouth, the genitals, or the anus
- Fever, chills, and other flu-like symptoms
- Aches and pains in the joints
- Swelling and redness in the throat that lasts for more than three weeks

DIAGNOSIS

The diagnosis of STDs depends to a large extent on the patient. Teenagers should learn the symptoms of various STDs. When they observe any of these symptoms in their own bodies, they should seek medical attention.

This principle is valuable advice for most diseases and disorders. But it is especially important in the case of STDs. People are often reluctant to talk about personal matters, such as sexual activity. They may prefer to ignore changes they observe in their genital areas or changes they know may be related to sexual activity. But timely treatment can stop STDs from becoming even more serious.

Most STDs are relatively easy to diagnose. The symptoms described above are easy to observe and quite characteristic of sexually transmitted diseases. Many of the diseases can be diagnosed with simple blood tests. The organism that causes the diseases can generally be detected and identified in the patient's blood.

Doctors often test for more than one STD at a time. A person who is infected with syphilis, for example, may also have gonorrhea at the same time.

Notification

Sexually transmitted diseases are regarded as a public health problem. That is, they do not involve a single person alone, but the health of the entire community. A person diagnosed with an STD was infected by someone else and is at risk of transmitting to others.

To cut down on the spread of STDs through a community, many states have reporting laws. These laws require that public health officials find and contact the partners of anyone diagnosed with an STD. The purpose of these laws is to reduce the spread of STDs through the community. In an ideal situation, patients themselves will contact all their partners. To make sure that happens, public health officials usually ask patients for the names and addresses of those partners. They then follow up with interviews to let those partners know that they may also be infected with an STD.

TREATMENT

All forms of STD should be treated by a medical professional. The type of treatment used differs from infection to infection. In some cases, antibiotics can cure a disease quickly and efficiently. (Antibiotics are substances derived from bacteria or other organisms that fight the growth of other bacteria or organisms.) The standard treatment for syphilis, gonorrhea, and chlamydial infections, for example, is a single injection of the common antibiotic penicillin or a series of pills.

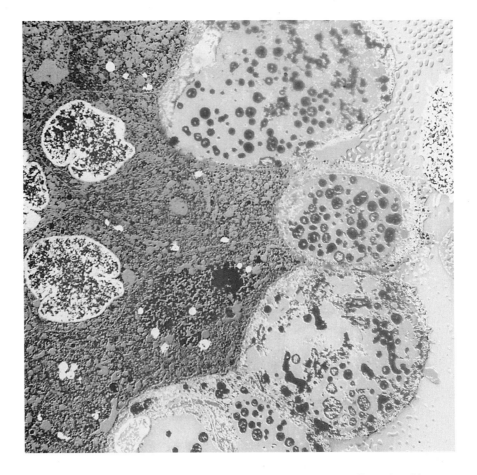

Chlamydia trachomatis bacterium which cause non-specific urethritis. (Reproduced by permission of Custom Medical Stock Photo)

Viral infections, like HIV infection and genital herpes, are more difficult to treat. There are not many effective medications for the treatment of viral infections.

PROGNOSIS

The prognosis for recovery from STDs varies from disease to disease. When properly treated in their earliest stages, many can be cured completely in a short period of time. Gonorrhea, NGU, NSU, and syphilis fall into this category.

In other cases, such as HIV infections, no cure is currently available. However, treatments are available to relieve the symptoms of non-curable STDs and to reduce the risk of serious complications.

Sexually transmitted diseases can be prevented in a number of ways, including the use of vaccinations, lifestyle choices, safer sex practices, and hygienic measures.

Vaccines

Vaccines have been developed for a few STDs, such as hepatitis A and hepatitis B. A vaccine (pronounced vak-SEEN) is a material that that causes the body's immune system to build up resistance to a particular disease. Individuals at risk for these infections should be vaccinated against them. Researchers are continually looking for vaccines against other sexually transmitted diseases.

Lifestyle Choices

The risk of contracting a sexually transmitted disease is very much related to choices one makes about one's sexual activity. Abstinence (avoiding sexual activity altogether) may be the best method of avoiding STDs.

In general, the larger the number of sexual partners a person has, the greater the risk he or she has of contracting an STD. Among sexually active people, the risk of contracting an infection is lowest for those who are in monogamous (pronounced muh-NOG-uh-muss) relationships (couples who have no sexual partners outside of their relationship).

It is also important to know the health status of a prospective sexual partner. Sexual activity with prostitutes or anonymous partners increases the risk of contracting STD. Discussing one's sexual health with a prospective partner is an important health precaution.

One can also choose to take part or not take part in intravenous drug use. Intravenous drug use often involves sharing needles with other people who may be infected with an STD. Some sexually transmitted infections are easily spread in blood passed from one person to another.

Use of Condoms and Other Contraceptives

The term safer sex is used to describe a number of techniques that can be used during sexual activity to avoid contracting an STD. The concept is that sexual activity can be both pleasurable and safe by taking a few simple precautions.

Perhaps the most effective precaution one can use during sexual activity is a condom. When properly used, a condom is very effective in preventing the transmission of bodily fluids from one person to another.

Spermicides (substances that kill sperm) and diaphragms are also somewhat effective in preventing the spread of STDs. But they are not totally effective and do not prevent the spread of some organisms, such as HIV. Either or both of these, when used with a condom, can decrease the chance of spreading and STD.

Hygienic Measures

Cleanliness is always an important factor in avoiding the spread of any disease. However, careful washing alone is not very effective against most organisms that cause STDs. The organisms are often able to penetrate far up into the body, where they will not be affected by soap and water.

See also: AIDS, and Herpes infections.

FOR MORE INFORMATION

Books

Dudley, William, ed. *Sexually Transmitted Diseases*. San Diego: Greenhaven Press, 1999.

Marr, Lisa. *Sexually Transmitted Diseases: A Physician Tells You What You Need to Know*. Baltimore: Johns Hopkins University Press, 1999.

Woods, Samuel G., and Ruth C. Rosen, eds. *Everything You Need to Know about STD*. New York: Rosen Publishing Group, 1997.

Organizations

Planned Parenthood Federation of America. 810 Seventh Ave. New York, NY 10019 (800) 230–7526. http://www.plannedparenthood.org.

National STD Hotline. (800) 227–8922.

Web sites

"Ask NOAH About: Sexually Transmitted Diseases." *NOAH: New York Online Access to Health*. [Online] http://www.noah.cuny.edu/stds/stds.html (accessed on October 31, 1999).

"Basic Facts about STDs." [Online] http://www.mcare.org/healthtips/homecare/basicfac.htm (accessed on May 23, 1998).

"Can STDs Be Prevented?" [Online] http://housecall.orbisnews.com/sponsors/asfp/topics/infections_d/stds/page5.html (accessed on May 23, 1998).

"1998 Guidelines for Treatment of Sexually Transmitted Disease." [Online] http://www.cdc.gov/nchstp/dstd/STD98T03.htm (accessed on May 23, 1998).

"The Challenge of STD Prevention in the United States." [Online] http://www.cdc.gov/nch.stp.dstd/STD_Prevention_in_the_United_States .htm (accessed on May 23, 1998).

SHAKEN BABY SYNDROME

DEFINITION

Shaken baby syndrome (SBS) refers to a combination of injuries that occurs when a baby or young child is violently shaken.

DESCRIPTION

Medical writers first described shaken baby syndrome in 1972. At first, doctors thought that shaken baby syndrome was caused by accidents. Later, they became more aware of patterns of child abuse and more cases of SBS were properly diagnosed.

Every year, about fifty thousand cases of SBS are reported. Boys make up more than 60 percent of those injured. The average SBS victim is six to eight months old, but children as old as five years or as young as a few days can be affected.

Some cases of SBS occur when a very angry or frustrated adult shakes an infant. In other cases, the injury is a result of ongoing abuse. Statistically, men inflict injury more often than women. These men tend to be in their early twenties. Men responsible for causing SBS are often either the baby's father or the mother's boyfriend. Data shows that women who injure babies are more likely to be babysitters or child care providers than the victim's mother.

CAUSES

Shaking is more likely to injure a baby than an older child or adult for three reasons. First, a baby's neck muscles are still weak. Second, its head is still relatively large and heavy, compared to its body size. Third, the baby's brain tissue and blood vessels are still quite fragile.

When a child is shaken violently, its head snaps back and forth. The brain is pushed first against one side of the skull, then against the other side. The bumping action can cause brain tissue to tear and blood vessels to break.

SYMPTOMS

Shaking may produce no visible symptoms in the baby even when extensive damage has occurred within the brain. Internal (inside) bleeding within the skull may cause the brain to swell. If the swollen brain pushes against the skull, damage to nerves and other parts of the brain may occur. Such damage can cause serious problems including blindness, hearing loss, paralysis, speech impairment, mental retardation, learning disabilities, and death. Nearly two thousand children die every year as a result of being shaken.

DIAGNOSIS

Shaken baby syndrome is often difficult to diagnose. There are usually no witnesses to the shaking. The baby may seem to be normal for a period of time after shaking. Babies who act abnormally may be diagnosed with some other medical disorder. Some changes in behavior that may suggest SBS include vomiting, seizures, or loss of consciousness. A baby may also have difficulty breathing, sucking, swallowing, or making sounds.

Additional clues about SBS sometimes come from interviews with the baby's parents. The parents may offer other reasons for the baby's unusual behavior. The explanations offered may not seem reasonable to a doctor.

A doctor who suspects SBS may look for several characteristic conditions that accompany the disorder. The first condition is bleeding at the back of both eyes. Shaking easily breaks blood vessels at the back of the eye. The bleeding is easy to see when the eyes are examined carefully.

Two other conditions often found with SBS are cerebral edema (pronounced suh-REE-bruhl ih-DEE-muh) and subdural hematoma (pronounced sub-DYOOR-uhl hee-muh-TOE-muh). These two terms refer to masses of blood in the brain caused when tissues swell and blood vessels break. The two conditions can be detected by using some form of imaging technique, such as a computed tomography (CT) scan (often also called a computerized axial tomography (CAT) scan), and magnetic resonance imaging (MRI). These techniques use X-ray photographs or electromagnetic fields to provide pictures of the interior of the brain without actually doing surgery.

TREATMENT

The type of treatment provided to an injured baby depends on the kind and extent of injuries. In mild cases, the injury may simply heal over time. In more serious cases, treatment may be

WORDS TO KNOW

Cerebral edema: Swelling of the brain caused by an accumulation of fluid.

Child abuse: Intentional harm done to infants and children, usually by parents or care givers.

Computed tomography (CT) scan: A technique in which X-ray photographs of a particular part of the body are taken from different angles. The pictures are then fed into a computer that creates a single composite image of the internal (inside) part of the body. CT scans provide an important tool in the diagnosis of brain and spinal disorders, cancer and other conditions.

Computerized axial tomography (CAT) scan: Another name for a CT scan.

Magnetic resonance imaging (MRI): A procedure that uses electromagnets and radio waves to produce images of a patient's internal tissue and organs. These images are not blocked by bones, and can be useful in diagnosing brain and spinal disorders and other diseases.

Subdural hematoma: An accumulation of blood in the outer part of the brain.

needed to deal with a specific symptom or injury, such as hearing loss or speech impairment.

Steps are often taken to protect the baby from further injury. The child may have to be placed in a foster home and/or the adult responsible for causing the injuries may be provided with counseling. Adults who cause SBS may also face criminal charges in the courts.

Alternative Treatment

There are no alternative treatments for SBS. A child who is not behaving normally should be taken to a hospital immediately.

PROGNOSIS

The prognosis for shaken baby syndrome is usually not good. A significant number of babies who are mistreated die. Many others suffer serious, long-term damage that will stay with them throughout their lives. Injuries that cause blindness, mental retardation, or loss of motor (muscular) control, for example, are permanent. They can not be repaired. Rehabilitation, however, can help a child learn to live and cope with their new disability.

THE PROGNOSIS FOR SHAKEN BABY SYNDROME IS NOT GOOD. SHAKING A BABY CAN CAUSE PERMANENT INJURIES SUCH AS BLINDNESS, MENTAL RETARDATION, OR LOSS OF MOTOR (MUSCULAR) CONTROL. IT CAN ALSO CAUSE DEATH.

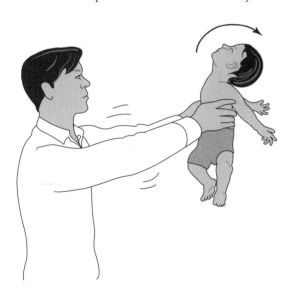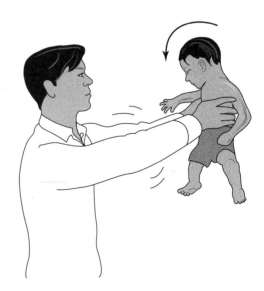

Shaking is more likely to injure a baby than an older child or adult because a baby's neck muscles are still weak, its head is still relatively large and heavy compared to its body size, and the baby's brain tissue and blood vessels are still quite fragile. (Reproduced by permission of Electronic Illustrators Group)

PREVENTION

Because this medical problem is caused by adults who intentionally and physically abuse a child, the only way to prevent shaken baby syndrome is by educating adults.

A common reason given by adults for this type of abuse is frustration with a crying baby. Parents and caregivers can be taught how to deal with this frustration. One general rule is to leave a crying baby alone until the adult has calmed down. Possible reasons for the baby's discomfort should then be considered. A warm bottle, dry diaper, soft music, a bath, or a ride in a swing may calm the child, which in turn may calm the adult.

Adults should also be aware that a baby who cries excessively may have a medical disorder and should be examined by a doctor.

FOR MORE INFORMATION

Books

Morey, Ann-Janine. *What Happened to Christopher: An American Family's Story of Shaken Baby Syndrome.* Carbondale, IL: Southern Illinois University Press, 1998.

Organizations

American Humane Association. Children's Division. 63 Inverness Drive East, Englewood, CO 80112. (303) 792–9900.

Shaken Baby Syndrome Prevention Plus. 649 Main Street, Suite B, Groveport, OH 43125. (800) 858–5222; (614) 836–8360. http://members.aol.com/sbspp/sbspp.html.

Web sites

"Ask NOAH About: Neurological Problems." *NOAH: New York Online Access to Health.* [Online] http://www.noah.cuny.edu/neuro/neuropg.html#Shaken (accessed on October 31, 1999).

SICKLE CELL ANEMIA

DEFINITION

Sickle cell anemia is an inherited blood disorder in which the body produces c-shaped red blood cells. Because of their shape, these cells may stick to each other or to the sides of blood vessels, and cause serious health disorders.

DESCRIPTION

Blood is made up of many kinds of cells, including red blood cells (RBCs). An important function of RBCs is to carry oxygen from the lungs to cells throughout the body. Red blood cells contain a molecule known as hemoglobin (pronounced HEE-muh-GLOW-bihn) that collects oxygen from the lungs then releases it when the RBC reaches other cells in the body.

Normally, red blood cells have a plump doughnut shape. In some cases, however, a person's body makes red blood cells that are curved with sharp points at the end. They are called sickle cells because they look like a sickle (a long farm tool with a curved blade that is used to cut grain).

Hemoglobin Genes

Sickle cell anemia is caused by defective genes. Genes are chemical units found in all cells that tell cells what functions to perform. For example, RBCs contain genes that tell the cell how to make hemoglobin molecules.

When a gene becomes damaged, the message it carries to the cell is incorrect. A damaged gene for hemoglobin tells the cell to make the wrong kind of hemoglobin. This defective hemoglobin creates a sickle shaped RBC rather than the correct doughnut-shaped RBC.

Genes are passed from both parents to their children. A person who receives a damaged hemoglobin gene from just one parent will not get sickle cell anemia. People who have only one defective hemoglobin gene are called carriers. Being a carrier of this particular defective gene may actually increase a person's resistance to malaria (see malaria entry), a dangerous infectious

---

WORDS TO KNOW

Anemia: A condition caused by a decrease in the number of red blood cells in the blood, characterized by fatigue, pale color of the skin, and shortness of breath.

Antibiotic: A substance derived from bacteria or other organisms that fights the growth of other bacteria or organisms.

Bone marrow: A spongy tissue in the center of bones where blood cells are produced.

Bone marrow transplantation: A process by which marrow is removed from the bones of a healthy donor and transferred to the bones of a person's with some kind of blood disorder.

Gel electrophoresis: A laboratory test that separates different types of molecules from each other.

Hemoglobin: A molecule found in blood that gives blood its red color. Hemoglobin is responsible for transporting oxygen through the blood stream.

Hydroxyurea: An experimental drug being tested for use with sickle cell anemia patients.

Red blood cell (RBC): Blood cells that transport oxygen and carbon dioxide through the blood stream.

Sickle cell: A red blood cell with an abnormal shape due to the presence of an abnormal form of hemoglobin.

disease. However, if a person receives a defective hemoglobin gene from both parents, he or she will develop sickle cell anemia.

Problems Associated with Sickle Cell Anemia

The presence of sickle cells in the blood can cause many health problems. For instance, sickle cells die more rapidly than normal cells. When this happens, the body often cannot produce new blood cells fast enough to replace the dying ones. Such a loss of RBCs can lead to anemia (pronounced uh-NEE-mee-uh; see anemia entry). Anemia is a disorder caused by an insufficient number of red blood cells.

Sickle cells can also cause health problems because of they tend to stick to each other and to the sides of blood vessels. As they clump or build up they can eventually block the flow of blood through a blood vessel. This blockage limits the flow of blood to cells, keeping them from getting the oxygen they need, and can eventually cause the cells to die.

Blockage can also lead to a stroke. If the clump of cells blocking a vessel breaks loose it may travel to the brain. If the clump blocks blood flow

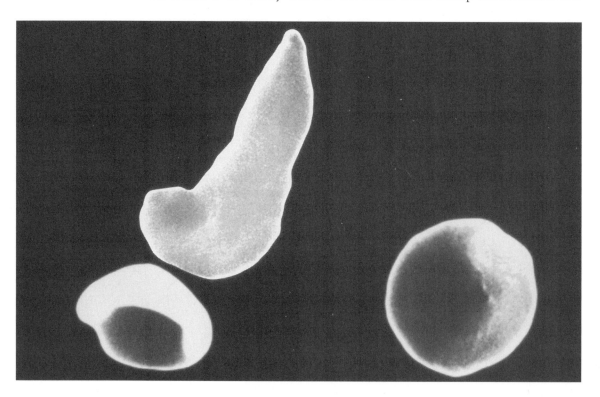

Healthy blood cells have a round, doughnut shape. Sickle cells are longer and narrow with sharp points at the ends. (Photograph by Dr. Gopal Burti, National Audubon Society. Reproduced by permission of Photo Researchers Inc.)

to the brain it can cause damage to the brain known as a stroke (see stroke entry).

Sickle cell anemia occurs primarily among people with African, Mediterranean, Middle Eastern, and Indian ancestry. Worldwide, about 250,000 children are born each year with sickle cell anemia. About two million Americans are thought to have at least one damaged hemoglobin gene. Approximately 72,000 Americans have two damaged hemoglobin genes and therefore have sickle cell anemia.

In the United States, the condition is most common among African Americans. About 1 in 12 African Americans is a carrier for sickle cell anemia. Hispanic Americans are also heavily affected. About 1 in every 1,000 to 1,400 Hispanic American babies are born with sickle cell anemia.

CAUSES

Sickle cell anemia is caused when a person receives a defective hemoglobin gene from both parents, causing the body to make abnormal red blood cells, which may clump and tend not to live as long as normal red blood cells. A person with sickle cell anemia may become anemic or develop other health problems.

SYMPTOMS

The symptoms of sickle cell anemia usually appear during the first year or two of life. However, some individuals do not develop symptoms until they become adults, and may not be aware for many years that they have the disorder. Some typical symptoms of sickle cell anemia include:

- **Anemia.** Anemia is caused by an inadequate number of red blood cells. It can result in fatigue, paleness, shortness of breath, headache, mild fever, and general ill health.
- **Painful crises.** Pain can strike the patient in any part of the body without notice. These attacks can occur as rarely as once a year or as often as every few weeks. They can also last for a variable period of time, from a few hours to a few weeks. Pain in the hands and feet are sometimes the earliest symptoms of sickle cell anemia in a child.
- **Enlarged spleen and infections.** Sickle-cell blockages can affect any of the body's organs. The organs do not receive the oxygen they need to grow normally. The spleen is especially at risk and may become enlarged or it may die completely. This can weaken the immune system and increase the chance that a patient will develop infections.
- **Delayed growth.** Children with sickle cell anemia usually do not grow as fast as other children. They may also reach puberty (sexual maturity) at a later age.

- **Stroke.** Blockages of blood vessels in the brain are especially dangerous. The brain may not get the oxygen it needs to function normally. When blockages occur, a person may become numb on one side of the body, may lose vision or the ability to speak, and may experience dizziness. Children between the ages of one and fifteen are at the highest risk for having a stroke due to sickle cell anemia.
- **Acute chest syndrome.** Acute chest syndrome is caused by blockage of blood vessels in the lungs. Symptoms of the condition include fever, cough, chest pain, and shortness of breath. The condition can reoccur many times and may cause permanent lung damage.

Other problems caused by blood vessel blockage include kidney damage, enlarged liver, vision problems, and priapism (a condition in which a man experiences repeated and painful erections of the penis not related to sexual arousal; pronounced PREE-uh-piz-um).

DIAGNOSIS

Anemia is easily diagnosed from its symptoms. Once a patient is diagnosed with anemia, a doctor will then try to trace the cause of the disorder. If the person is of African American or other high-risk heritage, sickle cell anemia may be suspected. This diagnosis can be confirmed by at least two laboratory tests. In the first test, a sample of the patient's blood is examined under the microscope where the presence of sickle cells is easy to see.

A doctor can confirm that sickle cells are present with a second test, called gel electrophoresis (pronounced jel ih-LEK-tro-fuh-REE-siss). Gel electrophoresis is a method for distinguishing similar kinds of molecules from each other and will show whether abnormal forms of hemoglobin are present in the blood.

TREATMENT

Sickle cell anemia cannot be cured. However, many of its symptoms can be treated. Its most serious complications can also be prevented. The important factor is to diagnose the disorder as early as possible and begin treatment immediately. Methods used to treat symptoms include:

- **Pain management.** Pain is a common problem with sickle cell anemia. Some patients get the relief they need from over-the-counter medication, such as aspirin and acetaminophen. Others need stronger painkillers. Care givers should be careful giving aspirin to children as it has been linked with development of Reye's syndrome (see Reye's syndrome entry).
- **Blood transfusions.** Blood transfusions are generally used only in extreme situations, such as severe anemia or especially bad episodes of pain.

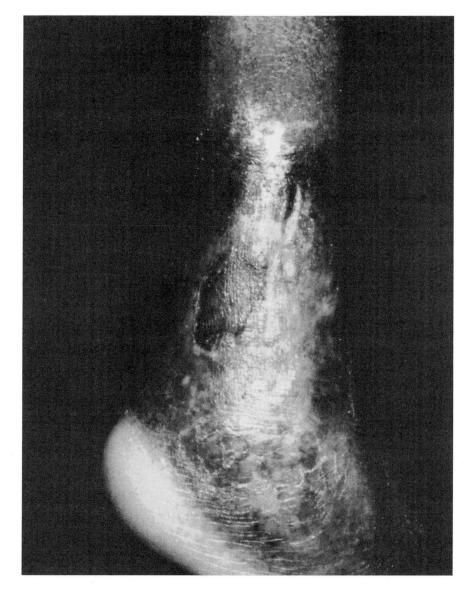

Dying tissue on a sickle cell patient's leg. (© 1995 Science Photo Library. Reproduced by permission of Custom Medical Stock Photo.)

- **Drugs.** Infants are often treated with antibiotics to prevent infections. (Antibiotics are substances derived from bacteria or other organisms that fight the growth of other bacteria or organisms.) Such treatments may last to the age of six. Research is constantly being conducted to develop drugs for the cure of sickle cell anemia. One promising candidate is hydroxyurea, which seems to reduce pain and acute chest syndrome and can limit the need for blood transfusions in some cases.

- **Bone marrow transplantation.** Bone marrow transplantation is used in only the most severe cases of sickle cell anemia. It is based on the fact that new blood cells are made in the marrow of bones. The marrow is soft tissue found in the center of bones. In a bone marrow transplant, marrow is removed from the bones of a healthy donor. It is then injected into the bones of a person with sickle cell anemia. If the procedure is successful, the donor marrow begins making normal, rather than sickle cell, RBCs. Bone marrow transplantation is a very risky procedure with only limited chances of success.

Alternative Treatment

Sickle cell anemia is best treated by conventional medical techniques. However, alternative treatments may help ease some symptoms of the condition. Relaxation techniques, application of warm compresses, and adequate hydration may increase a patient's comfort. Good nutrition, the avoidance of stress, and proper rest may also help prevent some complications of the disorder.

PROGNOSIS

The average life expectancy for men with sickle cell anemia in the United States is forty-two years. For women, it is forty-eight years. The prognosis for any one individual depends on many factors but in general, patients receiving proper medical care may learn to lead relatively normal lives with the disorder.

PREVENTION

Sickle cell anemia is a genetic disorder. There is no prevention for the disease other than genetic screening. Adults can have tests to find out if they carry the gene for sickle cell anemia. If they find they are carriers they can decide whether or not they want to have children. If they decide to have children, there is a known risk that the children may develop sickle cell anemia.

FOR MORE INFORMATION

Books

Bloom, Miriam. *Understanding Sickle Cell Disease.* Jackson, MS: University Press of Mississippi, 1995.

Beshore, George W., ed. *Sickle Cell Anemia.* New York: Franklin Watts, Inc., 1994.

Silverstein, Alvin, Virginia Silverstein, and Laura Silverstein Nunn. *Sickle Cell Anemia.* Hillside, NJ: Enslow Publishers, Inc., 1997.

Organizations

Sickle Cell Disease Association of America. 200 Corporate Point, Suite 495, Culver City, Ca 90230–7633. (310) 216–6363; (800) 421–8453. http://sicklecelldisease.org.

Sickle Cell Disease Program, Division of Blood Diseases and Resources. National Heart, Lung, and Blood Institute. 11 Rockledge Centre, 6701 Rockledge Dr., MSC 7950, Bethesda, MD 20892–7950. (301) 435–0055.

SKIN CANCER

DEFINITION

Skin cancer is a malignant growth on the outer layer of the skin. A malignant growth is one that has the potential to cause death. Skin cancers are often divided into two general groups: malignant melanomas and non-melanoma cancers.

DESCRIPTION

The outer layer of the skin (the epidermis) contains three kinds of cells. Most of those cells are squamous cells. Cells near the bottom of the epidermis are called basal cells. And cells that provide pigment (color) to the skin are known as melanocytes (pronounced MELL-uh-no-sites).

Each type of cell can become cancerous. The three types of skin cancers, therefore, are squamous cell cancer, basal cell cancer, and malignant melanoma (cancer of the melanocytes). Malignant melanoma is by far the most serious form of skin cancer.

Other forms of skin cancer occur, but they are quite rare. The most serious of these is Kaposi's sarcoma (see Kaposi's sarcoma entry). At one time, Kaposi's sarcoma was very rare. It occurred primarily in older men of Mediterranean ancestry. It now occurs commonly in individuals with AIDS (see AIDS entry).

Exposure to sunlight is thought to be the major cause of skin cancers. About eight hundred thousand cases of squamous and basal cell cancers alone are diagnosed each year in the United States. The risk for skin cancers increases the closer one lives to the equator.

All forms of skin cancer begin with a single cell. For reasons that are usually not known, the cell begins to grow very rapidly. Its growth is soon out of control. It divides into two new cells, which continue growing wildly. Eventually the cancerous cells spread through a larger area. They can also begin to grow downward towards inner layers of the skin.

Malignant Melanoma

Malignant melanoma is the least common type of skin cancer. It is also the most aggressive. It spreads to surrounding tissues very quickly. It also invades other parts of the body, especially the lungs and liver.

Melanomas are probably caused by exposure to the sun. But they are also caused by genetic factors. A person is more likely to develop a melanoma if someone else in his or her family has also had the disorder.

Melanomas can occur anywhere on the body. Among Caucasians, they appear most often on the head, neck, arms, legs, and trunk of the body. Among African Americans, they occur primarily on the palms of the hands and the soles of the feet.

Basal Cell Cancer

Basal cell cancer is the most common form of skin cancer. It accounts for about 75 percent of all skin cancers. Light-skinned people are more likely to get the disease than are dark-skinned people. It usually appears after the age of thirty. Basal cell cancers grow very slowly, making them easier to treat than melanomas.

Squamous Cell Cancer

Squamous cell cancer is the second most common type of skin cancer. It grows more quickly than basal cell cancer, but less quickly than a melanoma. It can spread to other parts of the body, especially the lymph nodes. Lymph nodes are small round or oval bodies that are part of the body's immune system. Squamous cell cancer occurs most often on the arms, neck and head. This form of skin cancer is usually not life-threatening. But it can cause serious scarring.

CAUSES

Heredity (the process by which genes are passed from one generation to another) is thought to be an important factor in the devel-

WORDS TO KNOW

Benign: Not dangerous.

Biopsy: Removal of a small piece of tissue for examination under a microscope.

Epidermis: The outer layer of skin.

Lesion: A change in the structure or appearance of a part of the body as the result of an injury or infection.

Lymph nodes: Small round or oval bodies within the immune system. Lymph nodes provide materials that fight disease and help remove bacteria and other foreign material from the body.

Malignant: Threatening to life.

Melanocyte: A specialized skin cell that produces melanin, a dark pigment (color) found in skin.

opment of melanomas. For all forms of skin cancer, exposure to sunlight is probably the most important environmental factor. Research suggests that sunburns received early in one's childhood can lead to skin cancer later in life. A cancer usually does not show up until ten to twenty years after the sunburn has been received. For this reason, skin cancers seldom develop before a person reaches his or her twenties.

Other factors may also lead to skin cancer. For example, people who work with certain chemicals may be at risk for the disease. Also, people with weakened immune systems, such as those who have AIDS, may be more likely to develop some kinds of skin cancer.

SYMPTOMS

All forms of skin cancer develop according to a similar pattern. The first sign of a cancer is usually a change in the appearance of an existing mole, the presence of a new mole, or a change in the appearance of an area of the skin.

Basal cell cancer usually appears as a small lesion (wound) in the skin that lasts for at least three weeks. The lesion (pronounced LEE-zhun) looks flat and waxy, with shiny, rounded edges. There may be a sore at the center of the lesion that makes it look like a dimple. The lesion slowly grows larger if it is not treated.

A squamous cell cancer generally begins as a small raised bump on the skin. The bump may have a sore at its center. It usually does not itch or cause pain.

A common symptom of melanoma is a change in an existing mole. The mole may change color, size or shape. It may become tender or itchy. If it starts to bleed, the cancer may already have begun to progress.

Specialists often recommend the ABCD rule in checking for melanomas. These letters come from the following steps:

• **A**symmetry. Moles are normally round. If a mole begins to take an unusual (asymmetric) shape, it may be cancerous.

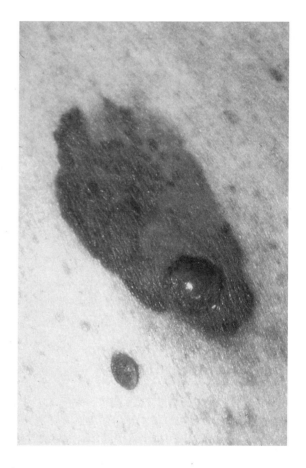

Malignant melanoma is the least common type of skin cancer. It is also the most aggressive. It spreads to surrounding tissues very quickly. (Reproduced by permission of Custom Medical Stock Photo)

- **B**order. A normal mole has a clear-cut border with the surrounding skin. A cancerous mole has an uneven border.
- **C**olor. Normal moles are tan or brown. A cancerous mole may be any mixture of red, white, blue, brown, purple, and/or black.
- **D**iameter. A normal mole is usually less than 5 millimeters (.25 inches) in diameter. Any mole that grows larger than that size may be cancerous.

DIAGNOSIS

Anyone who notices a suspicious-looking blemish on the skin should see a medical doctor. The doctor will ask about the history of the blemish, such as how long it has been there and whether it itches or bleeds, as well as other questions about the patient's health.

If a skin cancer is suspected, the doctor may take a biopsy of the blemish. A biopsy is a medical procedure in which a small sample of tissue is removed, usually with a thin needle. The tissue is then studied under a microscope. The presence of cancer cells can be detected with the microscope. The type of cancer present, if any, can be determined by the appearance of the cells.

It may also be necessary to determine how far the cancer has spread, if at all. Tests used to make this determination include X rays, blood tests, and various imaging tests. Imaging tests are tests used to study the composition and function of internal organs.

TREATMENT

The usual procedure for treating any form of skin cancer is surgery. The doctor cuts out the mole or diseased area of the skin with a scalpel. A small section of healthy tissue surrounding the cancer is also removed. The reason that healthy tissue is removed is to make sure that all cancer cells have been eliminated.

Other methods can be used to kill and/or remove a cancer also. For example, the cancer may be frozen with dry ice or liquid nitrogen. The dead tissue can then be easily removed. Radiation treatments are sometimes recommended for older people or in cases where surgery is not possible or desirable. Surgical removal of a cancer may be followed by cosmetic surgery to hide the scars left by cutting or freezing.

Basal cell cancer and squamous cell cancer are generally treated successfully by these methods. Advanced cases of melanoma may require more aggressive treatment. This is especially true if the cancer has begun to spread through the body. It may be necessary, for example, to remove a person's lymph nodes if they have become cancerous. Radiation therapy may also be recommended if the melanoma has spread to other parts of the body.

Alternative Treatment

There are no generally accepted alternative treatments for skin cancer. Some practitioners recommend therapies that may reduce one's risk for getting skin cancer. For example, they suggest a diet high in antioxidants, such as vitamins C and E. Antioxidants are chemicals that may slow down the growth of cancerous cells. Herbal remedies that may prevent skin cancer include natural antioxidants, such as bilberry, hawthorn, tumeric, and ginkgo.

PROGNOSIS

Both basal cell and squamous cell cancer are curable when treated promptly. The key to success is early detection and treatment of the conditions. The cure rate for both forms of cancer is nearly 100 percent.

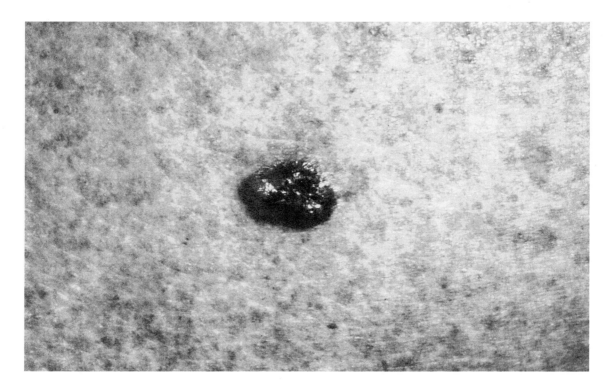

Basal cell cancers are the most common type of skin cancer. They grow very slowly, making them easier to treat than melanomas. (© 1995 SPL. Reproduced by permission of Custom Medical Stock Photo.)

The prognosis for melanoma depends on how far the disease has spread. If a melanoma is removed in its early stages, the cure rate may be as high as 95 percent. If the cancer has spread to other parts of the body, the cure rate drops dramatically. If it has reached the lymph nodes, for example, the survival rate after five years is about 50 percent. If the condition has gone beyond the lymph nodes, it may be considered incurable.

PREVENTION

Prevention is the best way to deal with all forms of skin cancer. The less one is exposed to sunlight, the less the risk of skin cancer. One way to avoid sunlight, of course, is simply to stay out of the sun. At the least, one should avoid the sun during the hottest part of the day, between 11 A.M. and 1 P.M. When one is in the sun, he or she should use sunscreen with a protective factor of fifteen or more.

Regular self-examinations can also be helpful. A person should check once a month for unusual moles or other growths on the skin. If such growths are found, medical advice should be sought.

FOR MORE INFORMATION

Books

Kenet, Barney J., and Patricia Lawler-Kenet. *Saving Your Skin: Prevention, Early Detection, and Treatment of Melanoma and Other Skin Cancers.* New York: Four Walls Eight Windows, 1998.

Lane, William I., and Linda Comac. *The Skin Cancer Answer.* Garden City Park, NY: Avery Publishing Group, 1999.

Robins, Perry. *Sun Sense: A Complete Guide to the Prevention, Early Detection and Treatment of Skin Cancer.* New York: Skin Cancer Foundation, 1990.

Organizations

American Academy of Dermatology. 930 N. Meacham Road, Schaumburg, IL 60173. (847) 330–0230; (888) 462–DERM (3376).

American Cancer Society. 1599 Clifton Rd., NE, Atlanta, GA 30329. (800) ACS–2345. http://www.cancer.org

National Cancer Institute. 31 Center Drive, Bethesda, MD 20892–2580. (800) 4–CANCER. http://www.nci.nih.gov.

Skin Cancer Foundation. PO Box 561, New York, NY 10156. (800) 754–6490.

Web sites

"Ask NOAH About: Skin Cancer." *NOAH: New York Online Access to Health.* [Online] http://www.noah.cuny.edu/cancer/nci/cancernet/201228.html (accessed on October 31, 1999).

Cancer Care News. [Online] http://www.cancercarinc.org (accessed on November 4, 1999).

SKIN DISORDERS

DEFINITION

Skin disorders include a variety of medical problems associated with the skin. Three common forms of skin disorder are dermatitis, psoriasis (pronounced suh-RY-uh-siss), and vitiligo (pronounced vit-ihl-EYE-go).

DESCRIPTION

Dermatitis

Dermatitis is a general term used to describe inflammation of the skin. Most types of dermatitis are characterized by a pink or red rash that itches. The most common form of dermatitis is contact dermatitis. This condition is caused by an allergic reaction to some material. It can occur on any part of the body, but appears most often on the hands, feet, and groin.

Contact dermatitis usually does not spread from one person to another. In some cases, however, it can be transferred from one part of the body to another. Poison ivy is an example. A person infected with poison ivy may first start scratching on the hands. But the infection may then be transferred to other parts of the body.

Other forms of dermatitis are less common. They include:

- Statis dermatitis, which is characterized by scaly, greasy-looking skin. This form most commonly affects the lower legs and ankles.
- Nummular dermatitis, which affects the hands, arms, legs, and buttocks. The condition occurs most commonly in men and women over the age of fifty-five.
- Atopic dermatitis, which usually occurs in early childhood. It is sometimes called infantile eczema. It usually occurs on the face, inside the elbows, and behind the knees.
- Seborrheic dermatitis (pronounced SEB-uh-REE-ick dur-muh-TY-tuhss), which may be dry or moist. It causes the formation of greasy scales and

yellow crusts. The body parts most affected are the scalp, eyelids, face, ears, underarms, breasts, and groin.

Psoriasis

Psoriasis is a chronic (long-lasting), non-contagious disease characterized by open sores in the skin that become covered with silvery-white scabs.

Psoriasis affects about four million Americans. The disease may develop at any age. About 10 to 15 percent of all cases are first diagnosed during childhood. The average age of diagnosis is twenty-eight.

Psoriasis occurs when skin cells start to grow very rapidly. Normally, the rates at which skin cells grow and die off are about the same. As old skin cells die, new ones replace them. In the case of psoriasis, new skin cells grow much more rapidly than old cells die off. As a result, new skin cells push older dead skin cells upwards. They form patches of dead skin on the arms, back, chest, elbows, legs, nails, and scalp. These patches are the scabs that are characteristic of psoriasis.

Vitiligo

Vitiligo is a condition in which smooth, white patches develop on the skin. It is caused when melanocytes die off. Melanocytes (pronounced MELL-uh-no-sites) are skin cells that give skin their color.

Vitiligo affects 1 to 2 percent of the world's population. It occurs equally among men and women. The disorder can first appear at any age. In about half of all cases, however, it starts before the age of twenty.

Vitiligo may appear as one or two well-defined white patches on the skin. Or it may cover large portions of the body. People with vitiligo often have other medical problems also, such as eye disorders, thyroid disease, diabetes mellitus, and pernicious anemia (see entries on visions disorders, diabetes mellitus, and anemias).

CAUSES

Dermatitis

Contact and atopic dermatitis are allergic reactions. Allergic reactions are caused by the body's immune system. The immune system is a

WORDS TO KNOW

Allergic reaction: A series of events initiated by the immune system against substances that are normally harmless to the body.

Chronic: A condition that continues for a long period of time.

Immune system: A network of organs, tissues, cells, and chemicals designed to fight off foreign invaders, such as bacteria and viruses.

Melanocyte: A specialized skin cell that produces melanin, a dark pigment (color) found in skin.

Rash: A spotted pink or red skin condition that may be accompanied by itching.

Steroids: A category of naturally occurring chemicals that are very effective in reducing inflammation and swelling.

Ultraviolet (UV) light: A naturally occurring part of ordinary sunlight that may, under some circumstances, have beneficial effects in curing certain medical disorders.

network of organs, tissues, cells, and chemicals designed to fight off foreign invaders, such as bacteria and viruses. Sometimes the immune system reacts to substances that are normally harmless to the body. It attacks the harmless material in the same way it would attack a disease-causing organism. Such responses are allergic reactions.

Allergic reactions can be caused by a great variety of objects, including:

- Flowers
- Herbs
- Vegetables
- Chlorine
- Household cleansers
- Detergents and soaps
- Fabric softeners
- Glues
- Perfumes
- Certain types of medications

Statis dermatitis is caused by poor circulation in the legs. Fluids collect in the lower legs, and they begin to swell. The swelling may cause a red, itchy rash.

The cause of nummular dermatitis is not known. A number of factors that can increase the risk for the disorder include hot or cold weather, stress, allergies, and bathing more than once a day.

Seborrheic dermatitis is cased by an over-production of oil glands in the skin.

Psoriasis

The cause of psoriasis is not known. However, researchers have identified a number of factors related to the occurrence of the disorder. These factors include:

- History of psoriasis in a person's family
- Stress
- Exposure to cold temperatures
- Injury, illness, or infection
- Use of steroids or certain other medications

Vitiligo

The cause of vitiligo is not fully understood. There appears to be a strong genetic factor involved. That is, the disorder seems to occur commonly in certain families. The condition is usu-

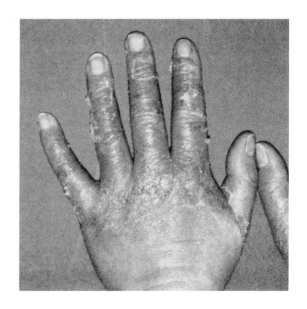

Dermatitis on the hand and fingers. (Reproduced by permission of Custom Medical Stock Photo)

ally triggered by some stressful event, such as an accident, job loss, death of a family member, severe sunburn, or serious illness.

SYMPTOMS

The symptoms of all forms of contact dermatitis and psoriasis are similar. They include a red, itchy rash that covers specific areas of the skin. In the case of vitiligo, the primary symptom is the loss of skin color. People with vitiligo may have other symptoms also, such as abnormal eye coloring.

DIAGNOSIS

All forms of skin disorders can be diagnosed fairly easily based on visual observation. The skin rashes associated with contact dermatitis and psoriasis are very distinctive. A doctor may scrape off a small sample of skin for examination under the microscope. That examination can usually provide positive identification of the specific condition bothering the patient.

TREATMENT

Contact Dermatitis

One step in treating the allergic reactions that cause contact dermatitis is to eliminate the substance that causes the reaction. For example, people who are allergic to certain household cleanser should not use those cleansers. They should find substitutes for them.

The itchiness and inflammation caused by dermatitis can be treated with a variety of products. The most effective products contain steroids. A doctor's advice should be sought, however, as some over-the-counter products can make a patient's condition worse. Antihistamines can also be taken to reduce an allergic reaction. These products act against the chemicals produced by the immune system that cause a rash.

Patients with other forms of dermatitis may require specialized treatments. For example, patients with statis dermatitis should elevate their legs whenever possible. They should sleep with a pillow under their lower legs.

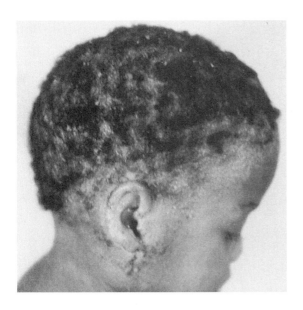

Seborrheic dermatitis, which may be dry or moist, causes the formation of greasy scales and yellow crusts on the skin. It appears most often on the scalp, eyelids, face, ears, underarms, breasts, and groin. (Reproduced by permission of Custom Medical Stock Photo)

Psoriasis

The treatment of psoriasis depends on the severity of a patient's condition. Mild cases may be treated in much the same way as contact dermatitis. Steroid creams often relieve the itchiness of rashes and scabs.

More serious cases of psoriasis may be treated with applications of ultraviolet light. Ultraviolet (UV) light is a naturally occurring part of ordinary sunlight. Under some circumstances, it can have beneficial effects in curing certain medical disorders. But it can also have serious side effects. It should be administered only under the direction of a medical professional. UV light may also be used in conjunction with steroids and other medications.

The most severe cases of psoriasis are difficult to treat. Various medications are available for use, but most have serious side effects. Methotrexate has become popular for the treatment of psoriasis, but it can damage the liver. A number of deaths have occurred among patients whose liver functions were not adequately checked by doctors.

Vitiligo

Vitiligo can not be cured, but it can be managed. The primary goal is to improve the appearance of the white areas caused by the condition. Careful use of cosmetics and selection of clothing can help. Patients may also need counseling about their condition. Extreme cases of vitiligo can be very unattractive. Patients may need help in learning how to live with their disorder.

Alternative Treatment

As with traditional medicine, the first step recommended for treating contact dermatitis is removal of the material that causes the allergy. Alternative practitioners then have a number of ways for relieving the redness and itchiness of a rash. These include:

- A warm oatmeal bath
- Clay or mud packs
- Herbal remedies, such as burdock root, calendula, chamomile, cleavers, evening primrose oil, nettles, and sassafras

Suggested treatments for psoriasis, in addition to the ones listed above, include:

- Soaking in a warm chamomile or salt water bath
- Drinking up to three cups a day of hot tea made from burdock root, dandelion root, Oregon grape, sarsaparilla, or balsam pear
- Eating a diet rich in fish, turkey, celery, parsley, lettuce, lemons, limes, fiber, and fruit and vegetables
- Drinking at least eight glasses of water a day
- Taking nutritional supplements, such as folic acid, lecithin, vitamin A, vitamin E, selenium, and zinc

PROGNOSIS

Contact dermatitis can be controlled in most cases if the agent that causes the reactions is avoided or eliminated. Future exposure to the agent is likely to cause a reoccurrence of the condition.

The symptoms of psoriasis can often be treated successfully. However, the disease can not be cured and may become worse over time. Patients with the most severe forms of the disorder may require counseling as well as medical advice. The condition can become very disfiguring and emotionally upsetting for the patient.

Vitiligo may become stable or slowly grow worse over time.

PREVENTION

Most cases of contact dermatitis can be prevented if the agent that causes the allergic response can be identified. If the agent can not be

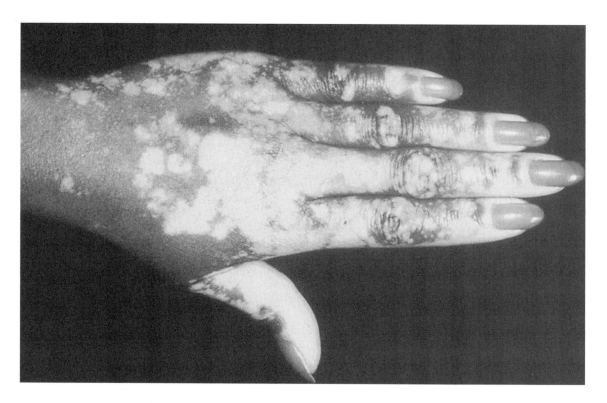

Vitiligo is a condition in which smooth, white patches develop on the skin. It is caused when melanocytes die off. (Reproduced by permission of Custom Medical Stock Photo)

avoided, other forms of prevention are possible. For example, a person who has to work with a chemical that causes a reaction should use gloves and protective clothing. People who accidentally come into contact with an agent that causes an allergy should wash thoroughly with soap and water as soon as possible.

Neither psoriasis nor vitiligo can be prevented. However, psoriasis has the potential to develop into more serious conditions. For that reason, patients should monitor the status of their condition. They should seek medical help if they develop a fever, begin to feel achy, feel unusually tired, or experience other unusual symptoms.

FOR MORE INFORMATION

Books

Editors of Time-Life Books. *The Medical Advisor: the Complete Guide to Conventional and Alternative Treatments.* Alexandria, VA: Time-Life, Inc., 1996.

Gottlieb, Bill, ed. *New Choices in Natural Healing.* Emmaus, PA: Rodale Press, 1995.

Organizations

American Academy of Dermatology. PO Box 681069, Schaumburg, IL 60618–4014. (703) 330–0230. http://www.aad.org.

American Skin Association. 150 E. 58th St., 3rd Floor, New York, NY 10155–0022. (212) 688–6547.

Frontier's Foundation for Vitiligo and Pigment Disorders. 4 Rozina Court, Owings Mills, MD 21117. (301) 594–0958.

National Foundation for Vitiligo and Pigment Disorders. 9032 South Normandy Dr., Centerville, OH 45459. (513) 885–5739.

National Psoriasis Foundation. 6600 SW 92nd Ave., Suite 300, Portland, OR 97223. (800) 723–9166. http://www.psoriasis.org.

National Vitiligo Foundation. PO Box 6337, Tyler, TX 75703. (903) 531–9767.

Web sites

"Ask NOAH About: Dermatology." *NOAH: New York Online Access to Health.* [Online] http://www.noah.cuny.edu/dermatology/derm.html#skininfections (accessed on October 31, 1999).

SLEEP DISORDERS

DEFINITION

Sleep disorders are a group of conditions characterized by disturbance in the amount, quality, or timing of a person's sleep. They also include emotional and other problems that may be related to sleep. There are about seventy different sleep disorders. Short-term, temporary changes in a person's sleep pattern are not included in sleep disorders.

DESCRIPTION

Sleep disorders are divided into two major categories. One category consists of disorders in which a person has trouble falling asleep or staying asleep. This category also includes disorders in which a person may fall asleep at inappropriate times. Conditions of these kinds are called dyssomnias. A second category of sleep disorders includes those in which people experience physical events while they are sleeping. Nightmares and sleepwalking are examples of these disorders. Conditions of this type are called parasomnias.

The following are some examples of each type of sleep disorder:

Dyssomnias

- **Insomnia.** Insomnia (see insomnia entry) is perhaps the most common of all sleep disorders. About 35 percent of all adults in the United States experience insomnia during any given year. People with insomnia have trouble falling asleep. Often people with this disorder worry or become anxious about not being able to sleep, which can make the problem even worse. Insomnia may begin at any time in a person's life. It tends to be most common in young adulthood and middle age.
- **Hypersomnia.** Hypersomnia is a condition in which a person is excessively sleepy during normal waking hours. The person may often fall asleep for lengthy periods during the day, even if he or she has had a good night's sleep. In some cases, patients have difficulty waking up in the morning. They may seem confused or angry when they awaken. About 5 to 10 percent of people who seek help for sleep disorders have hypersomnia. The condition is most common in young adults between the ages of fifteen to thirty.
- **Narcolepsy.** Narcolepsy is characterized by sleep attacks over which patients have no control. They may fall asleep suddenly with no warning. The sleep attack may last a few minutes or a few hours. The number of attacks patients experience can vary. People with narcolepsy usually feel refreshed after awakening from a sleep attack but they may become sleepy again a few hours later and experience another attack.

Three other conditions are often associated with narcolepsy: cataplexy, hallucinations, and sleep paralysis. Cataplexy is the sudden collapse of a person's muscles. The person may become completely limp and fall to the ground. A person may also experience hallucinations. Hallucinations are sounds and sights that a person experiences that do not exist in the real world. Sleep paralysis occurs when a person is just falling asleep or just waking up. The person may want to move, but is unable to do so for a few moments.

- **Sleep apnea.** Sleep apnea (pronounced AP-nee-uh) is a condition in which a person actually stops breathing for ten seconds or more. The most common symptom of sleep apnea is very loud snoring. Patients with this condition alternate between periods of snoring or gasping and periods of silence.
- **Circadian rhythm sleep disorders.** The term circadian (pronounced sir-CAYD-ee-uhn) rhythm refers to the usual cycle of activities, such as waking and sleeping that is common to any form of life. Most people are accustomed to falling asleep after it gets dark out and waking up when it gets light. In certain conditions, this pattern can be disrupted. A person may fall asleep as the sun comes up and wake up as the sun goes down. An example of a circadian sleep disorder is jet lag. People who fly suddenly across many time zones may have their sleep patterns disrupted. It may take a few days before those patterns return to normal.

WORDS TO KNOW

Apnea: A temporary pause in one's breathing pattern. Sleep apnea consists of repeated episodes of temporary pauses in breathing during sleep.

Brainstem: Portion of the brain that connects the spinal cord to the forebrain and the cerebrum.

Cataplexy: A sudden loss of muscular control that may cause a person to collapse.

Circadian rhythm: Any body pattern that follows a twenty-four-hour cycle, such as waking and sleeping.

Insomnia: Difficulty in falling asleep or in remaining asleep.

Jet lag: A temporary disruption of the body's sleep/wake rhythm caused by high-speed air travel through different time zones.

Narcolepsy: A sleep disorder characterized by sudden sleep attacks during the day and often accompanied by other symptoms, such as cataplexy, temporary paralysis, and hallucinations.

Polysomnograph: An instrument used to measure a patient's body processes during sleep.

Restless leg syndrome: A condition in which a patient experiences aching or other unpleasant sensations in the calves of the legs.

Sedative: A substance that calms a person. Sedatives can also cause a person to feel drowsy.

Stimulant: A substance that makes a person feel more energetic or awake. A stimulant may increase organ activity in the body.

Somnambulism: Also called sleepwalking, it refers to a range of activities a patient performs while sleeping, from walking to carrying on a conversation.

Parasomnias

- **Nightmare disorder.** Nightmare disorder is a condition in which a person is awakened from sleep by frightening dreams. Upon awakening, the person is usually fully awake. About 10 to 50 percent of children between the ages of three and five have nightmares. The condition is most likely to occur in children and adults who are under severe stress.
- **Sleep terror disorder.** Sleep terror disorder occurs when a patient awakens suddenly crying or screaming. The patient may display other symptoms, such as sweating and shaking. Upon awakening, the patient may be confused or disoriented for several minutes. He or she may not remember the dream that caused the event. Sleep may return in a matter of minutes. Sleep terror disorder is common in children four to twelve years of age. The condition tends to disappear as one grows older. Less than one percent of adults have the disorder.
- **Sleepwalking disorder.** Sleepwalking disorder is also called somnambulism (pronounced suhm-NAHM-byoo-LIHZ-uhm). The condition is characterized by a variety of behaviors, of which walking is only one. Sleepwalkers may also eat, use the bathroom, unlock doors, and carry on conversations. If awakened, sleepwalkers may be disoriented. They may have no memory of their sleepwalking experience. About 10 to 30 percent of children have at least one sleepwalking experience. The occurrence among adults is much lower, amounting to about 1 to 5 percent of all adults.

A few sleep disorders are related to some physical or mental disorder. The three conditions that fall into his category include:

- Sleep disorders related to mental disorders. Many types of mental illness can cause sleep disorders. People who have severe mental illness, for example, may develop chronic (long-lasting) insomnia.
- Sleep disorders due to physical conditions. Physical illnesses such as Parkinson's disease (see Parkinson's disease entry), encephalitis (see encephalitis entry), brain disease, and hyperthyroidism may cause sleep disorders.
- Substance-induced sleep disorders. The use of certain types of drugs can lead to sleep disorders. The most common of these drugs are alcohol and caffeine. Certain types of medications can also cause sleep disorders. Antihistamines, steroids, and medicines used to treat asthma are examples.

CAUSES

In many cases, the cause of a sleep disorder is not known. In other cases, researchers know at least part of the reason the disorder occurs. Some examples include:

- **Insomnia.** Insomnia may be caused by emotional experiences or concerns such as marital problems, problems at work, feelings of guilt, or concerns about health. A person may become so distraught that sleep is impossible. Insomnia often becomes worse when patients worry about the condition. In such cases, the worry itself becomes another cause for the disorder.

- **Hypersomnia.** One possible cause of hypersomnia is restless legs syndrome. Restless legs syndrome is the name given to cramps and twitches a person may experience in the calves of the legs during sleep. These sensations may keep a person awake and lead to sleep episodes during the day.
- **Narcolepsy.** The cause of narcolepsy is currently not known.
- **Sleep apnea.** The most common cause of sleep apnea is blockage of the airways. The condition occurs most commonly in people who are overweight. The snoring and gasping that are typical of apnea are caused by the person's trying to catch his or her breath. Less commonly, sleep apnea is caused by damage to the brainstem.
- **Circadian rhythm sleep disorders.** Circadian rhythm sleep disorders are caused when people are forced to adjust to new dark/light patterns. An example is a worker whose assignment is changed from the day shift to the night shift. The worker must learn how to sleep when it's light out and to work when it's dark out.

The causes of most parasomnias are not well understood. In some cases, severe stress may be responsible for the condition. In other cases, it is not clear what the cause for the disorder is.

SYMPTOMS

The symptoms of most sleep disorders are obvious from the descriptions above. A person with insomnia, for example, tends to be very tired during the day. A person with nightmare disorder displays the disturbed behavior typical of a person who has been awakened from sleep by a bad dream.

DIAGNOSIS

A beginning point in diagnosing sleep disorders is an interview with the patient and his or her family. From this interview may come a list of symptoms that suggests one or another form of sleep disorder. For example, very loud snoring may be an indication that the patient has sleep apnea. Sleepwalking is, itself, enough of a symptom to permit diagnosis of the condition.

Doctors use a number of other tools to diagnose the exact type of sleep disorder a patient has experienced. Some of these tools include:

- **Sleep logs.** Patients are asked to record everything about their sleep experiences they can remember. The log might include symptoms, time of appearance, severity, and frequency. Events in the person's life may also be recorded as possible clues to the cause of the disorder.

- **Psychological testing.** Some sleep disorders are caused by emotional problems in a person's life. Those problems may be identified by means of certain tests. Examples of these tests are the Minnesota Multiphasic Personality Inventory (MMPI), the Beck Depression Inventory, and the Zung Depression Scale.
- **Laboratory tests.** Techniques have now been developed to observe and record a patient's behavior during sleep. The most common device used is called a polysomnograph. this device measures a person's breathing, heart rate, brain waves, and other physical functions during sleep. Various types of sleep disorder can be identified based on these measurements.

TREATMENT

The choice of treatment for a sleep disorder depends on the cause of the disorder, if it is known. For example, some people develop insomnia be-

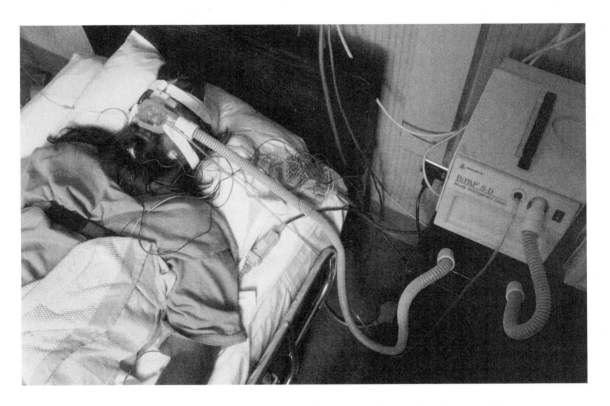

The most common device to used to test for sleeping disorders is called a polysomnograph. This device measures a person's breathing, heart rate, brain waves, and other physical functions during sleep. (Photograph by Russell D. Curtis. Reproduced by permission of the National Audubon Society Collection/Photo Researchers, Inc.)

cause they have become depressed. The solution to this problem is not to treat the insomnia, but to treat the depression (see depression entry). The patient may be given antidepressants or counseling to improve his or her emotional outlook. If this treatment is successful, the insomnia usually disappears on its own.

In many cases, however, the sleep disorder itself may be treated directly. The five forms of treatment that can be used are medications, psychotherapy, sleep education, lifestyle changes, and surgery.

Medications

One might expect that insomnia should be treated with a sedative (a substance that helps a person relax and fall asleep). But sedatives provide only temporary relief from insomnia. They do not cure the underlying cause for the disorder. In addition, some sedatives may be habit-forming or may interact with other drugs to cause serious medical problems.

Stimulants (substances that cause a person to feel more energetic or awake) are often effective in treating narcolepsy. The drug known as clonazepam is used to treat restless legs syndrome. Benzodiazepines are used for children with sleep terror disorder or sleepwalking because they help the child sleep more soundly.

Psychotherapy

Psychotherapy is used when sleep disorders are caused by emotional problems. Patients are helped to understand the nature of their problems and to find ways to solve or to live with those problems. To the extent this treatment is successful, the patient's sleep disorders may be relieved.

Sleep Education

Researchers now know a great deal about the sleep process. By learning about that process, and changing their behavior patterns, patients may overcome some forms of sleep disorder. Some general guidelines that can help people sleep better include the following:

- Wait until you are sleepy before going to bed.
- Avoid using the bedroom for work, reading, or watching television.
- Get up at the same time every morning, no matter how much or how little you have slept.
- Get at least some physical exercise every day.
- Avoid smoking and avoid drinking liquids that contain caffeine.
- Limit fluid intake after dinner.
- Learn to meditate or practice relaxation techniques.
- Do not stay in bed if you can't fall asleep. Get up and listen to relaxing music or read.

Lifestyle Changes

Some types of sleep disorders can be relieved by changing one's lifestyle. For example, people with sleep apnea should stop smoking if they smoke, avoid alcohol and drugs, and lose weight to improve the function of their airways. People who experience circadian rhythm sleep disorders should try to adjust their travel or work patterns to allow time to adjust to new day/night patterns. Children with nightmare disorder should not watch frightening movies or television programs.

Surgery

Surgery is the treatment of last resort for sleep apnea, perhaps the only type of sleep disorder that is life-threatening. Combined with other factors, such as obesity, it can cause death. In such cases, surgery may be required to open up the patient's airways and make breathing easier.

Alternative Treatment

Stress may be responsible for a number of forms of sleep disorder. Alternative treatments that teach people how to reduce stress in their lives can be very helpful. These treatments may include acupuncture, meditation, breathing exercises, yoga, and hypnotherapy. Homeopathic practitioners recommend a variety of substances to treat insomnia caused by various factors. They suggest *Nux vomica* for insomnia caused by alcohol or drugs, *Ignatia* for insomnia caused by grief, *Arsenicum* for insomnia caused by fear or anxiety, and *Passiflora* for insomnia related to mental stress.

Practitioners of Chinese medicine also have a range of herbs for the treatment of sleep disorder. The substance recommended depends on the particular type of disorder. For example, the magnetic mineral known as magnetite is recommended for insomnia caused by fear or anxiety.

Dietary changes may also help relieve some sleep disorders. Patients should avoid any food that contains caffeine or other stimulants. Such foods include coffee, tea, cola drinks, and chocolate. Some botanical remedies that may help a person relax and get a good night's sleep include valerian, passionflower, and skullcap.

PROGNOSIS

Prognosis depends on the specific type of sleep disorder. In most cases, children outgrow sleep disorders such as nightmares and sleep terror disorder. Other conditions tend to be chronic. Narcolepsy, for example, is a life-long condition. Relatively few forms of sleep disorder represent life-threatening medical conditions. Sleep apnea is one of the few examples.

See also: Insomnia.

FOR MORE INFORMATION

Books

Albert, Katherine A. *Get a Good Night's Sleep*. New York: Simon & Schuster, 1996.

Borysenko, Joan. *Minding the Body, Mending the Mind*. Reading, MA: Addison-Wesley Publishing Company, 1987.

Kabat-Zinn, Jon. *Full Catastrophe Living: Using the Wisdom of Your Body and Mind to Face Stress, Pain, and Illness*. New York: Bantam Doubleday Dell Publishing Group, 1990.

Zammit, Gary. *Good Nights: How to Stop Sleep Deprivation, Overcome Insomnia, and Get the Sleep You Need*. Kansas City, MO: Andrews McMeel Publishing, 1998.

SMALLPOX

DEFINITION

Smallpox is an infection caused by the virus called variola (pronounced vuh-RY-uh-luh). Throughout history, smallpox has been a greatly feared disease. It has been responsible for huge epidemics worldwide. The disease has caused great suffering and many deaths. Smallpox is now thought to have been eliminated from the Earth. In 1980 the World Health Organization (WHO) announced that the disease had been wiped out by a bold program of vaccination.

DESCRIPTION

The smallpox virus infected humans only. It did not infect other animals or insects. Neither could animals or insects transmit the virus from one human to another. The disease could be transmitted only by contact between humans. Sometimes a person came into contact with someone with skin lesions caused by the disease. Skin lesions are wounds produced by the virus. They were known as pox. A person also could catch the virus even if the infected person had no lesions.

CAUSES

Smallpox was a relatively contagious disease. The virus could be transferred from one person to another in a number of ways. A person could catch the virus by touching the lesions of an infected person. The virus could also be transferred in droplets of moisture produced during coughing or sneezing. And a person could get the virus from books, blankets, utensils, or other objects used by someone with the disease.

The virus usually entered the body through the respiratory (breathing) tract. It then passed through an incubation period of twelve to fourteen days. An incubation period is the time that passes after a person is infected before symptoms appear. During this time, the virus was multiplying within the body and moving through the bloodstream.

SYMPTOMS

The first symptoms of smallpox were fever and chills, muscle aches, and a flat, reddish-purple rash on the chest, abdomen, and back. These symptoms lasted for about three days. Then the rash faded and the fever dropped.

A day or two later, the fever would return. A bumpy rash would begin to appear on the feet, hands, and face. The rash then spread to the chest, abdomen, and back. The individual bumps in the rash filled with clear fluid. They eventually became filled with pus over a period of ten to twelve days. The bumps (pox) would eventually form scabs. When the scabs fell off, a small pit was left on the skin. People who survived a smallpox infection were often terribly scarred in this way.

Death from smallpox was usually caused by complications. For example, bacteria could easily get into the open skin lesions. Pneumonia, bone infections, or other diseases would result.

An especially severe form of smallpox was called sledgehammer smallpox. The name came from the fact that the infection struck very quickly and with great force. It caused massive, uncontrolled bleeding from the skin lesions, the mouth, nose, and other areas of the body. A person could die very quickly from sledgehammer smallpox.

Throughout history, people have been terrified by smallpox. One reason for their concern was the ease with which the disease spread through whole communities. The other reasons for worry was that no cure for the disease was ever found.

DIAGNOSIS

At one time, most doctors could diagnose smallpox simply by examining a patient. The

WORDS TO KNOW

Epidemic: An outbreak of a disease that spreads over a wide area in a relatively short period of time.

Lesion: A change in the structure or appearance of a part of the body as the result of an injury or infection.

Vaccine: A substance that causes the body's immune system to build up resistance to a particular disease.

Variola: The virus that causes small pox. The only two small samples of variola that remain on Earth are being stored in two separate research laboratories.

skin lesions had a very characteristic appearance. Doctors also knew what to look for when there was a smallpox epidemic in an area. In modern times, diagnosis could also be made by a blood test. A sample of the patient's blood could be examined under an electron microscope. An electron microscope is a very powerful type of microscope. The variola virus can actually be seen in the blood with this type of microscope.

TREATMENT

No cure for smallpox was ever found. The best that could be done was to keep a patient comfortable and wait for the disease to die off on its own.

PROGNOSIS

Death from smallpox ranged as high as 35 percent of those who were infected. In the case of sledgehammer smallpox, the death rate was nearly 100 percent. Patients who recovered from the disease almost always had severe scarring from skin lesions.

PREVENTION

A person who has had smallpox can never have the disease again. This fact was known as far back in history as the tenth century. Medical workers in China, India, and the Americas made use of this information. They often tried to protect people from smallpox with a simple form of vaccination. First, they removed the liquid material from the rash of a person infected with

THE END OF THE SMALLPOX VIRUS?

Smallpox has been eliminated as a human disease. But the virus has not. Two samples remain in scientific laboratories. They have been kept for the purpose of research. Has the time now come to destroy these last two samples of variola virus also?

The World Health Organization (WHO) thinks so. WHO is an international agency that deals with health problems throughout the world. It recommended in March 1986, December 1990, and September 1994 that the virus samples in Atlanta and Moscow be destroyed. The organiza-tion was worried that the virus might fall into the hands of terrorists. It could be used to reintroduce the world's most terrible infectious disease to human populations. That risk is too great, WHO believes.

Other scientists disagree. We should not intentionally eliminate *any* organism, they say, even one as terrible as variola. Besides, we can learn about other viruses by continuing to study the smallpox virus.

In the summer of 1999 the World Health Organization decided to delay destruction of the remaining samples of the smallpox virus until 2003.

smallpox. Then, they would make small scratches in the arm of the person to be vaccinated and place the liquid material from the infected person into the scratch.

This method had mixed results. Under the best circumstances, people who received this treatment developed a mild case of smallpox. They were then protected against the disease for the rest of their lives. However, the vaccinated person sometimes developed a full-blown case of smallpox. Instead of receiving protection from the disease, they would become ill from it.

In 1798 the English scientist Edward Jenner developed a variation on this procedure. He noticed that milkmaids sometimes caught a mild form of smallpox called cowpox. Cowpox was caused by a virus similar to, but less damaging than, the variola virus. Jenner used fluid from cowpox lesions to vaccinate people against smallpox. The cowpox fluid was much more likely to cause mild symptoms of the disease. But it still provided a person with protection against smallpox.

By the twentieth century a very effective smallpox vaccine was available. A vaccine (pronounced vak-SEEN) is a substance that causes the body's im-

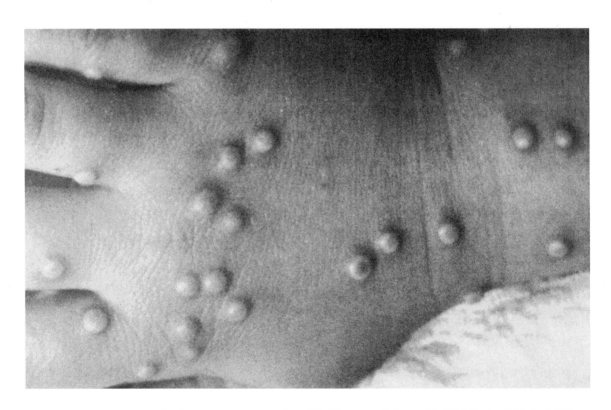

Smallpox causes a rash of pus-filled bumps called pox. (© 1991 National Medical Slide. Reproduced by permission of Custom Medical Stock Photo.)

mune system to build up resistance to a particular disease. Most young children in developed nations were routinely vaccinated against the disease and smallpox began to die out in some parts of the world. But it was still common in developing nations.

In 1967 WHO began a campaign to eliminate the variola virus completely. The organization watched carefully for outbreaks of smallpox throughout the world. When those outbreaks occurred, WHO workers were sent to the area where an epidemic was beginning. Everyone in the area was then vaccinated against the disease.

The program eventually worked. By 1980 WHO was able to announce that the disease no longer existed anywhere in the world. Today, samples of the variola virus exist in two research laboratories, one in Atlanta, Georgia, and one in Moscow, Russia. These samples are being saved for research purpose only. Some people worry that a relative of the variola virus may develop that can cause a smallpox-like infection. The variola samples might then be useful in developing a vaccine against the new infection.

FOR MORE INFORMATION

Books

Giblin, James Cross. *When Plague Strikes: The Black Death, Smallpox, AIDS.* New York: HarperCollins Children's Books, 1995.

Lyons, Albert A., and R. Joseph Petrucelli, II. *Medicine: An Illustrated History.* New York: Harry N. Abrams, 1987.

Stoffman, Phyllis. *The Family Guide to Preventing and Treating 100 Infectious Diseases.* New York: John Wiley and Sons, 1995.

Periodicals

Siebert, Charles. "Smallpox is Dead: Long Live Smallpox." *New York Times Magazine* (August 21, 1994): pp. 30+.

Wagner, Betsy. "Smallpox is Now a Hostage in the Lab." *Washington Post* (January 4, 1997): pp. WH8+.

SMOKE INHALATION

DEFINITION

Smoke inhalation is breathing in smoke. Smoke contains many substances that can cause damage to the human body.

DESCRIPTION

The most common cause of smoke inhalation is fire in a structure, such as a home, office, or factory. People trapped in a burning structure as well as firefighters may inhale smoke produced by the fire.

Cigarette smoking also produces the effects of smoke inhalation. People who smoke do not get as much smoke into their lungs at once as someone trapped in a structural fire. Over a long period of time, however, the effects of cigarette smoking can add up. And eventually the effects on a person's lungs from smoking can be as bad or worse than those caused by other forms of smoke inhalation.

Smoke inhalation is responsible for a large number of the deaths caused by structural fires each year. In many cases, patients do not show symptoms of smoke inhalation until twenty-four to forty-eight hours after the fire. Because of this, they may not be diagnosed correctly and their medical problem may not be treated soon enough or by the correct methods.

CAUSES

The smoke a person inhales can cause damage to the body in three different ways. First, the smoke may actually cause burns. The smoke is carried in by hot air that can damage or destroy tissues in the mouth, nose, and upper respiratory (breathing) system.

Smoke can also cause damage by irritating tissues. The materials found in smoke can be toxic (poisonous) to cells or they can cause physical damage by rubbing across tissues.

Finally, smoke can harm the body because it cuts off the supply of oxygen. Cells need oxygen in order to remain alive and function normally. If too much smoke is present in the body, it can prevent oxygen from reaching cells. Cells and tissues then begin to die from oxygen starvation.

SYMPTOMS

Some symptoms of smoke inhalation are visible to the naked eye. For example, nose hairs may be burned and there may be burns on the throat and inside the nose. The throat may also begin to swell up.

WORDS TO KNOW

Bronchodilator: A substance that causes muscles in the respiratory system to relax.

Bronchoscope: A device consisting of a long thin tube with a light and camera on the end for looking into a patient's airways and lungs

Pulmonary: Pertaining to the lungs.

Respiratory system: The nose, tonsils, larynx, pharynx, lungs, and other structures used in the process of breathing.

Toxic: Poisonous.

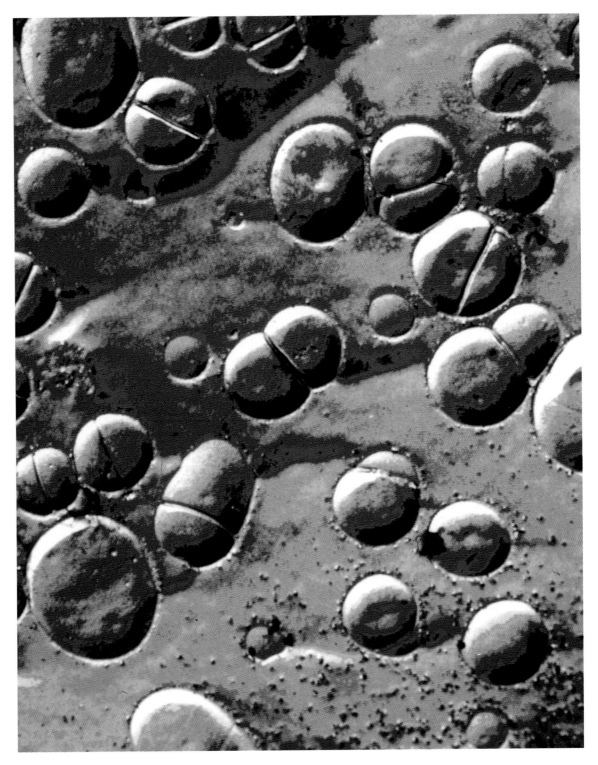

Group A B streptococcus bacteria, magnified 7000 times. (© 1991. Reproduced by permission of Custom Medical Stock Photo.)

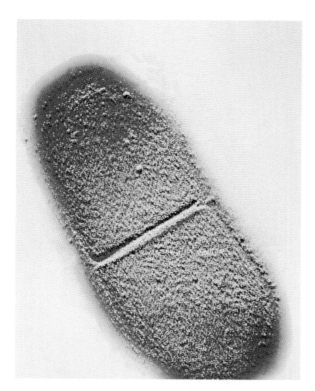

Group A Streptococcus bacterium. (© 1998 J.L. Carson. Reproduced by permission of Custom Medical Stock Photo.)

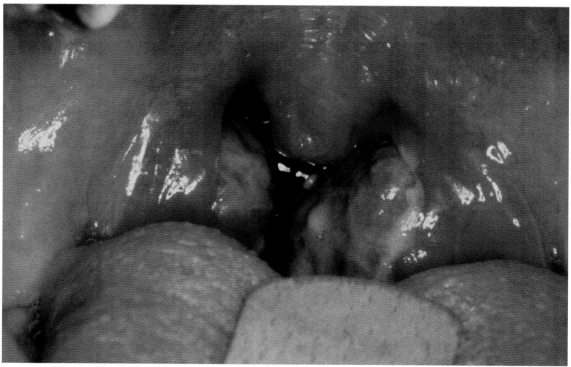

Tonsillitis is an infection and swelling of the tonsils. The tonsils are oval-shaped masses of lymph gland tissue located on both sides of the throat. (© 1993 NMSB. Reproduced by permission of Custom Medical Stock Photo.)

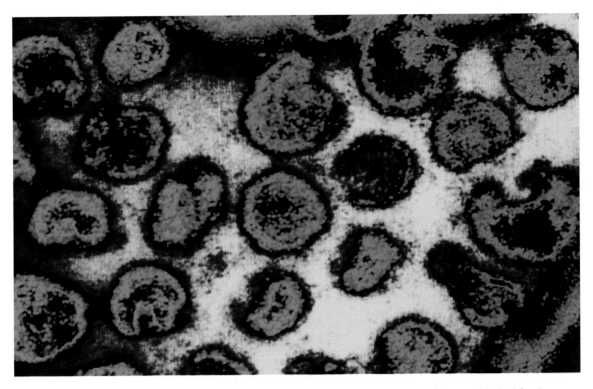

Rubella virus particles, magnified 300,000 times. (© 1994. Reproduced by permission of Custom Medical Stock Photo.)

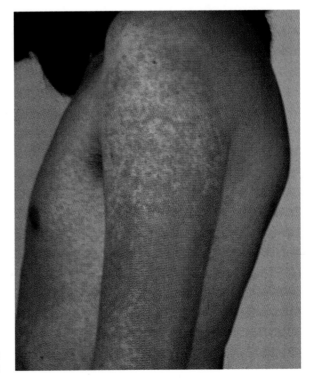

A rubella rash. (Reproduced by permission of Custom Medical Stock Photo.)

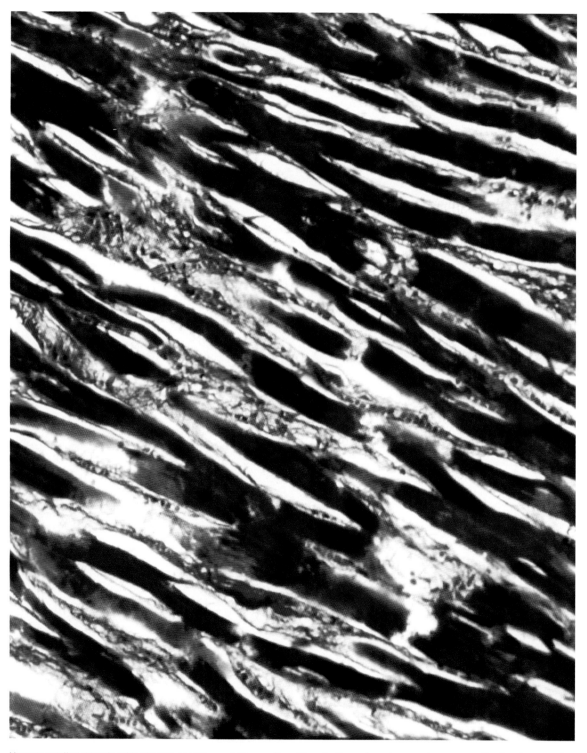

Human cardiac muscle with chronic carditis, or inflammation. Muscle fibers (purple areas) are normally closely spaced. White and blue areas are spaces between the muscle fibers that fill with fluid, causing inflammation. (© 1995 Astrid & Hanns-Frieder Michler/Science Photo Library. Reproduced by permission of Custom Medical Stock Photo.)

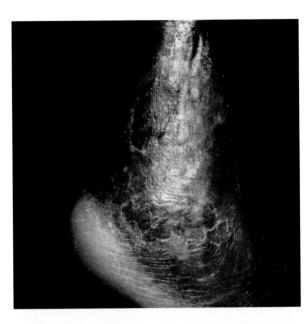

Dying tissue on a sickle cell anemia patient's leg. (© 1995 Science Photo Library. Reproduced by permission of Custom Medical Stock Photo.)

A magnified image of a healthy blood cell (round) and a sickle cell (narrow with sharp point at the end). (Photograph by Dr. Gopal Burti, National Audubon Society. Reproduced by permission of Photo Researchers, Inc.)

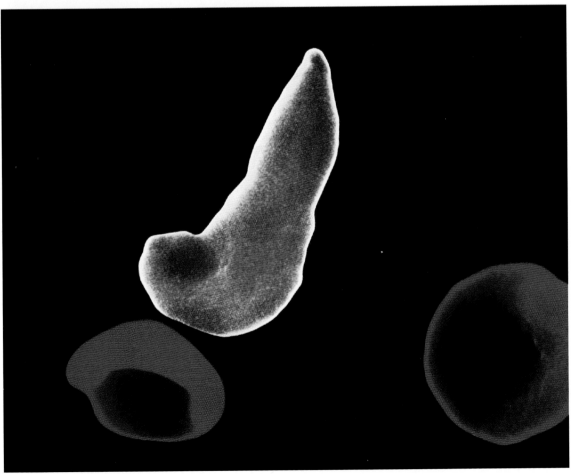

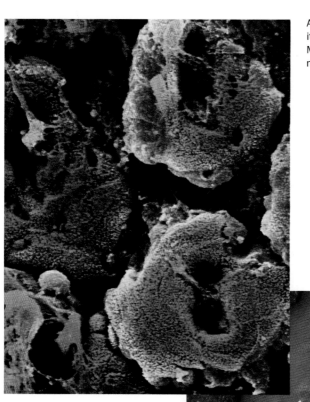

A magnified image of a human colon with ulcerative colitis. (© 1995 Professors P.M. Motta and F.M. Magliocca/Science Photo Library. Reproduced by permission of Custom Medical Stock Photo.)

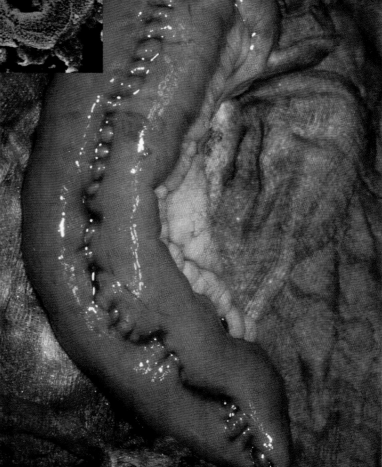

A specimen of a colon with ulcerative colitis. (Reproduced by permission of Photo Researchers, Inc.)

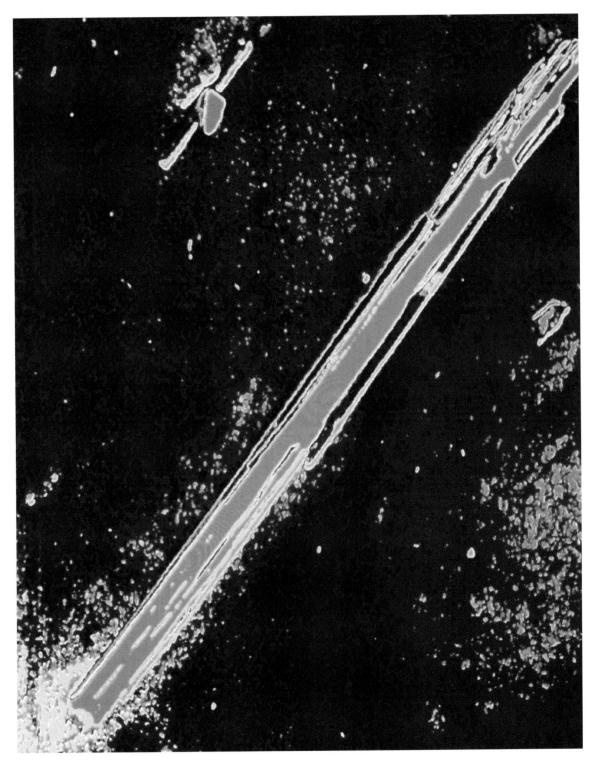

A magnified image of a pertussis toxin crystal which causes whooping cough. (© 1992. Reproduced by permission of Custom Medical Stock Photo.)

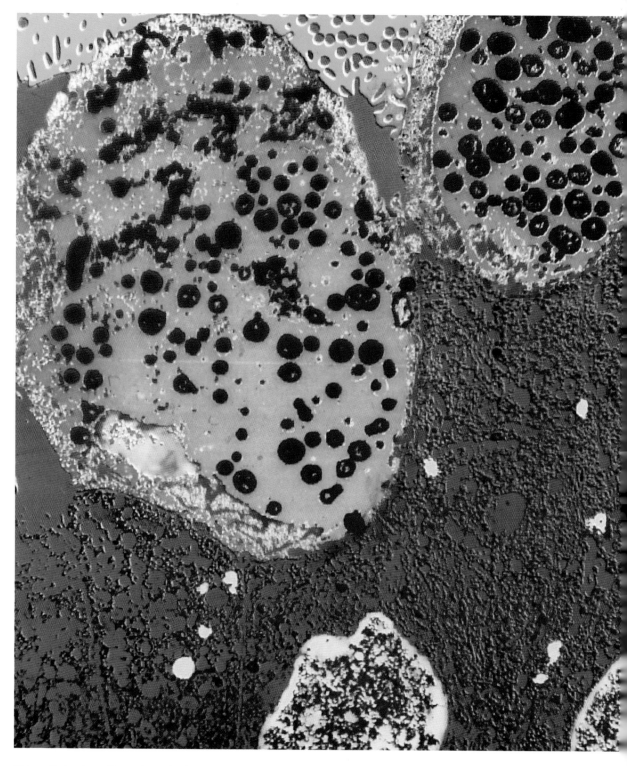

Chlamydia trachomatis are bacteria that cause non-specific urethritis. (Reproduced by permission of Custom Medical Stock Photo.)

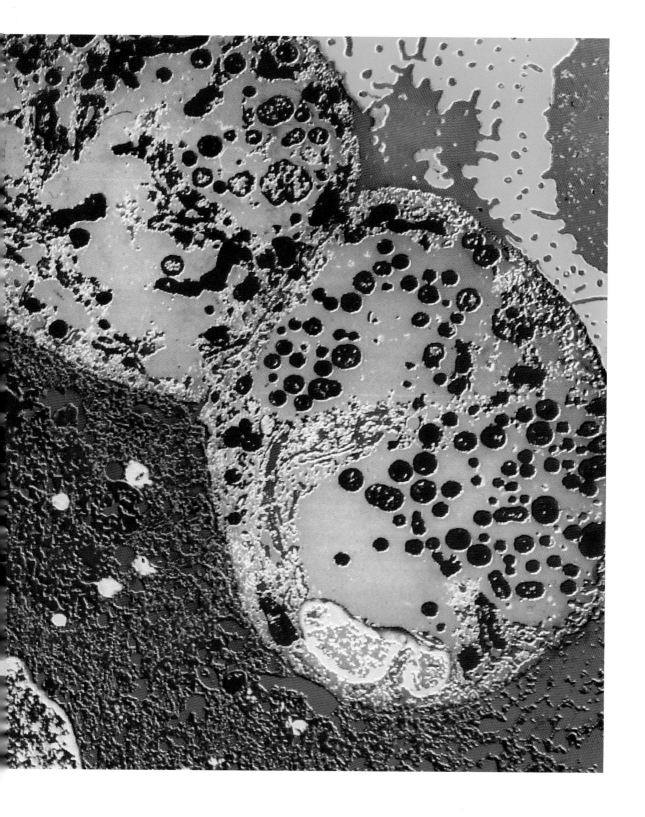

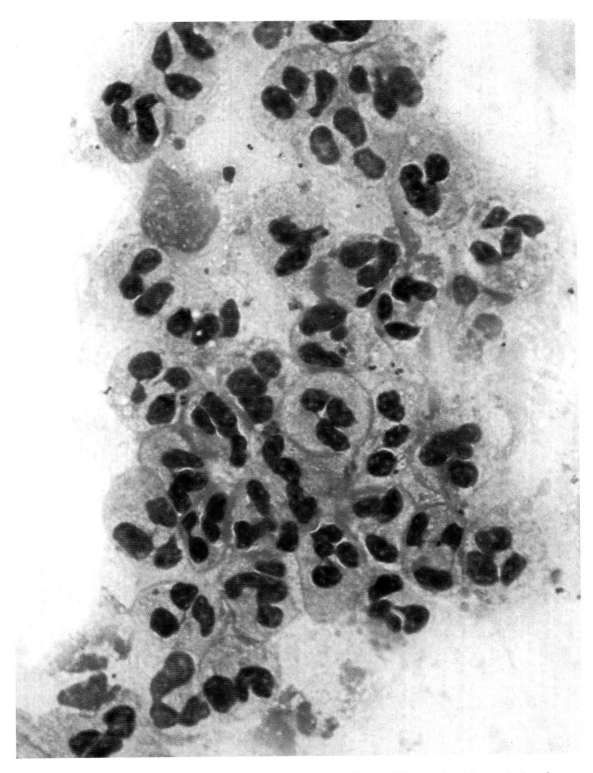

A magnified image of the bacteria that cause gonorrhea. (© 1992 Mike Peres, RBP. Reproduced by permission of Custom Medical Stock Photo.)

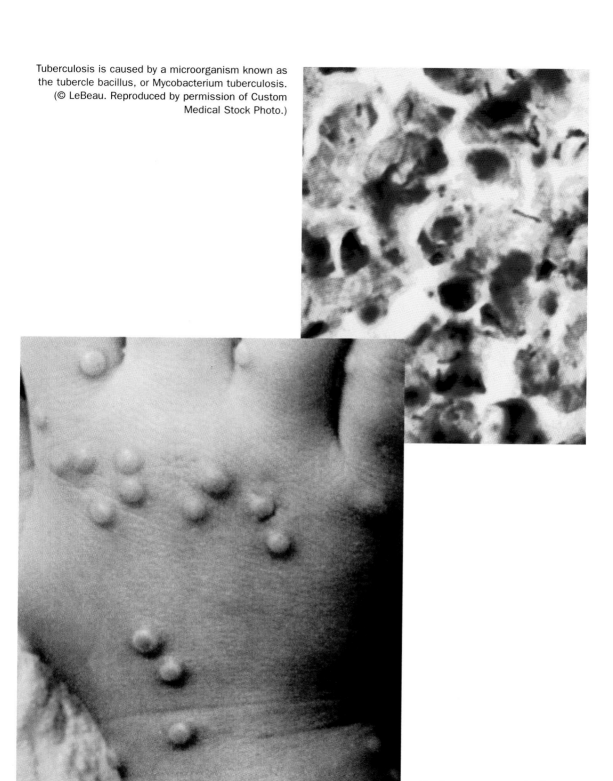

Tuberculosis is caused by a microorganism known as the tubercle bacillus, or Mycobacterium tuberculosis. (© LeBeau. Reproduced by permission of Custom Medical Stock Photo.)

Smallpox causes a rash of pus-filled bumps called pox. (© 1991 National Medical Slide. Reproduced by permission of Custom Medical Stock Photo.)

An illustration of side-to-side spinal curvature that occurs with scoliosis. (© 1994 J. McDermott. Reproduced by permission of Custom Medical Stock Photo.)

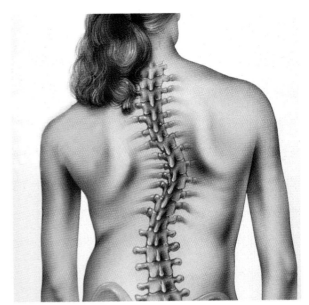

Spina bifida occurs when the spine of a fetus does not close properly. Some portion of the spinal column may protrude from the newborn baby's back and form a sac. (Biophoto Associates. Reproduced by permission of the National Audubon Society Collection/Photo Researchers, Inc.)

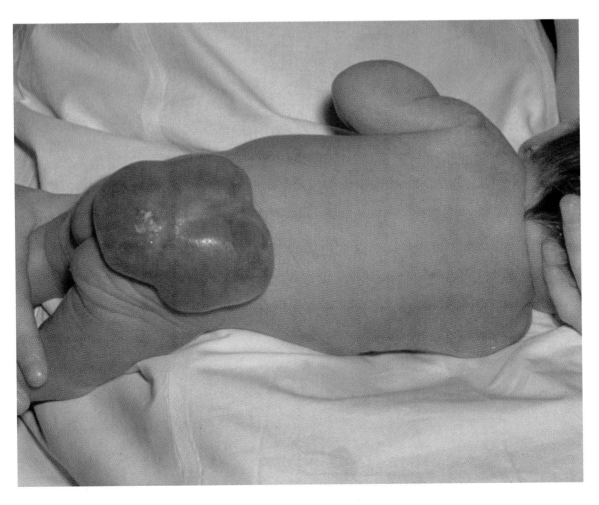

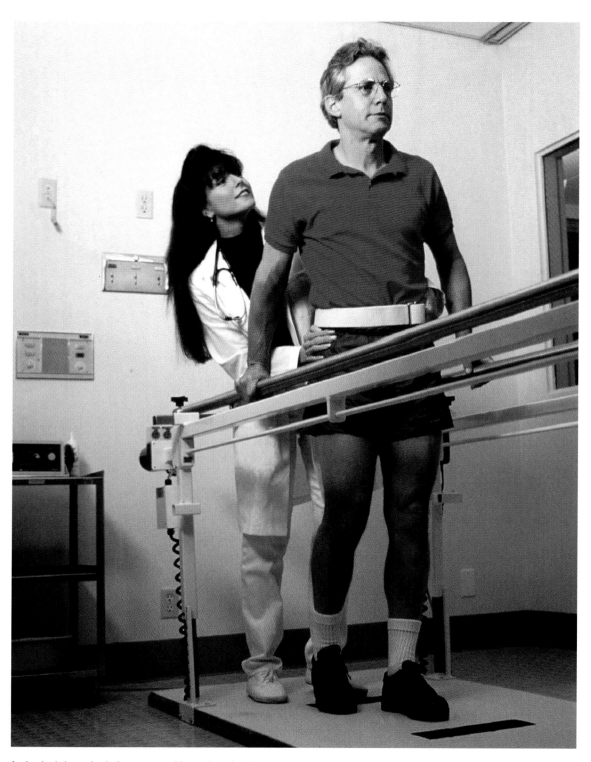

A physical therapist helps a man with stroke rehabilitation. Physical therapy is used to help patients recover as much of their original body functions as possible. (© 1993 ATC Productions. Reproduced by permission of Custom Medical Stock Photo.)

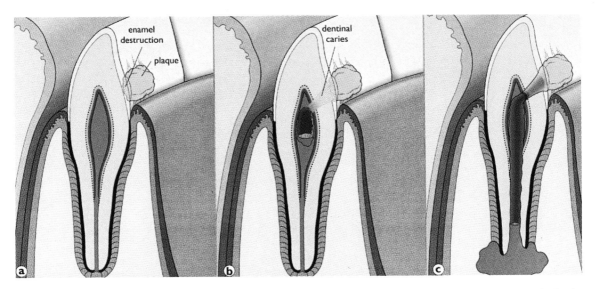

An illustration of the development of dental cavities in three stages. Tooth decay is caused when sweet or starchy food particles remain on the teeth. Bacteria that live on the surface of teeth break the sugar down into lactic acid which soaks into tiny holes and weak spots in the tooth enamel, creating a hole. If the hole penetrates into the dentin, the tooth becomes sensitive to touch and temperature. Decay can even penetrate to the center of the tooth, the pulp. In that case, the inner tooth may become inflamed and begin to ache. (Reproduced by permission of Biophoto Associates/Science Source/Photo Researchers, Inc.)

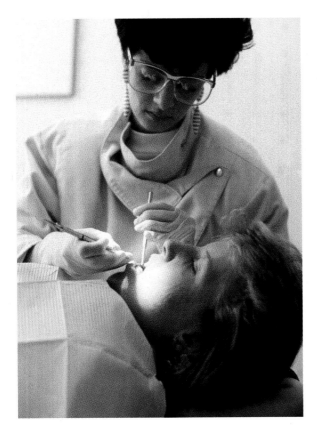

Regular visits to the dentist for a check-up and cleaning make it possible to catch tooth decay before it becomes too serious. (© 1991. Reproduced by permission of Custom Medical Stock Photo.)

Malignant melanoma is the least common type of skin cancer. It is also the most aggressive. It spreads to surrounding tissues very quickly. (© 1994 Michael English, M.D. Reproduced by permission of Custom Medical Stock Photo.)

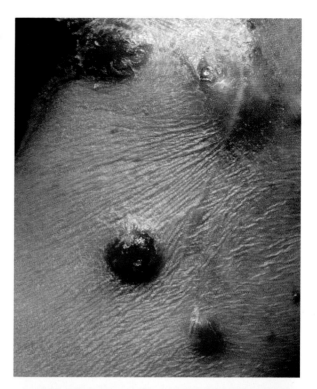

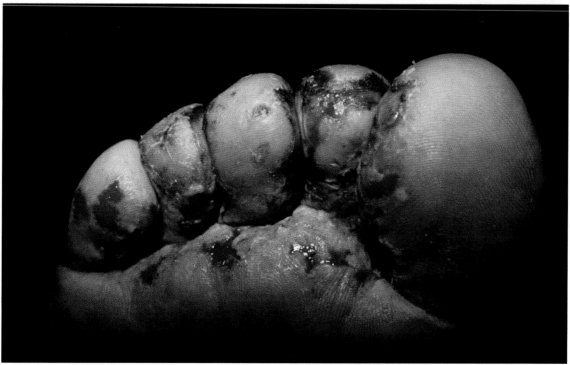

Ringworm infection on the underside of toes. The disease is actually caused by a fungus, not a worm. (© 1988. Reproduced by permission of Custom Medical Stock Photo.)

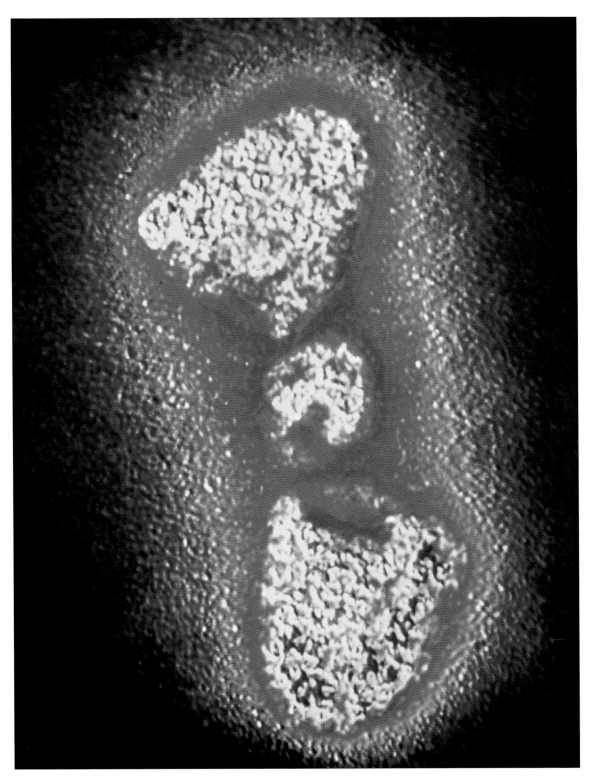

Rabies virus as seen through a microscope. (Reproduced by permission of Custom Medical Stock Photo.)

Smoke inhalation causes other obvious symptoms including noisy breathing, coughing, hoarseness, black or gray saliva (spit), and fluids in the lungs. A person who is not receiving enough oxygen may become short of breath and may develop a bluish-gray or cherry-red skin color. As the condition becomes worse, the patient may lose consciousness or stop breathing.

DIAGNOSIS

Diagnosis of smoke inhalation is based on personal history and physical examination. In most cases, the patient will visit a doctor because he or she has been present at a structural fire. The possibility of smoke inhalation will be clear. In the case of a smoker, this connection may not be so obvious.

A physical examination may reveal some or all of the symptoms listed above. In addition, the doctor can listen to the patient's chest and take his or her pulse rate. Smoke inhalation may cause abnormal chest sounds and a decreased pulse rate.

Blood tests may also be taken. A blood test can show the amount of oxygen in the blood. It can also show if toxic gases from the smoke are present in the blood. A chest X ray will not show damage to the respiratory system but it may show the presence of fluids in the lungs.

Damage to the patient's airways and lungs can be viewed directly with a bronchoscope. A bronchoscope is a device that consists of a long thin tube that can be inserted into the patient's respiratory system. The doctor can look through the tube directly into the windpipe and lungs to see if damage has occurred to tissues.

FIRE SPRINKLER SYSTEMS

The first fire sprinkler system was built in 1874 by the American inventor Henry S. Parmalee. He developed the system to protect the factory in which he built pianos.

Sprinkler systems soon became popular in large factories and warehouses. But they did not seem to have any use in the large majority of office buildings and other structures. They were much too expensive to build.

Attitudes about sprinkler systems began to change in the 1940s. A number of horrible fires were responsible for this change. Perhaps the most important was a fire that struck the Coconut Grove Night Club in Boston in 1942. In that fire, 492 people were killed, many by smoke inhalation.

Before long, city governments began to insist on sprinkler systems in all new office and apartment buildings. For example, New York City requires such systems in all high-rise buildings. The city of Chicago requires sprinkler systems in all nursing homes. Some communities even require sprinkler systems in private homes. San Clemente, California, is one such community.

TREATMENT

smoke inhalation The primary goal in treating smoke inhalation is to make sure that the patient is getting enough oxygen. Two steps may be necessary to achieve this objective. First, the patient's airway has to be kept open. In some cases, the patient may be breathing easily and normally. This condition suggests that the airway is open and functioning normally. In that case, all that may be necessary is to give the patient oxygen through a mask that delivers pure oxygen or air enriched with oxygen to his or her body.

If the patient is wheezing, his or her airway may be constricted (narrowed) or blocked. In that case, the first step is to open up the airways. One way to do this is to give the patient a bronchodilator (pronounced brahng-KO-DI-lay-tor). A bronchodilator is a substance that causes muscles in the respiratory system to relax. As they relax, the tubes through which air gets

Even with special training and protective gear firefighters sometimes suffer from smoke inhalation while fighting fires. (Reproduced by permission of AP/Wide World Photos)

into the lungs become larger. The patient is able to breathe more easily. At this point, oxygen may also be given.

In some cases it may be necessary to insert a tube into the patient's respiratory system through the nose. Oxygen can then be provided through the tube.

Other forms of treatment may be necessary also. For example, the smoke inhaled may have contained certain toxic substances. Blood tests will often show the presence of these toxic substances in the blood. They can then be treated with other substances that will react with the toxic materials and make them harmless.

PROGNOSIS

The key to complete recovery from smoke inhalation is often prompt treatment. People with relatively moderate symptoms who receive early treatment tend to recover completely from the experience. In some cases, however, patients may develop chronic respiratory or pulmonary (lung) disorders. Patients most at risk for such disorders are those who had respiratory problems such as asthma (see asthma entry) before exposure to smoke. Those patients are likely to experience more severe symptoms of their disorder than they did before the smoke inhalation.

PREVENTION

Avoiding smoke inhalation may be difficult because, of course, people usually do not choose to be present in a burning building. The best way to avoid smoke inhalation, then, is to prevent the structural fires that create the problem. Structural fires are best prevented by the use of safe electrical wiring, proper storage of flammable materials, maintenance of clean, well-ventilated chimneys and wood stoves, and other basic fire safety practices.

The damage caused by structural fires can often be reduced dramatically by the installation of smoke detectors and sprinkler systems. Studies have shown that more than 98 percent of all potentially disastrous fires can be prevented by properly installed sprinkler systems.

Finally, fire fighters should be provided with and trained in the use of proper protective gear to avoid the problems of smoke inhalation.

FOR MORE INFORMATION

Web Sites

"Fire Sprinkler Facts." [Online] http://www.waycool.com/southwest/intro.html (accessed on November 5, 1999).

"Homeowners Guide to Fire Sprinkler Systems." *National Fire Sprinkler Association Home Page.* [Online] http://www.nfsa.org/homeown.html (accessed on November 5, 1999).

Johnson, Norma Jean. "Smoke Inhalation." [Online] http://www.emedicine.com/EMERG/topic538.htm (accessed on November 5, 1999).

SORE THROAT

DEFINITION

Sore throat is a painful inflammation of the pharynx. The pharynx (pronounced FAAR-ingks) is the part of the throat that lies between the mouth and the larynx (pronounced LAAR-ingks), or voice box. It is associated most commonly with the common cold (see common cold entry) or influenza (the flu; see influenza entry). While most sore throats heal without complications, in some cases, they develop into a serious illness.

DESCRIPTION

Almost everyone gets a sore throat at one time or another. Children tend to have them more often than adolescents or adults. Sore throats are most common during the winter months. Infections of the upper respiratory (breathing) tract are more common then and these infections can cause a sore throat.

Sore throats can be either acute or chronic. An acute sore throat comes on suddenly and usually lasts three to seven days while a chronic sore throat lasts much longer.

CAUSES AND SYMPTOMS

Sore throats have many different causes. Proper treatment depends on understanding the cause of the sore throat.

Viral Sore Throat

Viruses cause 90 to 95 percent of all sore throats. Cold and flu viruses are usually responsible for the condition. These viruses cause an inflammation of the throat and sometimes the tonsils. Symptoms of a viral infection include a runny nose, cough, congestion, hoarseness, and fever. The level of pain varies considerably. It may be quite mild or very severe. In the worst cases, a patient may not be able to eat, breathe, swallow, or speak.

Another group of viruses that cause sore throat are the adenoviruses (pronounced AD-nn-oh-VY-russ-ez). The adenoviruses usually cause infections of the lungs and ears. In addition to those symptoms described above, adenoviruses may cause white bumps on the tonsils and throat, diarrhea, vomiting, and a rash. Sore throats caused by these viruses last about a week.

A third type of virus responsible for causing sore throat is the coxsackie virus. This virus causes a disease known as herpangina (pronounced hur-pan-JI-nuh). Herpangina occurs most commonly among children under the age of ten. The disease is most common during the summer. It is sometimes called summer sore throat.

Summer sore throat can be quite severe. Symptoms include a high fever and the presence of tiny grayish-white blisters on the throat and mouth. These blisters break open and become very painful. People with this form of sore throat may vomit, have abdominal pain, and, generally, feel very sick.

A fourth type of virus that causes sore throat is the Epstein-Barr virus, (EHP-stine BAR) which also causes mononucleosis (see infectious mononucleosis entry). Mononucleosis is a very common disease. About 80 to 95 percent of all Americans have had the disease by age forty. Symptoms are mild and the disease usually clears up quickly. It can, however, produce a very painful sore throat.

There is no simple way to distinguish a viral sore throat from a bacterial sore throat. Viral sore throats are quite contagious. They can be spread by personal contact and by coughing or sneezing.

Bacterial Sore Throat

About 5 to 10 percent of all sore throats are caused by bacteria. The most common bacterial sore throat is caused by a bacterium called group A *Streptococcus* (pronounced strep-tuh-KOK-us). This type of sore throat is usually called strep throat (see strep throat entry). Bacterial sore throats can also be caused by the *Gonococcus* bacterium (pronounced GAHN-uh-KOCK-us). This bacterium also causes the sexually transmitted disease gonorrhea (see sexually transmitted diseases entry). Bacterial sore throats are also contagious.

Noninfectious Sore Throat

Not all sore throats are caused by infection. For example, people with allergies often have

WORDS TO KNOW

Adenoviruses: A group of viruses that usually cause infections of the lungs and ears.

Antibiotic: A substance derived from bacteria or other organisms that fights the growth of other bacteria or organisms. Useful in treating bacterial sore throats, antibiotics are not effective against viral sore throats.

Coxsackie virus: A virus that causes a disease known as herpangina.

Gonorrhea: A sexually transmitted disease caused by the *Gonococcus* bacterium.

Larynx: The voice box.

Lymph nodes: Small round or oval bodies within the immune system. Lymph nodes provide materials that fight disease and help remove bacteria and other foreign material from the body.

Mononucleosis: A highly infectious disease caused by Epstein-Barr virus. Characterized by fever, swollen lymph nodes and sore throat.

Pharynx: The part of the throat that lies between the mouth and the larynx, or voice box.

sore throats. The sore throat is caused by fluids dripping from the back of the person's nose into the throat. These fluids irritate the pharynx.

Many materials in the environment can also irritate the pharynx. Such irritants include cigarette smoke, polluted air, chemical fumes, and dry air. These forms of sore throat are not contagious.

DIAGNOSIS

Sore throats are easy to diagnose from a patient's symptoms. However, the type of sore throat is usually difficult to diagnose. Most sore throats clear up quickly on their own, so a detailed diagnosis as to exact cause is usually not necessary. However, sore throats can sometimes continue for a relatively long time. In that case, medical advice should be sought. Some types of sore throat can develop into serious diseases.

Diagnosis of sore throat begins with a medical history and a physical examination. In the medical history, the doctor will try to find out if the patient has been near someone with a cold or the flu. If so, the patient may have contracted the sore throat by way of that contact.

The physical examination may provide further information. The doctor may discover a sinus infection, bronchitis, or some other infection of the upper respiratory tract. Any one of these infections could be the cause of the sore throat. If the doctor suspects strep throat, laboratory tests may be ordered. These tests will tell whether the *Streptococcus* bacterium is present or not.

COUGH DROPS

Coughing serves an important function in the human body. It provides a way of expelling (getting rid of) harmful materials that get into the body. But coughing is an annoying, and sometimes crippling, pattern.

Throughout history, humans have used all kinds of natural products to relieve coughing. Today, one of the most popular cough treatments is the cough drop. The cough drop is similar to liquid cough medicine, except that it is prepared in a more convenient form.

The first commercial cough drops were prepared by James Smith, of Poughkeepsie, New York, in the mid-1850s. Smith made his cough drops in a pot on his kitchen stove. He then began selling them as the *James Smith and Sons Compound of Wild Cherry Cough Candy* in 1852. He claimed that the product would relieve coughs, colds, hoarseness, and sore throat.

Later, Smith's sons joined their father in the business. When other companies also began to make cough drops, the Smiths decided they needed to make their product distinctive. They began to package their cough drops in boxes with pictures of the two sons on the front. They also protected the name of their product by putting the words "Trade Mark" on the package. The two words, "Trade" and "Mark," appeared below the pictures of the two sons. Very soon, people who bought cough drops began to think of the two boys as "Trade" and "Mark." Many never knew that their real names were William and Andrew.

A simple, quick, and inexpensive test is available for mononucleosis. If the doctor suspects that the patient has this disease, the test can be performed in the office.

TREATMENT

For the vast majority of sore throats, there are no treatments to cure the disease. These cases of sore throat are caused by viruses, against which there are few medications. Antibiotics may be prescribed for bacterial sore throats. But they will have no effect on viral sore throats.

The usual medication prescribed for bacterial sore throats is penicillin. Penicillin can be given either as a single injection or a series of pills. The pills must be taken for ten days. If a patient does not take the full course of pills the infection may return.

A number of treatments are available for the symptoms of sore throat. These include rest, a healthy diet, plenty of fluids, restrictions on heavy exercise, and a variety of drugs. The drugs that are usually recommended are aspirin, acetaminophen (trade name Tylenol), or ibuprofen (trade names Advil, Motrin). These medications reduce pain and fever that accompany a sore throat.

Chronic sore throat requires a somewhat different treatment. In many cases, the sore throat is not caused by an infection. Instead, it may be produced by some environmental condition. People who work around chemicals, for example, may have chronic sore throats. In such cases, it may be necessary to change the patient's working conditions in order to provide relief for the sore throat.

Home Care for Sore Throat

Sore throat is usually not a very serious disease. It can be treated most effectively with some simple remedies available in the home, including:

- Taking aspirin, acetaminophen, or ibuprofen for pain. But children should not be given aspirin because of the risk of Reye's syndrome (see Reye's syndrome entry).
- Gargling with warm tea or warm salt water
- Drinking plenty of fluids but avoiding fruit juices
- Eating soft, nutritious foods, such as noodle soup, and avoiding spicy foods
- Refraining from smoking

Viruses cause 90 to 95 percent of all sore throats which cause an inflammation of the throat and sometimes the tonsils. (Reproduced by permission of Custom Medical Stock Photo)

- Resting until the fever is gone
- Increasing the humidity of a room with a room humidifier
- Avoiding the use of antiseptic lozenges and sprays, which are likely to make the condition more uncomfortable

Alternative Treatment

Alternative practitioners recommend a variety of natural products for the treatment of sore throat. For example, aromatherapists recommend inhaling the fragrances of lavender, thyme, eucalyptus, sage, and sandalwood. Herbalists recommend taking osha root, ginger, or slippery elm. Some practitioners suggest gargling with a mixture of water, salt, and tumeric. Homeopathic practitioners treat sore throats with very dilute solutions of *Lachesis, Belladonna, Phytolacca,* yellow jasmine, or mercury. Nutritionists recommend vitamins and minerals such as vitamins A or C and the mineral zinc.

PROGNOSIS

Sore throat caused by a viral infection usually clears up on its own within one week with no complications. The one exception is mononucleosis. Most cases of mononucleosis also clear up on their own but the recovery period may be much longer. Among adults, it may take up to six months to recover completely from mononucleosis. In rare cases, mononucleosis may lead to complications, such as swollen tonsils, adenoids, and lymph nodes. Lymph nodes are small round or oval bodies that are part of the body's immune system. If this happens, the patient should seek emergency medical care.

Patients with bacterial sore throat usually begin to feel better about 24 hours after starting on antibiotics. An antibiotic is a substance derived from bacteria or other organisms that fights the growth of other bacteria or organisms. Strep throat is the most serious form of sore throat since it can lead to serious complications. These complications include scarlet fever (see scarlet fever entry), kidney damage, and rheumatic fever. Treatment with antibiotics during the early stages of sore throat can usually avoid these complications.

PREVENTION

It is difficult to avoid getting a sore throat. People carrying the viruses and bacteria that cause the disease are all around us. The chance of being infected can be reduced, however. Some simple rules to follow include the following:

- Wash hands frequently and well.
- Avoid close contact with someone who has a sore throat.
- Do not share food and eating utensils with anyone.

- Do not smoke.
- Stay out of polluted air.

FOR MORE INFORMATON

Web sites

"Ask NOAH About: Pain." *NOAH: New York Online Access to Health.* [Online] http://www.noah.cuny.edu/pain/pain.html#S (accessed on October 31, 1999).

National Institute of Allergy and Infectious Diseases. "Infectious Mononucleosis Fact Sheet." [Online] http://www.niaid.nih.gov/factsheets/infmono.htm (accessed September 1, 1997).

SPINA BIFIDA

DEFINITION

Spina bifida (pronounced SPI-nuh BIFF-ih-duh) means an open or severed spine and it is one of the most serious of all birth defects. The condition may affect a small region of the spine or a much larger area. In case of spina bifida, portions of the spinal column are pushed outward, making them vulnerable to injury or infection.

DESCRIPTION

The rate of spina bifida differs considerably among various populations. It occurs in about 1 of every 700 births among whites in North America. Among African-Americans, the rate is about 1 in every 3,000 births. In some parts of Great Britain, the rate may be as high as 1 in every 100 births.

Spina bifida occurs when the spine of a fetus does not close properly. Some portion of the spinal column may protrude (stick out) from the newborn baby's back. The protrusion may form a sac that includes some part of the spine. The spinal material present in the sac can vary considerably. In some cases, it consists of the membranes that cover the spinal cord. In other cases, part of the spinal cord itself is present in the sac. In the most extreme cases, the entire spine may be exposed.

The severity of spina bifida depends on a number of factors. These factors include which part of the spine has failed to close, how badly the spine is distorted, and what other medical problems the baby may have.

CAUSES

Spina bifida is a genetic disorder that is caused by a combination of defective genes. It is one of a group of genetic disorders known as neural tube defects. The neural tube is a structure that forms very early in the life of a fetus. It eventually develops into the central nervous system of the body. The central nervous system includes the brain and the spinal cord.

Neural tube defects often appear very early, sometimes within the first three or four weeks after conception. Spina bifida occurs when the neural tube does not develop normally and the covering for the spinal cord fails to wrap completely around the spine. Open spaces develop, allowing part of the spine to stick out.

SYMPTOMS

The symptoms of spina bifida depend on the location and size of the opening. Most patients have some degree of weakness in the legs. In the most extreme cases, there may be complete paralysis. The higher up the spine the defect occurs, the more severe the disabilities a person will have.

People with spina bifida often have severe bowel and bladder problems related to the spinal cord's inability to send the signals necessary for emptying them. Difficulty in emptying the bladder can lead to serious, even life-threatening infections of the kidney.

WORDS TO KNOW

Amniocentesis: A medical procedure in which a sample of the fluid surrounding the fetus in a woman's womb is withdrawn and examined.

Catheter: A thin tube inserted into the body to allow fluids to be sent into or taken out of the body.

Cerebrospinal fluid (CSF): The fluid that surrounds tissues in the brain and spinal column.

Computed tomography (CT) scan: A technique in which X-ray photographs of a particular part of the body are taken from different angles. The pictures are then fed into a computer that creates a single composite image of the internal (inside) part of the body. CT scans provide an important tool in the diagnosis of brain and spinal disorders, cancer and other conditions.

Computerized axial tomography (CAT) scan: Another name for a CT scan.

Genetic disorder: A medical problem caused by one or more defective genes.

Hydrocephalus: An abnormal accumulation of cerebrospinal fluid (CSF) in the brain.

Myelograph: A test in which a dye is injected into the spinal column to allow examination of the spine with X rays or a CT scan.

Neural tube: A structure that forms very early in the life of a fetus and eventually develops into the central nervous system of the body.

Ultrasound test: A medical procedure in which a sound wave is transmitted into a pregnant woman's womb. The reflections produced from the sound wave can be studied for the presence of abnormalities in a fetus.

Another complication of spina bifida may be hydrocephalus (pronounced (HI-droh-SEF-uh-luss). Hydrocephalus is also known as water on the brain. The fluid present in hydrocephalus is not water, but cerebrospinal fluid (CSF). CSF is a liquid that surrounds tissues in the brain and spinal cord. Spina bifida may force large amounts of CSF into the brain. The excess fluid causes pressure on the brain, damaging brain tissue.

Many children with spina bifida also have other problems with bone structure. These problems may include clubfeet, hip dislocation, and abnormal curves and bends in the spinal column.

Intelligence in patients with spina bifida varies widely. Though people with the disease might have normal intelligence, in some cases the disease can cause severe mental retardation.

DIAGNOSIS

The sac formed as a result of spina bifida may be quite large or very small. In the mildest cases, it may be confused with a tumor. When the sac is not obvious, other clues to the disorder include the presence of a birthmark on the spine (called a port wine stain) or growth of hair in the injured region. Babies with spina bifida may also exhibit weak muscles and poor reflexes.

Tests are available for confirming the presence of spina bifida. One such test is a myelograph. In a myelograph, a dye is injected in the area around the spinal cord. The spinal cord is then observed with an X ray or a computed tomography (CT) scan, which can create a picture of internal organs. Either test will show the structure of the spinal cord in detail and gaps in the spine usually show up clearly.

GENETIC TESTING

Spina bifida is one of many genetic disorders. Such disorders develop before a child is ever born. What difference would it make if parents knew that their child had a genetic disorder before the child was born?

Until recently, there was no point in asking that question. Doctors had no way of knowing whether or not a baby would be born with a genetic disorder.

But that situation has changed. Today, it is possible to identify many genetic disorders while a fetus is still in the womb. For example, a small sample of the fluid surrounding the fetus can be withdrawn. Certain tell-tale "markers" in the fluid indicate whether or not a genetic disorder is present. Today, parents can know in advance whether or not their baby will have spina bifida.

How should parents use this knowledge? Some people want to have their baby born, no matter what health problems it may have. Other people feel differently. They do not want to subject their child to even a few weeks or days of pain and suffering.

Genetic testing can be an invaluable source of information for parents. But it can also raise some of the most difficult questions they will ever have to answer.

Spina bifida can now be diagnosed before birth. The mother is given a blood test for a substance known as alpha-fetoprotein (AFP). AFP is always present in the blood of a pregnant woman but the presence of an abnormal fetus causes an increase in the level of AFP.

Additional tests can determine whether the abnormality involves the neural tube. During an amniocentesis (pronounced AM-nee-oh-sehn-TEE-siss) test for instance, fluid surrounding the fetus is removed and examined in order to gain further information as to the likelihood of a neural tube defect.

Finally, the fetus can be examined by ultrasound. In an ultrasound test, a sound wave is sent into the pregnant woman's womb. The sound wave bounces off the fetus. Its reflection forms a picture of the fetus that can be studied for the presence of neural tube defects. The combination of blood

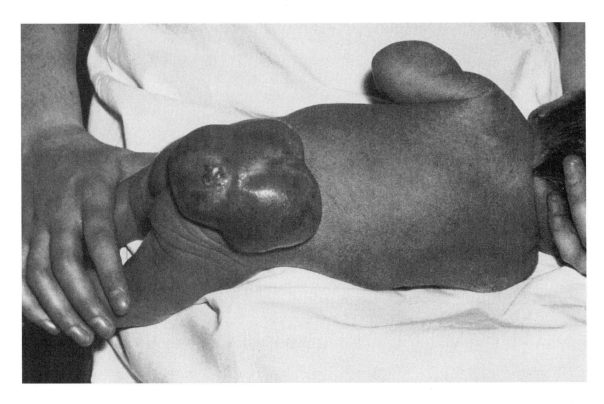

Spina bifida occurs when the spine of a fetus does not close properly. Some portion of the spinal column may protrude from the newborn baby's back. The protrusion may form a sac that includes some part of the spine, such as the membranes that cover the spinal cord or parts of the cord itself. (Biophoto Associates. Reproduced by permission of the National Audubon Society Collection/Photo Researchers, Inc.)

tests, amniocentesis, and ultrasound tests can now diagnose over 90 percent of all neural tube defects.

TREATMENT

The first goal in treating spina bifida is to close the gap in the patient's spinal column. The decision as to how and when to perform this surgery can be very difficult, however. It depends on a number of factors, including the extent and location of injury.

Patients with spina bifida may require other operations to deal with complications of the disorder. Surgery may be needed to correct clubfeet, hip dislocations, and other disorders of the skeleton. In addition, children with hydrocephalus may require the installation of a drainage tube in the brain to relieve fluid pressure.

Children with spina bifida may also require the insertion of a catheter. A catheter is a thin tube inserted into the bladder, which can empty the bladder when the patient can not. Problems with bowel movements may require high-fiber diets, laxatives, or enemas to avoid blockage of the bowel.

PROGNOSIS

The outlook for children with spina bifida varies widely depending on the severity of the condition. Improved surgical procedures have saved the lives of many children. In many cases patients can live relatively normal, well-adjusted lives.

On the other hand, the prognosis is not very promising for children with severe forms of spina bifida. The children most at risk are those who are completely paralyzed, have serious infections of the spinal cord, or have hydrocephalus or other birth defects.

PREVENTION

There is no known way to prevent spina bifida. Some research suggests, however, that the risk for neural tube defects can be reduced with folic acid therapy. Folic acid is a member of the vitamin B family. Studies have shown that pregnant women who take small amounts of folic acid have reduced risk for having children with neural tube defects.

Spinal bifida can also be prevented if parents make birth decisions based on blood tests, amniocentesis, and ultrasound tests. These tests can determine with a high degree of reliability if a fetus has neural tube defects. Parents can use this information to make decisions about the future of the fetus.

FOR MORE INFORMATION

Books

Lutkenhoff, Marlene, ed. *Spinabilities: A Young Person's Guide to Spina Bifida.* Bethesda, MD: Woodbine House, 1997.

Sandler, Adrian. *Living With Spina Bifida: A Guide for Families and Professionals.* Chapel Hill: University of North Carolina Press, 1997.

Periodicals

Kolata, Gina. "Vitamin Can Avert Birth Defect, But Message Goes Unheeded." *New York Times* (March 4, 1995): pp. 5+.

Organizations

March of Dimes Birth Defects Foundation. 1275 Mamaroneck Ave., White Plains, NY 10605. (800) 367–6630.

Spina Bifida Association of America. 4590 MacArthur Blvd., NW, Suite 250, Washington, DC 20007–4266. (800) 621–3141.

SPINAL CORD INJURY

DEFINITION

Spinal cord injury is damage to the spinal cord that causes loss of sensation (feeling) and motor (muscular) control.

DESCRIPTION

About ten thousand new spinal cord injuries (SPI) occur each year in the United States. About 250,000 people currently have this condition. Spinal cord injury can happen to anyone at any time of life. The typical patient, however, is a man between the ages of nineteen and twenty-six. The most common causes of SPI are motor vehicle accidents (which are responsible for 50 percent of all cases), a fall (20 percent), an act of violence (15 percent), or a sporting accident (14 percent). Alcohol or drug abuse is involved in many of the accidents that result in spinal cord injuries.

About 6 percent of those who suffer injury to the lower spine die within a year while approximately 40 percent of those who suffer injury to the upper spine die within a year.

CAUSES

The spinal cord is a long rope-like piece of nervous tissue. It runs from the brain down the back. It is contained within the spinal column. The spinal column consists of a set of bones known as vertebrae (pronounced VUR-tuh-bray).

Pairs of nerves travel from the spinal cord to muscles in the arms, legs, and other parts of the body. Messages travel from muscles to the spinal cord and then to the brain along one set of nerves. Messages travel in the opposite direction, from brain to spine to muscles, along the other set of nerves.

Each pair of nerves is connected to the spinal cord in the space between two adjacent vertebrae. The nerves are named for the vertebrae where they enter the spinal cord. The five sets of nerves connecting to the spinal cord are defined as follows:

- C1-8 nerves enter the spine near the eighth cervical vertebrae, located in the neck.
- T1-12 nerves enter the spine near the thoracic vertebrae, located in the chest.
- L1-5 nerves enter the spine near the lumbar vertebrae, in the lower back.
- S1-5 nerves enter the spine through the sacral vertebrae, located in the pelvis region.
- The coccygeal nerves (pronounced kock-SIHJ-ee-uhl) enter the spine through the coccyx, or tailbone.

Injury to the spinal cord may damage any one or more of these nerves. When nerves are damaged, messages can not travel from the brain to the body's muscles, or from the muscles to the brain. For example, a person may lose their sense of touch if nerve messages are not able to travel from the fingers to the brain. Or a person may lose the ability to walk if nerve messages can not travel from the brain to leg and foot muscles. Other functions, such as urination, sexual function, sweating, and blood pressure, may also be affected.

The spinal cord can be damaged in many ways. A sudden and violent jolt can cause a temporary spinal concussion. The symptoms of a concussion usually disappear completely in a few hours. Or the spinal cord can suffer a contusion. A contusion is a bruise that can cause bleeding in the spinal column. Such bleeding can produce pressure on nerve cells that can cause those cells to die.

WORDS TO KNOW

Autonomic responses: Bodily responses that occur automatically, without the need for a person to think about it.

Contracture: Permanent tightening and shortening of a muscle.

Contusion: A bruise.

Motor function: A body function controlled by muscles.

Spasticity: The permanent tightening of a joint into an abnormal position.

Spinal cord: A long rope-like piece of nervous tissue that runs from the brain down the back.

Spinal transection: A complete break in the spinal column.

Vertebrae: Bones that make up the spinal column.

Spinal compression is caused when an object such as a tumor or abnormal growth puts pressure on the spinal column. This compression can cause the death of nerve cells.

Some injuries can cause a laceration (tear) in the spinal column. In the most serious cases, the spinal cord can be torn apart. This type of injury is known as a spinal transection. A spinal cord injury can consist of any one or combination of these types of damage.

SYMPTOMS

The symptoms of SCI depend on two factors: where the damage occurs and how serious it is. For example, damage below the T1 nerves causes loss

Former Texas Christian University football player Matt Moore suffered a paralyzing spinal injury during football practice. About 14 percent of spinal cord injuries are caused by sporting accidents. (Reproduced by permission of AP/Wide World Photos)

of feeling and paralysis in the legs and the lower body. The T1 nerves lie at the base of the ribs. Arm and upper body movement is not affected by this kind of injury.

Damage to nerves below the C3 level of nerves may cause loss of feeling and paralysis of the arms as well as the legs and upper body. The C3 nerves are located in the middle of the neck. This kind of injury may also damage a person's chest muscles, making breathing difficult, but not impossible.

Damage above the C3 level may cause loss of feeling and paralysis throughout the body below the neck. A person with this kind of damage is not able to breathe on his or her own.

A spinal transection causes complete loss of feeling and muscle control. A person is completely paralyzed in the part of the body below the injury. For example, a person whose spinal cord is severed at T1 will be unable to move his or her legs or the lower part of the body. If the spine is injured but not severed, some feeling may remain.

Spinal cord injuries can cause many other kinds of symptoms, including:

- Blood clots. Blood clots may form in veins when an arm or leg has been inactive for a long time. The clot may break loose and cause damage to the heart or lungs.
- Pressure ulcers. Pressure ulcers are sores that develop when a person can not move for long periods of time.
- Muscle stiffness. Spinal cord damage may make it impossible to move muscles normally. After a while, the muscles tend to become tight and shortened. This process is called a contracture. Eventually, the muscles become frozen in an abnormal and awkward position. When this happens, the muscle is said to be spastic.
- Calcium deposits in muscles and tendons. Spinal cord injury may cause the growth of bone-like material in muscles and tendons. This growth may produce swelling, redness, heat, and stiffness in a muscle.
- Failure of autonomic responses. Some body organs regulate themselves. The heart is an example. It automatically increases or decreases its rate of beating based on outside conditions, such as temperature. A person doesn't have to think about making these changes. They occur automatically. They are known as autonomic (self-controlling) responses. SCI can damage these systems. An organ may not respond the way it is supposed to. For example, pressure on the skin can cause organs to produce wild and uncontrolled responses. The patient may experience terrible headaches, nausea, anxiety, seating, and goose bumps. In extreme cases, these abnormal responses may lead to seizures, loss of consciousness, and even death.
- Loss of bladder and bowel control. Bladder and bowel control are maintained by the use of certain muscles. Young children have to learn how to use these muscles when they become toilet-trained. SCI can cause damage

to the nerves that control these muscles. A person may urinate or defecate without wanting to, or may not be able to urinate or defecate when he or she needs to.

- Sexual dysfunction. Maintaining an erection requires control over muscles in the penis. If nerves are damaged, this control may not be possible. A man may not be able to have an erection. Sexual intercourse may become impossible. Women with spinal cord injuries, however may still be able to become pregnant, and can usually deliver a child with proper medical care.

DIAGNOSIS

Symptoms such as those listed above may suggest the presence of spinal cord injury. A final diagnosis is usually made using some form of imaging technique. An imaging technique is any method for studying the structure of an internal organ. For example, X rays may show the location and extent of damage to the spinal cord.

TREATMENT

The first step in treating spinal cord injuries is immobilization. Immobilization involves the use of splints, braces, or a cast to prevent the patient from moving. It keeps a spinal tear or injury from becoming worse. Steroid injections (shots) may be given to the patient as well. Steroids reduce inflammation and swelling, and this can prevent further damage to cells and tissues in the spinal cord. Immobilization and drug injections have greatly reduced the severity of spinal cord injuries in the last few decades.

There are currently no treatments that will make a spinal cord grow back to its normal condition. The most that can be done is to help people with spinal cord injuries avoid complications and to make the best use of those bodily functions they still control. Programs of this type often require a variety of professional workers, including a neurologist (specialist in nerve disorders), psychiatrist or psychologist, physical therapist and occupational therapist. Depending on the type of injury, a patient might also need the help of a respiratory therapist, speech-language specialist, nutritionist, special education teacher, or recreation therapist. Support groups also provide important information, advice, and emotional support for SCI patients. Support groups are made up of other individuals who have the same medical problem.

Some specific forms of rehabilitation (recovery) treatment include the following:

Paralysis and loss of feeling

Many patients with SCI can recover at least some of their ability to move. Physical therapists can teach patients how to use muscles that are still functional to take over for those that are not. The therapist can also help with exercises that will strengthen muscles that can still move. He or she also suggests equipment that may aid the patient's ability to move, such as braces, canes, or wheelchairs.

An occupational therapist teaches patients how to perform normal daily activities, such as eating and caring for oneself. The therapist may suggest changes in the person's home or work to make routine activities easier to perform.

A respiratory therapist helps SCI patients learn how to function with a weakened breathing system. For example, patients may learn new methods of coughing to make sure that disease-causing agents are eliminated from the lungs.

Pressure ulcers

Pressure ulcers (bedsores) often develop when a person is confined to bed for long periods of time. The sores can be prevented by turning the patient every two hours. Special chairs and mattresses are available that make pressure ulcers less likely.

Contracture and spasticity

Patients can be taught exercises that keep their muscles from becoming too stiff. In some cases, drug injections can help relax the muscle tissue. In extreme cases, surgery may be necessary to cut and/or replace tendons that have become too stiff.

Abnormal calcium deposits

A drug known as etidronate disodium (Didronel) helps control the way calcium is used in the body. When injected into SCI patients, it prevents calcium from depositing in muscles and tendons. In some cases, doctors may decide to remove abnormal calcium deposits by surgery.

Failure of autonomic responses

Patients and their families should learn to detect signs that autonomic responses are failing.

If not treated quickly, these failures can cause serious damage or death. Patients may need to be protected from conditions, such as exposure to the sun and pressure on the skin that may cause abnormal responses.

Sexual dysfunction

Counseling may help SCI patients to learn other forms of sexual behavior than traditional forms of intercourse. These alternative sexual behaviors can often be as satisfying as those with which the patient was familiar.

PROGNOSIS

The prognosis for spinal cord injury depends on two factors: the location of the injury and its extent. Injuries of the neck above the C4 nerves are the most dangerous. Patients often lose the ability to breathe on their own. The infection of the respiratory (breathing) tract that can result is the leading cause of death among patients with this type of spinal cord injury.

Overall, 85 percent of SCI patients who survive the first twenty-four hours after being injured are still alive ten years after the injury. How much control over bodily functions a patient recovers is impossible to predict. There more moderate the injury to the spinal cord, the greater chance for recovery.

PREVENTION

The vast majority of spinal cord injuries occur during accidents. As a result, it is difficult to prevent such injuries. Perhaps the most important step one can take is to use safety precautions that are available. For example, one should always wear a seat belt when traveling in a car. Also, one should wear protective equipment, such as helmets, when engaging in certain types of sports such as bike riding, roller-blading, and mountain climbing.

FOR MORE INFORMATION

Books

Reeve, Christopher. *Still Me*. New York: Random House, 1998.

Senelick, Richard C., and Karla Dougherty. *The Healthsouth Spinal Cord Injury Handbook for Patients and Their Families*. Birmingham, AL: Healthsouth Corporation, 1998.

Williams, Margie. *Journey to Well: Learning to Live After Spinal Cord Injury*. Newcastle, CA: Altarfire Publishing, 1998.

Organizations

The National Spinal Cord Injury Association. 8300 Colesville Road, Silver Springs, MD 20910. (301) 588–6959. http://www.erols.com/nscia.

Other

"Ask NOAH About: Spinal Cord and Head Injuries." *NOAH: New York Online Access to Health*. [Online] http://www.noah.cuny.edu/neuro/spinal.html (accessed on October 31, 1999).

STREP THROAT

DEFINITION

Strep throat is an infection of the pharynx (pronounced FAAR-ingks). The pharynx is the part of the throat that connects the mouth and the larynx (pronounced LAAR-ingks), or voice box. Strep throat is caused by a group of bacteria known as the streptococcal (pronounced strep-tuh-KOK-uhl) bacteria. If untreated, a strep throat can lead to serious complications, such as rheumatic fever (see rheumatic fever entry).

DESCRIPTION

Strep throat accounts for 5 to 10 percent of all sore throats. Anyone can get the disease but it is most common among school age children and certain groups of adults. Adults at higher risk include smokers, people who are unusually tired, and those who live in damp, crowded conditions.

Strep throat occurs most often between November and April. The disease passes directly from person to person and coughing, sneezing, or close contact can transfer it from one person to another. If someone in a household has strep throat there is a one in four chance that another person in the household will get the infection, too.

CAUSES

Strep throat is caused by various types of bacteria called Group A *streptococcal* bacteria. These bacteria cause other common infections also, such as tonsillitis and scarlet fever.

SYMPTOMS

The first symptoms of strep throat appear one to five days after a person is infected. The symptoms are no different from any other kind of sore throat (see sore throat entry). They include fever, chills, headache, muscle aches, nausea, a feeling of tiredness, and swollen lymph glands. (Lymph nodes are small round or oval bodies that are part of the body's immune system.) The patient's tonsils will be swollen and have bright red with white or yellow patches on

WORDS TO KNOW

Antibiotic: A substance derived from bacteria or other organisms that fights the growth of other bacteria or organisms.

Lactobacillus acidophilus: A bacterium found in yogurt that changes the balance of bacteria in the intestine in a beneficial way.

Lymph nodes: Small round or oval bodies within the immune system. Lymph nodes provide materials that fight disease and help remove bacteria and other foreign material from the body.

Throat culture: A sample of tissue taken from a person's throat for analysis. The culture is often taken by swiping a cotton swab across the back of the throat.

Tonsillitis: An infection and swelling of the tonsils.

them. A person with strep throat often has bad breath. Strep throat can often spread and cause an infection to the tonsils (see tonsillitis entry).

Some people with the disease may have few or no symptoms of strep throat. Many young children may get a headache or stomachache, but show no signs of having a sore throat. Other patients develop a high fever along with a sunburn-like rash on the face and upper body, and their tongues may become right red. This form of the infection is known as scarlet fever (see scarlet fever entry). Scarlet fever is no more dangerous than strep throat and both illnesses are treated the same way.

A serious complication of strep throat is rheumatic fever. Rheumatic fever (pronounced roo-MAT-ick FEE-vur) occurs most often in children between the ages of five and fifteen. However, rheumatic fever is relatively rare and is seldom a problem if strep throat is treated properly and quickly.

DIAGNOSIS

The first steps in diagnosing strep throat are a patient history and physical examination. The doctor will ask if the patient has been around other people with the infection. He or she will also examine the patient's throat and chest. The doctor will also try to eliminate other potential causes of the symptoms, such as bronchitis (see bronchitis entry) or sinus infection.

Two kinds of tests are available for strep throat. Both involve taking a throat culture, which is done by using a cotton swab to remove a sample of tissue from the sore area in the throat. The sample can then be used for a rapid strep test or a culture.

The rapid test shows whether streptococcal bacteria are present in the throat. The results are available in about twenty minutes. The advantage of the test is the speed with which a diagnosis can be made. Its disadvantage is its high rate of error. The results are wrong in about 20 percent of all cases.

For this reason, the throat culture is often used for a second test. In this test, the sample obtained from the throat is allowed to grow in a warm, moist place for a period of twenty-four to forty-eight hours. During this period, the bacteria reproduce and grow. They reach a size where they can be studied under a microscope to see what types of bacteria are present. This test produces a much higher rate of accuracy in determining whether a patient has strep throat.

TREATMENT

Strep throat is treated with antibiotics. Antibiotics are substances derived from bacteria or other organisms that fight the growth of other bacteria or organisms. Penicillin is the most common antibiotic used. The penicillin is usually given orally (by mouth). The usual treatment lasts for ten days. Patients are advised to be sure that they take all of the medication given. If they stop too soon, the infection may return. Penicillin is sometimes be given by injection. A long-lasting form of the drug (Bicillin) may have the same effect as a 10-day treatment with pills.

About 10 percent of the time, penicillin is not effective against the strep bacteria. In that case, another antibiotic is prescribed. People who are allergic to penicillin may also require an alternative. Other antibiotics used in such cases include amoxicillin, clindamycin, erythromycin, or cephalosporin.

Though strep throat usually gets better on its own after four or five days, antibiotics are usually prescribed anyway, to prevent complications such as rheumatic fever from developing.

Home Care for Strep Throat

Some simple home care treatments can be used to make a patient with strep throat more comfortable. These treatments are used in addition to, not in place of, antibiotics. These home treatments include:

- Pain killers, such as acetaminophen or ibuprofen. Aspirin should not be given to children because of the risk of Reye's syndrome (see Reye's syndrome entry).
- Gargling with double strength tea or warm salt water
- Drinking plenty of fluids, excepting for acidic fluids such as orange or grapefruit juice
- Eating soft, nutritious foods, such as noodle soup
- Avoiding smoking and second hand smoke
- Resting until the fever is gone and then resuming normal activities gradually
- Using a room humidifier

Most throat lozenges and sprays available in drug stores should be avoided. They are likely to make a strep throat worse.

Alternative Treatment

Most alternative treatments are designed to ease the symptoms of strep throat. They do not help to cure the infection. One recommended treatment is the use of the bacterium that occurs in yogurt, *Lactobacillus acidophilus,* (pronounced LACK-toe-buh-SILL-us as-ih-DOFE-uh-luhss) to counteract the effects of antibiotics on bacteria that occur naturally in the intestines.

Other suggested treatments include:

- Inhaling the fragrances of certain herbs, such as lavender, thyme, eucalyptus, sage, and sandalwood
- Gargling with a mixture of water, salt, and tumeric, alum, sumac, sage, or bayberry
- Taking a tea made from osha root, sage, Echinacea, or cleavers

PROGNOSIS

Patients with strep throat usually begin feeling better about twenty-four hours after first taking antibiotics. Symptoms rarely last longer than five days.

People remain contagious until they have been taking antibiotics for twenty-four hours. Children should not return to school until they are no longer contagious. Food handlers should not work during the same time period. People who are not treated with antibiotics may continue to spread strep bacteria for several months.

PREVENTION

The risk of passing strep throat from one person to another can be reduced by some simple actions, such as:

- Washing hands frequently and well, especially after nose blowing or sneezing and before handling foods
- Disposing of used tissues properly

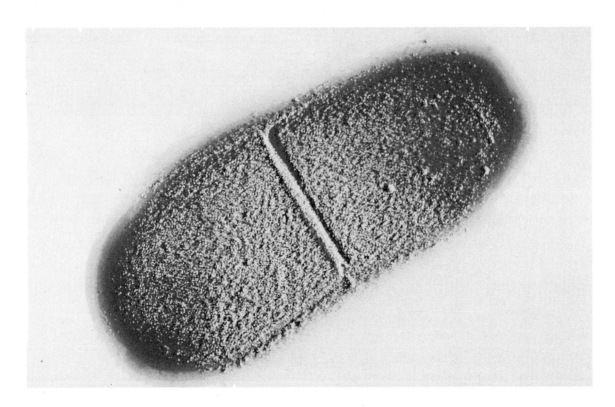

Group A Streptococcus bacterium. (© 1998 J.L. Carson. Reproduced by permission of Custom Medical Stock Photo.)

- Avoiding close contact with someone who has strep throat
- Not sharing food and eating utensils with other people
- Not smoking

FOR MORE INFORMATION

Web sites

"Ask NOAH About: Respiratory Disorders." *NOAH: New York Online Access to Health.* [Online] http://www.noah.cuny.edu/respiratory/resp.html#STREP (accessed on October 31, 1999).

National Institute of Allergy and Infectious Diseases. "A Group of Streptococcal Infection." *NIAID Fact Sheet.* [Online] http://www.niaid.nih.govfactsheets/strep.htm (accessed on February 1, 1999).

STROKE

DEFINITION

A stroke is the sudden death of cells in a limited part of the brain caused by a reduced flow of blood to the brain.

DESCRIPTION

Blood brings oxygen and nutrients to brain cells and also removes waste products from cells. A stroke occurs when blood flow is interrupted to part of the brain. Without blood, brain cells quickly begin to die. The effects of a stroke depend on the part of the brain affected. A stroke may cause paralysis, speech problems, loss of memory or reasoning ability, coma, or death.

More than half a million people in the United States experience a stroke each year. Stroke is the third leading cause of death in this country and the leading cause of disability. Two-thirds of all strokes occur in people over the age of sixty-five. They affect men more often than women, and blacks more often than whites.

Stroke is a medical emergency that requires immediate medical attention. The sooner treatment is received, the better the chances of survival. At one time, nine out of ten people died after a stroke. Because of improved treatment methods, less than three out of ten people who suffer a stroke die from the experience.

stroke

There are four main types of strokes. They are:

- Cerebral thrombosis
- Cerebral embolism
- Subarachnoid hemorrhage
- Intracerebral hemorrhage

Cerebral thrombosis and cerebral embolism account for about three-quarters of all strokes.

Cerebral thrombosis occurs when a blood clot forms inside the brain, stopping the flow of blood to or from the brain. The medical term for blood clot is thrombosis. The most common cause for the formation of a blood clot is the hardening of the arteries, or atherosclerosis (see atherosclerosis entry).

A cerebral thrombosis occurs most often at night or early in the morning. It is often preceded by a transient ischemic attack (TIA), which is also referred to as a mini-stroke. A TIA may act as a warning sign that a full stroke is likely to occur.

Cerebral embolism is also caused by a blood clot. The clot, however, forms elsewhere in the body then travels through the bloodstream to the brain. Once in the brain, it produces effects like those of cerebral thrombosis.

Subarachnoid hemorrhage and intracerebral hemorrhage are caused when blood vessels in the brain break. Blood vessels sometimes develop weak spots in their walls. These weak spots are called aneurysms (pronounced AN-yu-RIHZ-umz; see cerebral aneurysm entry). When an aneurysm breaks, blood flows out of the blood vessel into the surrounding tissue and brain cells begin to die rapidly. An intracerebral hemorrhage takes place inside the brain. A subarachnoid (pronounced sub-uh-RAK-noyd) hemorrhage occurs on the surface of the brain.

WORDS TO KNOW

Aneurysm: A weak spot in a blood vessel that may break open and lead to a stroke.

Cerebral embolism: Blockage of a blood vessel in the brain by a blood clot that originally formed elsewhere in the body and then traveled to the brain.

Cerebral thrombosis: Blockage of a blood vessel in the brain by a blood clot that formed in the brain itself.

Intracerebral hemorrhage: Bleeding that occurs within the brain.

Subarachnoid hemorrhage: Bleeding that occurs on the surface of the brain.

Tissue plasminogen activator (tPA): A substance that dissolves blood clots in the brain.

SYMPTOMS

The symptoms of a stroke caused by an embolism usually appear suddenly and are most intense right after the stroke occurs. With a thrombosis, the stroke comes on more slowly. In either case, symptoms include:

- Blurring or decreased vision in one or both eyes

- Severe headache, often described as "the worst headache of my life"
- Weakness, numbness, or paralysis of the face, arm, or leg. These symptoms usually occur on one side of the body only
- Dizziness or loss of balance or coordination

DIAGNOSIS

Rapid diagnosis is essential in successful treatment of stroke. A doctor will first look for symptoms. He or she will then look at the patient's medical history for the presence of risk factors in the patient's background and a description of when and how symptoms appeared.

If stroke is suspected, more sophisticated tools are used for diagnosis. Imaging techniques will show whether the stroke was caused by a blood clot or a hemorrhage. This information is needed to begin the correct type of treatment. Blood and urine tests are also carried out. Other tests used to determine if a stroke has occurred include an electrocardiogram, angiography, or ultrasound tests.

TREATMENT

Immediate Intervention

Stroke treatment usually occurs in two phases. The first phase involves immediate steps to save the patient's life. In many cases, this involves dissolving the blood clot. The most effective substance currently available for this step is tissue plasminogen activator, or tPA. In order to be effective, tPA must be given to the patient within three hours of the stroke. In such cases, tPA goes to the blood clot and begins dissolving it immediately. The normal flow of blood to the brain is restored.

Some patients can not be given tPA. For example, the doctor may not know exactly when the stroke occurred. In these cases, other blood-thinning agents can be used. The substance known as heparin is often used. Even ordinary aspirin can be effective in dissolving the blood clot.

The primary goal in treating brain hemorrhages is to relieve pressure on the brain. Cer-

RISK FACTORS FOR STROKE

The factors that determine a person's risk of having a stroke include age, sex, heredity, lifestyle choices, and other medical problems:

- **Age and sex.** The risk of stroke increases with increasing age. Men are more likely to have a stroke than women.

- **Heredity.** Blacks, Asians, and Hispanics all have higher rates of stroke than do whites. People with a family history of stroke are also at greater risk.

- **Lifestyle choices.** Lifestyle choices that increase a person's risk for stroke include smoking, low level of physical activity, excessive alcohol consumption, or use of cocaine or other illegal drugs.

- **Other medical problems.** Stroke risk is higher for people with diabetes, heart disease, high blood pressure, previous stroke, obesity, high cholesterol level, or high red blood count.

tain drugs can be used for this purpose. They include urea, mannitol, and the corticosteroids.

In some cases, surgery can be used to treat brain hemorrhages. A surgeon can close off blood vessels that have ruptured (broken open) in order to stop bleeding and help reduce pressure on the brain.

Rehabilitation

Once a patient's condition has been stabilized, rehabilitation can begin. Rehabilitation refers to a variety of methods for helping a patient recover normal functions to the extent possible. The patient may also need to learn how to use existing functions to take the place of those lost by the stroke.

About 10 percent of all patients who survive a stroke recover completely. Another 10 percent suffer severe disability and require institutional care for the rest of their lives. The remaining 80 percent of stroke survivors are able

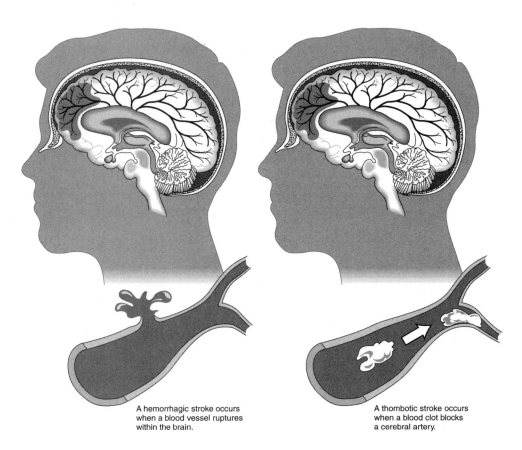

A hemorrhagic stroke occurs when a blood vessel ruptures within the brain.

A thombotic stroke occurs when a blood clot blocks a cerebral artery.

A hemorrhagic stroke (left) compared to a thrombotic stroke (right). (Reproduced by permission of Hans & Cassady, Inc.)

to return to their homes and their daily routines. However, they may require additional therapy and support services.

PREVENTITIVE REHABILITATION. A program of rehabilitation consists of two parts. The first objective is to prevent medical complications of stroke. People who have had a stroke are at high risk for other serious medical problems including a second stroke.

Another possible complication is deep venous thrombosis (a blood clot in a vein). This condition may develop when a limb has become paralyzed and blood is no longer flowing normally in the limb. In such cases, the chance that a blood clot will develop greatly increases. If a blood clot forms and then breaks loose, it may travel to the lungs. In the lungs, it may cause a pulmonary embolism, (a blot clot in the lungs) that can very quickly lead to death.

Stroke patients may be kept on a special program of medication to prevent this complication. The program includes the use of drugs that thin blood out and reduce the chance that blood clots will form.

Once a patient's condition has been stabilized, rehabilitation can begin. Rehabilitation refers to a variety of methods for helping a patient recover normal functions to the extent possible. (© 1993 Mike Moreland. Reproduced by permission of Custom Medical Stock Photo.)

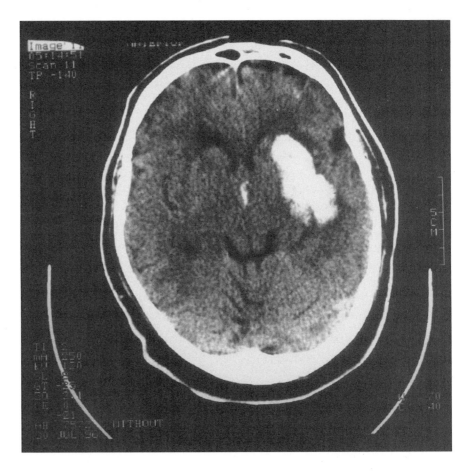

CAT scan of a brain showing a stroke resulting in hemorrhage (white area). (© 1996 Bates, M.D. Reproduced by permission of Custom Medical Stock Photo.)

Another complication of stroke is caused by damage to throat muscles. A stroke patient may find it difficult to swallow normally. Food may get into the lungs, causing pneumonia or other infections. This condition can be treated with breathing exercises and temporary use of soft foods in the diet.

Depression is another side effect of stroke. Depression can be treated with drugs and with counseling that helps patients cope with the conditions caused by the stroke.

REHABILITATIVE THERAPY. Brain cells killed by stroke do not grow back. The functions those cells control may be seriously damaged or lost. For example, cells in one part of the brain control the ability to speak. If those cells are killed, the patient may lose the ability to speak.

Fortunately, surviving brain cells can sometimes be trained to take on new functions and patients may recover some or all of the function lost during the stroke. For instance, areas of the brain that were not previously responsible for a patient's ability to speak may learn how to control speech.

Rehabilitative therapy draws primarily on four types of treatment:

- Physical therapy is used to help patients recover as much of their original body functions as possible. Treatment may involve exercises that help patients regain strength and become better able to move around. A physical therapist can provide advice on aids such as wheelchairs, braces, and canes.
- Occupational therapy helps patients improve self-care skills, such as feeding, bathing, and dressing. The occupational therapist may also help the patient redesign his or her living area or work area to make movement easier. A specialist in speech and language may also be needed to help patients relearn the ability to speak and swallow correctly.
- Mental health professionals treat mental problems, such as depression and loss of memory and thinking skills. They may also provide counseling to help patients deal with the new physical conditions resulting from stroke. Social workers and home caregivers may be needed to help patients adapt to the new challenges of dealing with tasks of everyday lives.
- Support groups can provide an important source of information, advice, and comfort for stroke patients and their families. A support group consists of other individuals who have the same medical problem as the patient.

PROGNOSIS

Prognosis depends on both sex and ethnicity. The highest rate of fatalities occurs in black males (52 percent) and the lowest in white females (23 percent). People who survive stroke may experience a wide variety of disabilities.

PREVENTION

Stroke prevention involves two separate issues. One issue is keeping the patient alive after a stroke. If a stroke patient is treated quickly, chances of survival are much greater. Everyone should become familiar with the symptoms of stroke. When those symptoms appear, a person should seek medical advice as quickly as possible. In many cases, local 911 services may need to be called immediately.

A second issue in prevention is reducing one's risk for the condition. Some steps that one can take to this end include:

- Stop smoking.
- Bring blood pressure under control.

- Get regular exercise.
- Keep body weight down.
- Avoid excessive alcohol consumption.
- Get regular medical checkups and follow the doctor's advice regarding diet and medicines.

FOR MORE INFORMATION

Books

Caplan, L.R., M.L. Dyken, and J.D. Easton. *American Heart Association Family Guide to Stroke Treatment, Recovery, and Prevention.* New York: Times Books, 1996.

Warlow, C. P., et al. *Stroke: A Practical Guide to Management.* Boston: Blackwell Science, 1996.

Weiner, F.M., H.M. Lee, and H. Bell. *Recovering at Home After a Stroke: A Practical Guide for You and Your Family.* Los Angeles: The Body Press/Perigee Books, 1994.

Organizations

National Stroke Association. 96 Inverness Drive East, Suite I, Englewood, CO 80112–5112. (303) 649–9299. http://www.stroke.org.

American Heart Association. 7272 Greenville Ave., Dallas, TX 75231–4596. (800) AHA–USA1 (242–8721). http://www.amhrt.org.

Web sites

"Ask NOAH About: Heart Disease and Stroke." *NOAH: New York Online Access to Health.* [Online] http://www.noah.cuny.edu/heart_disease/heartdisease.html#S (accessed on October 31, 1999).

SUDDEN INFANT DEATH SYNDROME

DEFINITION

Sudden infant death syndrome (SIDS) is the unexplained death of an apparently healthy infant, usually during sleep. The condition is also known as crib death.

DESCRIPTION

Sudden infant death syndrome strikes 1 to 2 infants in every 1,000. It is the leading cause of death in newborn children. SIDS accounts for about 10 percent of deaths occurring during the first year of life.

SIDS most commonly strikes babies between the ages of two and six months. It almost never occurs in babies younger than two weeks or older than eight months. Most SIDS deaths occur between midnight and 8 A.M.

More than 4,800 babies died of SIDS in 1992. That number dropped to 3,279 deaths in 1995. One reason for this decrease was better education about the disorder. Parents were being taught to place babies on their backs or sides when put to bed, which is thought to reduce the risk of SIDS. In spite of this progress, doctors still have not determined the cause of SIDS.

CAUSES

While the exact cause or causes of SIDS are still unknown, one important factor may be infection of the respiratory (breathing) tract. Some studies show that many babies who die of SIDS had recently been treated for a cold or other respiratory illness. Most SIDS deaths occur during the winter and early spring. These seasons are the peak times for respiratory infections. Research suggests that the following factors may increase the risk of SIDS for a baby:

- The baby sleeps on his or her stomach.
- The baby's mother smoked during pregnancy.
- The mother was under the age of twenty at pregnancy.
- The mother abuses drugs.
- The mother received little or no prenatal (before birth) care.
- The baby was born prematurely (early) or with a low birth weight.
- The baby lives in house where someone smokes.
- The baby is male (SIDS is more common for infant boys that girls).
- Baby is a member of a minority or low-income family.
- Baby's family has a history of Sudden Infant Death Syndrome.

Theories about SIDS

Researchers have long been puzzled as to the actual cause of SIDS. While there are a number of theories to explain the condition, none of them have been proven. Doctors are often unable even to determine whether a baby died because of a heart problem or because it suddenly lost the ability to breathe.

WORDS TO KNOW

Autopsy: A medical examination of a dead body.

Crib death: Another name for sudden infant death syndrome.

Secondhand Smoke: One person's exhaled cigarette smoke that is breathed in by another person nearby.

Generally the theories focus on either medical disorders or the baby's physical surroundings.

MEDICAL DISORDERS. One theory about the cause of SIDS is that the baby's upper airway gets blocked. The baby suffocates because it can not get oxygen. Another theory is that the baby's blood has the wrong composition and may not contain enough of certain chemicals needed to keep the brain functioning.

RESEARCHERS HAVE LONG BEEN PUZZLED AS TO THE ACTUAL CAUSE OF SIDS. WHILE THERE ARE A NUMBER OF THEORIES TO EXPLAIN THE CONDITION, NONE OF THEM HAVE BEEN PROVEN.

A third theory is that SIDS babies have a faulty nervous system. Normally, infants have a mechanism that wakes them up when their oxygen supply is low. It could be that SIDS babies don't have that mechanism. Other theories blame SIDS on a faulty immune system or the buildup of certain chemicals called fatty acids in the baby's blood.

PHYSICAL SURROUNDINGS. Some researchers think SIDS may be caused by the way a baby sleeps. For example, it may be that a baby sleeps with its face in soft bedding or that the baby may be wrapped too tightly in blankets. Either of these situations can stop the baby from breathing properly or getting enough oxygen.

SYMPTOMS

SIDS does not have any warning symptoms. Death occurs suddenly and unexpectedly.

TEN LEADING CAUSES OF INFANT DEATH (U.S.)

Congenital anomalies
Pre-term/Low birthweight
Sudden Infant Death Syndrome (SIDS)
Respiratory Distress Syndrome
Problems related to complications of pregnancy
Complications of placenta, cord, and membrane
Accidents
Perinatal infections
Pneumonia/Influenza
Intrauterine hypoxia and birth asphyxia

Source: *Monthly vital Statistical Report*, 46, no. 1, Supplement, 1996. (Reproduced by permission of Stanley Publishing)

DIAGNOSIS

The diagnosis of SIDS is usually a diagnosis of exclusion. That means that all other possible causes of death are first ruled out. If no other cause of death can be found, then SIDS may be diagnosed.

Certain diagnosis of SIDS can be made only with an autopsy. An autopsy is a medical examination of a dead body. In about 20 percent of all SIDS cases, an autopsy shows a specific cause for death, such as suffocation. Parents sometimes reject the idea of having an autopsy on their baby, but the procedure can help explain how the baby died. Knowing the actual cause of death can help parents understand that the baby's death was no fault of their own.

TREATMENT

There is no treatment for SIDS. The best that can be done is to take action to prevent babies from dying of the condition. A baby's parents may, however, benefit from treatment including counseling and support from groups of other SIDS parents.

PREVENTION

At least some cases of sudden infant death syndrome can be prevented. Parents can take a number of actions that will reduce the risk of SIDS for their babies. These actions include the following:

- **Sleep position.** At one time, parents were taught to put their babies on their stomachs when they went to bed. That position was thought to prevent the baby from choking in its sleep. Experts now suggest that babies

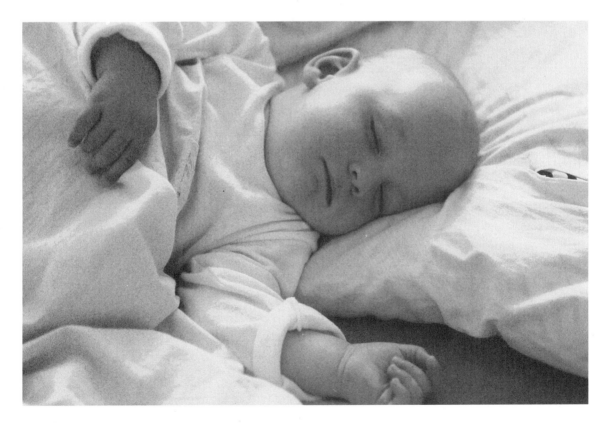

Experts now suggest that babies sleep on their backs or their sides. In these positions, they are less likely to have their faces covered in pillows and blankets. (© 1993 Jan Halaska. Reproduced by permission of Photo Researchers, Inc.)

sleep on their backs or their sides. In these positions, they are less likely to have their faces covered in pillows and blankets.

- **Good prenatal care.** Women should get the best possible medical care while they are pregnant. This care will ensure that they are themselves healthy. Expectant mothers should be warned about the risks of smoking, alcohol intake, and drug use. A healthy mother's body is the best protection the newborn baby can have. Good prenatal care also involves education for the mother. She should be taught the best techniques for caring for her new baby.

- **Proper bedding.** Soft bedding, such as beanbags, waterbeds, and soft mattresses, increase the risk for SIDS. Babies should sleep on firm mattresses with no soft or fluffy materials near by. Soft stuffed toys should not be placed in a crib while the baby sleeps.

- **Room temperature.** A baby's room should be kept at a temperature that is comfortable for the parents. A baby who becomes too warm may sleep too deeply and may find it more difficult to wake up if it has trouble breathing.

- **Diet.** Some studies show that babies who are breast-fed are at lower risk for SIDS. Mother's milk may provide additional protection against infections that can cause SIDS in infants.

- **Bed sharing with parents.** Opinions differ as to whether bed sharing between mother and baby increases or decreases the risk of SIDS. Bed sharing may encourage breast-feeding, which decreases the risk of SIDS. Parents who bed share may also be more aware of any problems their baby has breathing. On the other hand, some studies show that bed-sharing increases the risk of SIDS. In any case, parents should remember cautions about the use of bedding if their babies sleep with them. They should also remember that an adult's bed does not have the same safety features of an infant's crib.

- **Secondhand smoke.** The baby's room should be kept free of tobacco smoke at all times.

- **Electronic monitoring.** Electronic devices are now available that allow parents to listen in while their baby is sleeping. These devices sound an alarm if the baby stops breathing. So far, however, there is no scientific evidence that electronic devices reduce the risk of SIDS. The U.S. National Institutes of Health recommends their use only for babies known to be at risk for SIDS. These babies include premature infants, infants who have had previous breathing problems, or infants with siblings who have died of SIDS.

FOR MORE INFORMATION

Books

Horchler, Joan Nelson, and Robin Rice Morris. *The SIDS Survival Guide: Information and Comfort for Grieving Family and Friends and Professionals Who Seek to Help Them.* Hyattsville, MD: SIDS Educational Services, 1997.

Sears, William. *SIDS: A Parent's Guide to Understanding and Preventing Sudden Infant Death Syndrome.* Boston: Little Brown & Company, 1996.

Organizations

Association of SIDS and Infant Mortality Programs. 630 West Fayette Street, Room 5–684, Baltimore, MD 21201. (410) 706–5062.

National Institute of Child Health and Development/Back to Sleep. 31 Center Drive, MSC2425, Room 2A32, Bethesda, MD 20892–2425. (800) 505–CRIB. http://www.nih.gov/nichd.

National SIDS Resource Center. 2070 Chain Bridge Road, Suite 450, Vienna, VA 22181. (703) 821–8955.

IDS Alliance. 1314 Bedford Avenue, Suite 210, Baltimore, MD 21208. (800) 221–7437.

Web sites

Child Secure. [Online] http://www.childsecure.com (accessed on November 4, 1999).

TAY-SACHS DISEASE

DEFINITION

Tay-Sachs disease (pronounced tay-SACKS) is a genetic disorder that can lead to paralysis, blindness, convulsions, mental retardation (see mental retardation entry) and death. A genetic disorder is a medical problem passed down from one generation to the next. The disorder occurs because of a faulty gene. Genes are the chemical units in all cells that tell cells what functions they should perform. When those genes are absent or faulty, cells do not function properly and a medical disorder results.

DESCRIPTION

Gangliosides (pronounced GANG-glee-uh-SIDES) are fatty substances needed for the proper development of the brain and nerve cells. Under normal conditions, gangliosides are continuously broken down so that the correct amount of gangliosides is always present.

The chemical required to break down gangliosides is an enzyme. Enzymes are chemical compounds present in all cells. These compounds make possible thousands of different reactions needed to keep cells operating normally. In a person with Tay-Sachs disease, the enzyme needed to break down gangliosides is missing. As a result, gangliosides continue to build up in the brain. When the brain becomes clogged with this fatty material it is no longer able to function normally.

Tay-Sachs is especially common among Jewish people of eastern European and Russian origin, sometimes referred to as Ashkenazic Jews. About 1 in every 3,600 babies born to Ashkenazic Jewish couples will have Tay-Sachs disease. The disease is also relatively common among certain French-Canadian and Cajun French families. Tay-Sachs disease is quite rare in families of other ethnic backgrounds.

CAUSES

Every child receives two sets of genes, one from its mother and one from its father. These genes may be either dominant or recessive. A dominant gene is "stronger" than a recessive gene and controls the way a cell is going to function.

If a recessive gene is paired with a dominant gene, the recessive gene has no effect on the way a cell functions. The dominant gene overcomes the recessive gene. The only way a recessive gene has any effect on a cell if it is paired with another recessive gene. In such cases, the two recessive genes work together to direct a cell's operation.

Tay-Sachs is caused by a recessive gene. A child with one recessive gene shows no effect as a result of having the gene. The child is a carrier for the disease. A carrier is a person who has one recessive gene for a characteristic. The carrier can pass the gene on to his or her children even though the carrier does not have the disease.

A child with a pair of these recessive genes, however, will show the symptoms of Tay-Sachs disease because the child will lack a normal gene to makes the enzyme needed to break down gangliosides.

SYMPTOMS

Tay-Sachs disease normally shows up at about the age of six months. Prior to that time, the baby acts normally. Once the symptoms of Tay-Sachs begin to appear the baby stops interacting with other people. It may develop a staring gaze. Normal levels of noise tend to startle the baby to an abnormal degree.

By the time the baby is one year old, it has weak, floppy muscles. The baby may be completely blind, and will usually have a large head. Seizures become a problem between the ages of one and two years and the baby usually dies by the age of four.

WORDS TO KNOW

Dominant gene: A form of a gene that predominates over a second form of the same gene.

Enzymes: Chemicals present in all cells that make possible the chemical reactions needed to keep a cell alive.

Ganglioside: A fatty substance found in brain and nerve cells.

Gene: A chemical unit that carries instructions as to the functions a cell should perform.

Genetic disorder: A medical problem caused by one or more defective genes.

Recessive gene: A form of a gene that does not operate in the presence of a dominant form of the same gene.

DIAGNOSIS

A preliminary diagnosis for Tay-Sachs disease can usually be made by looking into the baby's eyes. If a baby has Tay-Sachs a characteristic cherry-red spot can be seen at the back of the eye.

In order to confirm this diagnosis, blood tests are performed that measure the amount of enzyme needed to break down gangliosides. If the level is very low, the baby has Tay-Sachs disease.

TREATMENT

There is currently no treatment for Tay-Sachs disease. Scientists hope to develop some type of treatment eventually. The treatment would involve providing babies with Tay-Sachs disease new genes. These genes would take

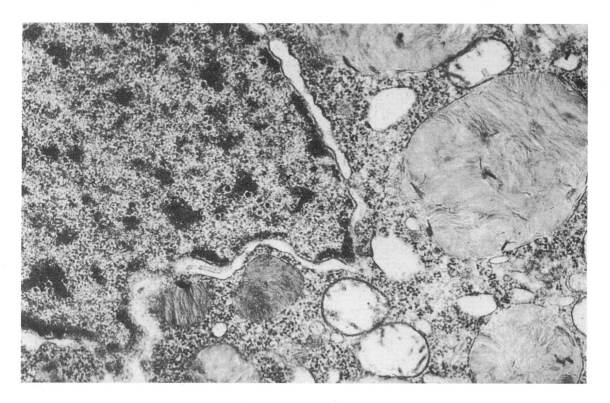

Tay-Sachs disease causes the abnormal buildup of gangliosides, a fatty material required for the normal development of the brain. When the brain becomes clogged with this fatty material it is no longer able to function normally. (© 1992 IMS Creative. Reproduced by permission of Custom Medical Stock Photo.)

over the job of making the enzyme the babies currently lack. While this technology is now being investigated, no technique has yet been shown to work satisfactorily.

PROGNOSIS

At the present time, the prognosis for a baby born with Tay-Sachs disease is certain death. Nothing can be done to keep the baby alive.

PREVENTION

Once a baby receives recessive genes from both parents, it is destined to develop Tay-Sachs disease. The only way to prevent this condition from happening, then, is to make sure no baby receives two recessive genes.

Parents from ethnic groups at risk for Tay-Sachs have the option of being tested for recessive genes. If only one parent has a recessive gene, the baby will not develop Tay-Sachs disease. If both parents have the recessive gene, the child will develop the disorder. Couples can use this kind of information to decide whether or not to have children.

Prenatal testing can also provide information about Tay-Sachs disease. A pregnant woman can be tested to see if her child has Tay-Sachs disease. She and her partner can then decide whether or not to continue with the pregnancy.

FOR MORE INFORMATION

Organizations

Late Onset Tay-Sachs Foundation. 1303 Paper Mill Rd., Erdenheim, PA 19038. (800) 672–2022.

March of Dimes Birth Defects Foundation. National Office. 1275 Mamaroneck Ave., White Plains, NY 10605. http://www.modimes.org.

National Tay-Sachs and Allied Diseases Association, Inc. 2001 Beacon St., Suite 204, Brookline, MA 02146. (800) 672–2022.

Web sites

"Ask NOAH About: Neurological Problems." *NOAH: New York Online Access to Health.* [Online] http://www.noah.cuny.edu/neuro/neuropg.html# TAYSACHS (accessed on October 31, 1999).

TEMPOROMANDIBULAR JOINT DISORDERS

DEFINITION

Temporomandibular joint disorder (TMJ) is a group of symptoms that involve pain in the head, face, and jaw. Symptoms of TMJ include headaches, soreness in the chewing muscles, and clicking or stiffness of the joints. The disorder can be caused by psychological as well as physical factors. TMJ is also known as temporomandibular joint syndrome.

DESCRIPTION

The temporomandibular joint (pronounced TEM-pu-roh-man-DIBB-yuh-lur) connects the jawbone (the mandible) with the lower part of the skull (the temporal bone). The joint is located in front of the ear. It allows the jaw to move up and down, back and forth, and forward and backward. Various factors can alter the shape or motion of the temporomandibular joint, which may then put pressure on facial nerves. This pressure can result in pain in various parts of the head. Most cases of TMJ occur in women between the age of twenty and fifty.

CAUSES

TMJ syndrome has several possible physical causes:

- **Muscle tension.** Overuse of jaw muscles can cause tightness in the temporomandibular joint. A common cause of muscle tightness is stress. People who are overly worried may clench or grind their teeth excessively, which can cause muscle tension.
- **Injury.** A direct blow to the jaw or the side of the head can cause TMJ. The blow can break a bone, bruise soft tissue, or dislocate the temporomandibular joint itself.
- **Arthritis** (see arthritis entry). Arthritis is a disease of joints caused by a number of factors. Arthritis in the region of the temporomandibular joint can cause TMJ.

WORDS TO KNOW

Arthrography: An imaging technique in which a dye is injected into a joint to make X-ray pictures of the inside of the joint easier to study.

Internal derangement: A condition in which the regular arrangement of parts in a system is disturbed. Some cases of TMJ are caused by a particular internal derangement in which the disc in the temporomandibular joint slips out of its normal position.

Mandible: The scientific term for the lower jaw.

Temporal bones: The bones that form the right and left sides of the skull.

- **Internal derangement.** The temporomandibular joint contains a small piece of cartilage called a disc, which keeps the jawbone and the temporal bone from rubbing against each other. Sometimes the disc slips out of place creating what is known as an internal derangement. Often this condition can be detected by a clicking or popping sound caused by the disc moving in and out of its correct position. On rare occasions, the disc can become permanently displaced, and a patient may lose the ability to move his or her jaw in all normal ways.
- **Hypermobility.** Hypermobility is a condition in which ligaments in the temporomandibular joint become loose. Ligaments are pieces of tissue that hold bones together. In cases of hypermobility, the jaw may slip entirely out of its socket.
- **Birth abnormalities.** Children are sometimes born with defects in the temporomandibular joint. For example, the top of the jawbone may be too small. Such causes of TMJ are relatively rare.

SYMPTOMS

The symptoms of TMJ depend in part on its cause. The most common symptoms include the following:

- Facial pain in front of the ears
- Headaches
- Sore jaw muscles
- A clicking sound when chewing
- A grinding feeling when opening and closing the mouth
- Temporary locking of the jaw

Some patients also report a buzzing or ringing in the ears. In most cases, the temporomandibular joint itself is not painful.

DIAGNOSIS

TMJ is most commonly diagnosed by a dentist. The dentist can often tell simply by touching a patient's face if the temporomandibular joint is out of place. Manipulation of the jaw provides additional information. It may be possible to see that the patient's teeth do not close together properly. Looseness in the jaw may indicate hypermobility as well.

Imaging Studies

Imaging studies are used to obtain pictures of the interior of a person's body. X rays are probably the best-known form of imaging studies. In most cases, imaging studies are not very helpful in diagnosing TMJ because the temporomandibular joint will look normal in such studies. Arthrography (pronounced arr-THRAHG-ruh-fee) is one form of imaging that can be useful, however. In arthrography, a dye is injected into the patient's temporomandibular joint. The joint is then observed while being X-rayed. Any abnormal movement of the jaw can be observed by this method.

TREATMENT

The pain associated with TMJ usually goes away on its own without treatment. About 80 percent of patients with the disorder improve in six months without treatment.

Medications

The minor discomfort of TMJ can be treated with pain relievers such as aspirin or acetaminophen. Muscle relaxants may help if the condition is caused by muscle tension. Instances when TMJ is caused by arthritis can be treated with corticosteroids, methotrexate, gold sodium, or other anti-arthritic medications.

Physical Therapy and Mechanical Devices

Some patients experience serious problems with clenching and grinding of their teeth at night. For these patients a plastic splint called a nightguard can be prescribed. The nightguard is placed over the teeth before going to bed. Splints can also be used to hold the jaw and disc in place when these factors are responsible for the disorder.

THE PAIN ASSOCIATED WITH TMJ USUALLY GOES AWAY ON ITS OWN WITHOUT TREATMENT. ABOUT 80 PERCENT OF PATIENTS WITH THE DISORDER IMPROVE IN SIX MONTHS WITHOUT TREATMENT.

TMJ can also be treated by a variety of other techniques, such as ultrasound, biofeedback, stretching exercises, electrical nerve stimulation, stress management techniques, or massage.

Surgery

Surgery can be used to place the temporomandibular joint back into its correct position. This approach is used almost exclusively in cases of TMJ caused by birth deformities or internal derangement.

PROGNOSIS

The prognosis for recovery from TMJ is excellent for almost all patients. Most patients do not need any form of long-term treatment. Surgical procedures used to treat TMJ are usually quite successful. The prognosis for cases of TMJ caused by arthritis depends on the progress of the arthritis itself.

PREVENTION

There is no way to prevent TMJ that is caused by physical factors. Stress-induced TMJ can be prevented by learning stress management techniques before the problem starts.

FOR MORE INFORMATION

Books

Shankland, Wesley E. *TMJ: Its Many Faces,* 2nd edition. Columbus, OH: Anadem, Inc., 1998.

Taddey, John J. *TMJ: The Self Help Program.* La Jolla, CA: Surrey Park Press, 1990.

Uppgaard, Robert O. *Taking Control of TMJ: Your Total Wellness Program for Recovering from Tempromandibular Joint Pain, Whiplash, Fibromyalgia, and Related Disorders.* Oakland, CA: New Harbinger Publications, 1999.

TENDINITIS

DEFINITION

Tendinitis (pronounced tehn-duh-NI-tiss) is the inflammation of a tendon. Tendons are tough, rope-like tissue that connect muscle to bone.

DESCRIPTION

Tendinitis usually occurs in middle or old age. The condition develops when people have used the same motion over and over again for a long time. When tendinitis occurs in younger people, it is usually caused by performing the same motion very frequently over a short period of time.

A classical example of tendinitis is tennis elbow. Tennis elbow gets its name because it occurs most commonly among tennis players. Tennis players may use the same swing of their arm over and over again many times during a few hours or few days. At the end of many weeks of play, the tendon at the player's elbow may become sore and inflamed.

Tendinitis occurs most commonly in three parts of the body. They are:

- Tendons of the hand
- Tendons of the upper arm that connect with the shoulder

- Tendons that run across the top of the foot and the Achilles tendon. The Achilles tendon connects the muscles in the calf of the leg with the heel bone in the foot

CAUSES

Tendons can be injured in two ways; by sudden stretching or repeated use. In either case, the tendon may be pulled, twisted, torn, or otherwise damaged.

SYMPTOMS

When the body tries to heal injured tendons it increases the blood flow to the injured tissues and sends nutrients to the tissues to help them heal. It also sends chemicals designed to fight possible infection to the damaged area.

These steps all help the tendon to get better. But they may also produce swelling, pain, heat, and redness in the damaged tissue, as well as discomfort in the injured area.

DIAGNOSIS

Tendinitis is usually easy to diagnose. The discomfort described by the patient provides the first clue as to the disorder. The doctor will also ask about the patient's work and recreational experiences. Activities that are repeated over and over again in the injured area also suggest the possibility of tendinitis. Tennis elbow is an example of a condition that can be diagnosed by studying the patient's daily activities. The doctor can usually confirm a diagnosis by applying pressure on an injured area or trying to move a sore joint.

TREATMENT

Tendinitis is best treated by a series of steps known as RICE. The four letters in this acronym stand for:

- Rest
- Ice
- Compression
- Elevation

WORDS TO KNOW

Antioxidant: A substance that prevents oxidation from taking place. Oxidation is a chemical reaction that can create heat, pain, and inflammation in the body.

RICE: The term stands for the program of rest, ice, compression, and elevation that is recommended for treating tendinitis.

Tendon: A tough, rope-like tissue that connects muscle to bone.

Tennis elbow: A form of tendinitis that occurs among tennis players and other people who engage in the same movement of the elbow over and over again.

The best way to apply ice is with ice water in a bag. The water insures that the cold will be applied directly to the skin. Chemical ice packs are not advised. They are too cold to use directly on the skin.

An elastic wrap, such as an Ace bandage, can be used to provide compression. Compression is a means of reducing swelling and keeping the joint in its proper position. In some cases, a splint may be used to keep the joint from moving.

Nonsteroidal anti-inflammatory drugs (NSAIDs) can also be used to reduce pain and swelling. Common NSAIDs are aspirin, acetaminophen (trade name Tylenol), and ibuprofen (trade names Advil, Motrin). When these medications are not effective, corticosteroids drugs may be used. Corticosteroids also reduce inflammation and swelling but are usually injected directly into the joint that has been damaged.

In extreme cases, surgery may be necessary. One purpose of surgery is to remove and/or reconstruct the damaged tendon. Another purpose of surgery may be to remove calcium buildups in the joint. Calcium tends to

A classical example of tendinitis is tennis elbow, caused by repetitive swinging of the arm. (© 1994 Jerry Wachter. Reproduced by permission of Photo Researchers, Inc.)

collect in joints that are chronically (continuously) affected with tendinitis and may restrict the joint's ability to move normally.

Alternative Treatment

Hydrotherapy is sometimes effective in treating tendinitis. Warm water helps injured tissue to relax and begin healing. Acupuncture has also been used to treat the disorder. Very gentle forms of massage may also relieve pain and increase mobility in the joint. Finally, increasing the intake of certain foods that are rich in anti-oxidants (such as carrots) may help reduce inflammation.

PROGNOSIS

Injured tendons tend to heal by themselves if given sufficient time and rest. The four elements of RICE treatment can help speed up this process. Healing also occurs sooner if the patient discontinues the activities that caused the problem in the first place.

PREVENTION

Tendinitis can be prevented if a person avoids the kinds of activities that causes injuries to tendons. This instruction is easy to give, but not so easy to follow. An automobile worker, for example, may find it difficult not to perform a particular movement over and over again if that movement is part of his or her regular job. Workers and employers can often work together to arrange conditions so that tendinitis is less likely to occur.

FOR MORE INFORMATION

Books

O'Shea, Kate S. *Healing Hip, Joint, and Knee Pain: A Mind-Body Guide to Recovering from Surgery and Injuries.* Berkley, CA: North Atlantic Books, 1998.

Pinsky, Mark A. *The Carpal Tunnel Syndrome Book: Preventing and Treating CTS, Tendinitis and Related Cumulative Trauma Disorders.* New York: Warner Books, 1993.

Scott, W. Norman, Robert S. Gotlin, and Johanna Warshaw. *Dr. Scott's Knee Book: Symptoms, Diagnosis, and Treatment of Knee Problems, Including: Torn Cartilage, Ligament Damage, Arthritis, Tendinitis, and Arthritis.* New York: Fireside, 1996.

Villar, Richard. *Knee Problems: A Patient's Guide to Treatment and Recovery.* London: Thorsons Publications, 1996.

Organizations

American College of Rheumatology. 1800 Century Place, Suite 250, Atlanta, GA 30345. (404) 633–3777. http://www.rheumatology.org.

Web sites

American College of Rheumatology. "Tendinitis and Bursitis." *HealthTouch Online.* [Online] http://www.healthtouch.com/level1/leaflets/ACR/ACR035.htm (accessed on November 5, 1999).

"Tendonitis." [Online] http://www.yourhealth.com/ahl/2109.html (accessed on November 5, 1999).

TETANUS

DEFINITION

Tetanus (pronounced TET-n-uhss) is an infection of the central nervous system (the brain and spinal cord). The disease is rare, but often fatal. It is caused when the bacterium *Clostridium tetani* (pronounced claw-STRID-ee-um TEHT-uh-nee) enters the body. The bacterium often enters the body through wounds or cuts exposed to soil. Tetanus can easily be prevented through vaccination.

DESCRIPTION

Tetanus is rare in the United States. For many years, a vaccine (pronounced vak-SEEN) has been available to protect against the disease and the vast majority of American children receive the vaccine. A vaccine is a substance that causes the body's immune system to build up resistance to a particular disease. Cases of tetanus usually occur in adults who were never vaccinated against tetanus.

Only about one hundred cases of tetanus are reported in the United States each year. Of this number, about 70 percent occur in people over the age of fifty. Most of those who die of tetanus are over the age of sixty.

Tetanus causes muscular spasms (tightening of the muscles) that can cause paralysis of the respiratory (breathing) system and lead to death.

WORDS TO KNOW

Central nervous system: A system of nerve cells in the brain and the spinal cord.

Clostridium tetani: The bacterium that causes tetanus.

Spasm: A contraction of the muscles that can cause paralysis and/or shaking.

Toxin: A poison.

Vaccine: A substance that causes the body's immune system to build up resistance to a particular disease.

The disease is sometimes called lockjaw. The name comes from a common symptom of tetanus in which the jaw muscles become tight and rigid and a person is unable to open his or her mouth.

Sometimes tetanus affects only one part of the body but usually the infection spreads throughout the body until the entire body becomes paralyzed. The incubation period for tetanus is anywhere from two to fifty days. The incubation period is the time between infection and the first appearance of symptoms. When symptoms occur early, the chance of death is increased.

CAUSES

Tetanus is caused by a bacterium called *Clostridium tetani*. Bacterial spores (the inactive form of the bacterium) are found in soil, street dust, and animal feces. The spores are transmitted to humans through cuts in the skin. Once inside the body, the spores become active. As they grow, they release a toxin (poison) into the blood stream.

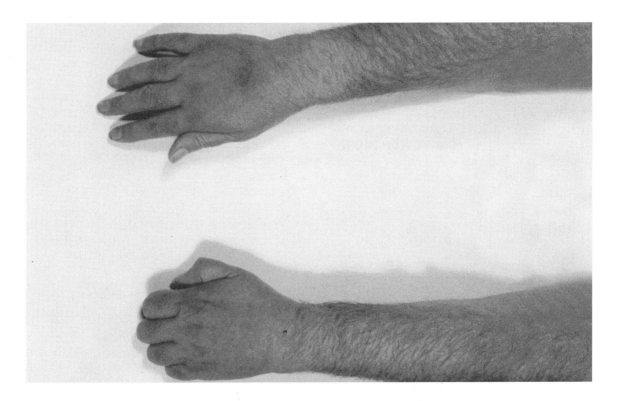

Tetanus causes muscles to permanently contract. Sometimes tetanus affects only one part of the body but usually the infection spreads throughout the body until the entire body becomes paralyzed. (Reproduced by permission of Custom Medical Stock Photo)

Cuts that have not been thoroughly cleaned are the major source of infection. But the disease can be transmitted in other ways also, such as animal scratches and bites, surgical wounds, and dental work.

SYMPTOMS

The first symptom of tetanus is often a stiff or locked jaw. The patient is unable to open his or her mouth or to swallow. Stiffness soon spreads to the neck and other muscles of the body. The patient often goes into uncontrollable spasms (shaking). The spasms can become so severe as to cause broken bones. Other symptoms of tetanus include irritability, restlessness, loss of appetite, and drooling.

DIAGNOSIS

The symptoms of tetanus are quite distinctive and a doctor can usually diagnose the disease simply by observing the patient. Knowing whether or not the patient has had a tetanus vaccination also helps a doctor make their diagnosis.

TREATMENT

Tetanus is a life-threatening disease. It requires immediate hospitalization. Treatment consists of two main steps. First, the patient is given antibiotics to kill the bacteria. Second, injections of antitoxin are also given. An antitoxin is a substance that reacts with and destroys the bacterial toxin.

EMIL ADOLF VON BEHRING

The vaccine against tetanus was discovered by the German bacteriologist Emil Adolf von Behring (1854–1917) in 1890. Behring was working at the time in the laboratory of the great bacteriologist Robert Koch. One of Behring's colleagues in Koch's laboratory was the Japanese bacteriologist Shibasaburo Kitasato.

Behring and Shibasaburo were especially interested in two terrible diseases, diphtheria and tetanus. Behring had an idea that a vaccine against both diseases might be possible by producing an "antitoxin" against them. He made the antitoxin in the following way:

First, he injected the bacteria that cause tetanus into an experimental animal, such as a rabbit. Then, he removed blood from the infected animal. Next, he injected that blood into a second animal, such as a horse. Finally, he removed blood from the second animal. From this blood, he made a vaccine to be used with humans.

Behring's idea was later developed more fully by his colleague Paul Ehrlich. The vaccine developed by Behring and Ehrlich later became part of the DPT (diphtheria/tetanus/pertussis) vaccine that nearly all young children receive today. For his invention of the vaccine, Behring was awarded the first Nobel Prize in medicine in physiology in 1901.

Patients may also need medication to control muscle spasms. In severe cases, the patient may have to be placed on artificial respiration. Recovery takes six weeks or more. After a patient is better, he or she should receive the tetanus vaccine to protect against future episodes of the disease.

PROGNOSIS

Up to 30 percent of people with tetanus in the United States die. Early diagnosis and treatment improves the chance of survival. The death rate among young babies who develop the disease is more than 90 percent.

PREVENTION

Tetanus can easily be prevented through vaccination. The usual method uses a combination of vaccines that protect against three diseases: tetanus, diphtheria, and pertussis (whooping cough; see whooping cough entry). The vaccine is given in five doses at the ages of two months, four months, six months, fifteen to eighteen months, and four to six years.

Adults should receive a booster shot against tetanus every ten years. A booster shot is a dose of the vaccine that renews a person's resistance to the disease. Adults who have never received a tetanus vaccination should begin one as soon as possible. The adult series consists of three injections over a six to twelve month period.

Side effects of the tetanus vaccine are minor. They include soreness, redness, and swelling at the site of the injection. The symptoms disappear with a few days.

Another way to prevent tetanus infections is to make sure that wounds and scratches are thoroughly cleaned. The tetanus bacterium grows only where there is no oxygen present. So a thorough cleaning of a wound will kill all bacteria. A wound should also be treated with an antibiotic cream and covered with a bandage. Wounds that don't heal should be examined by a doctor.

FOR MORE INFORMATION

Periodicals

Zamalu, Evelyn. "Adults Need Tetanus Shots, Too." *FDA Consumer* (July/ August 1996): pp. 14–18.

Web sites

"Childhood Infections: Tetanus." *KidsHealth*. [Online] http://www.KidsHealth .org (accessed December 10, 1997).

"Shots for Safety." [Online] http://www.nih.gov/nia/health/pubpub/shots.htm (accessed December 7, 1997).

"Taking Care of Cuts, Scrapes, and Minor Wounds: What Mom May Not Have Told You." [Online] http://www.mayo.ivi.com (accessed December 9, 1997).

"Tetanus & Diphtheria (Td) Vaccine." [Online] http://www.healthtouch.com/level1/leaflet/cdc181.htm (accessed December 10, 1997).

TONSILLITIS

DEFINITION

Tonsillitis (pronounced tahn-suh-LIE-tiss) is an infection and swelling of the tonsils. The tonsils are lymph nodes, or oval-shaped masses of lymph gland tissue, located on both sides of the throat that are part of the body immune system.

DESCRIPTION

The tonsils normally help prevent infections in two ways. They act like filters to trap bacteria, viruses, and other materials that enter the body through the mouth and sinuses. They also produce antibodies to help fight off infections. An antibody is a chemical produced by blood cells to fight off specific kinds of foreign bodies, such as bacteria and viruses.

While a person can get tonsillitis at any age, the infection occurs most commonly among children between the ages of five and ten years.

CAUSES

Tonsillitis is caused by viruses or bacteria that infect the tonsils. They cause the tonsils to become inflamed and swollen. One of the first symptoms of tonsillitis is a severe sore throat (see sore throat entry). Other symptoms include fever, chills, tiredness, muscle aches, earache, swollen glands in the neck, and pain or discomfort when swallowing. Very young children with tonsillitis may become fussy and stop eating.

WORDS TO KNOW

Antibiotic: A substance derived from bacteria or other organisms that fights the growth of other bacteria or organisms.

Lymph nodes: Small round or oval bodies within the immune system. Lymph nodes provide materials that fight disease and help remove bacteria and other foreign material from the body.

Tonsillectomy: A surgical procedure to remove the tonsils.

Tonsils: Oval-shaped masses of lymph gland tissue located on both sides of the back of the throat.

SYMPTOMS

Tonsillitis may cause the tonsils, which are visible at the back of the throat, to look red and enlarged. The tonsils may also have visible white or yellow spots or a thin coating. The symptoms of tonsillitis usually last four to six days.

DIAGNOSIS

Tonsillitis can be diagnosed from visible symptoms and a physical examination. A doctor will examine the patient's eyes, ears, nose, and throat and look for signs of swelling, redness, or discharge.

The doctor may also take a throat culture. To do a throat culture, the doctor wipes a cotton swab across the tonsils and back of the throat. The swab is then tested for the presence of bacteria and viruses that cause tonsillitis.

Some tests can be performed quickly. A doctor may suspect the presence of certain disease-causing bacteria almost immediately. He or she can then prescribe antibiotics to treat the infection. An antibiotic is a substance derived from bacteria or other organisms that fights the growth of other bacteria or organisms.

But a longer waiting period is needed for more reliable tests. The cotton swab may need to be incubated for twenty-four to forty-eight hours. During incubation the swab is kept in a warm, moist environment. Bacteria and viruses grow well in this environment. A researcher can then study the material on the swab under a microscope and determine which bacteria and/or viruses are present. With this information, the doctor can make a sound diagnosis of the patient's condition.

A doctor may decide to conduct exclusionary tests also. An exclusionary test is one performed to find out if some condition other than tonsillitis is present. For example, the patient's sore throat might be caused by diphtheria. Blood tests will often rule out infections other than those that cause tonsillitis. If no other infections are present, the doctor may decide that the patient's problem really is tonsillitis.

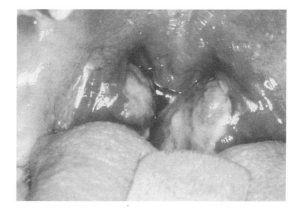

Tonsillitis is an infection and swelling of the tonsils. The tonsils are oval-shaped masses of lymph gland tissue located on both sides of the throat. (© 1993 NMSB. Reproduced by permission of Custom Medical Stock Photo.)

TREATMENT

Treatment for tonsillitis depends on the agent that caused the infection. If the infection is bacterial, antibiotics can help cure the disease. If the infection is viral, there are no drugs that will cure the disease.

Most doctors will recommend treatments designed to keep a patient comfortable while the disease runs its course. These treatments include bed rest, drinking extra fluids, gargling with warm salt water, and taking pain relievers to reduce fever. Eating frozen juice bars or drinking either cold fruit drinks or warm tea or broth can also bring some relief of sore throat pain.

In many cases, doctors decide to treat tonsillitis with surgery. This treatment may be recommended for children who have severe cases of tonsillitis more than once. In a tonsillectomy, the tonsils are surgically removed.

Alternative Treatment

Alternative practitioners recommend a variety of natural products for the treatment of tonsillitis. These products include dietary supplements, such as vitamin C and beta-carotenes, and certain herbal remedies. The herbs that are suggested include calendula, cleavers, echinacea, astragalus, goldenseal, myrrh, bitter orange, *Lomatium dissectum,* and *Ligusticum porteri.* Some of these

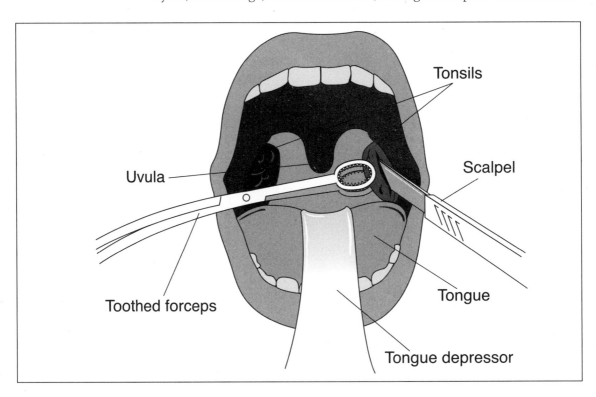

In a tonsillectomy, the tonsils are surgically removed. This treatment may be recommended for children who have severe cases of tonsillitis more than once. (Reproduced by permission of Electronic Illustrators Group)

herbs are thought to strengthen the immune system. Others are believed to kill bacteria or viruses.

Some homeopathic remedies suggested for tonsillitis include *Belladonna, Phytolacca, Mercurius, Lycopodium, Lachesis, Hepar sulphuris, Arsenicum,* and *Rhus toxicodendron.*

PROGNOSIS

Tonsillitis usually gets better on its own within a few days. Treating the symptoms of sore throat and fever will make the patient more comfortable. In cases where the fever lasts for more than forty-eight hours or reaches a temperature of more than 102°F (38°C) the patient should be seen by a doctor.

Any medication that has been prescribed should be taken until all of it has been taken. Patients sometimes stop taking their medications when they feel better, but though the symptoms may have cleared up, the infection may not have been cured. The infection may spread to other parts of the upper respiratory (breathing) system. The ears and sinuses are especially subject to such infection. In rare cases, much more serious conditions, such as rheumatic fever (see rheumatic fever entry) or pneumonia (see pneumonia entry) may develop.

PREVENTION

The bacteria and viruses that cause tonsillitis are easily transmitted from person to person. The infection often spreads quickly among members of a family or students in a classroom. Avoiding contact with anyone who has the symptoms of tonsillitis can reduce the risk of infection.

Drinking glasses and eating utensils should never be shared. A person who has had tonsillitis should throw out his or her toothbrush to avoid re-infection. People who are caring for a person with tonsillitis should take special precautions and wash their hands often to prevent spreading the infection to other people.

FOR MORE INFORMATION

Books

Inlander, Charles B., and the staff of the People's Medical Society, eds. "Tonsilitis." In *The Consumer's Medical Desk Reference.* New York: Stonesong Press, 1995.

Shaw, Michael, ed. "Tonsilitis." In *Everything You Need to Know about Diseases.* Springhouse, PA: Springhouse Corporation, 1996.

Web sites

"Childhood Infections: Tonsillitis." *KidsHealth.* [Online] http://kidshealth.org/ parent/common/tonsillitis.html (accessed on November 5, 1999).

TOOTH DECAY

DEFINITION

Tooth decay is the destruction of the enamel (outer surface) of a tooth. Tooth decay is also known as dental cavities or dental caries. Decay is caused by bacteria that collect on tooth enamel. The bacteria live in a sticky, white film called plaque (pronounced PLAK). Bacteria obtain their food from sugar and starch in a person's diet. When they eat those foods, the bacteria create an acid that attacks tooth enamel and causes decay.

DESCRIPTION

Tooth decay is the second most common health problem after the common cold (see common cold entry). By some estimates, more than 90 percent of people in the United States have at least one cavity; about 75 percent of people get their first cavity by the age of five.

Anyone can get tooth decay. However, children and the elderly are the two groups at highest risk. Other high-risk groups include people who eat a lot of starch and sugary foods; people who live in areas without fluoridated water (water with fluoride added to it); and people who already have other tooth problems.

Tooth decay is also often a problem in young babies. If a baby is given a bottle containing a sweet liquid before going to bed, or if parents soak the baby's pacifier in sugar, honey, or another sweet substance, bacteria may grow on the baby's teeth and cause tooth decay.

CAUSES

Tooth decay occurs when three factors are present: bacteria, sugar, and a weak tooth sur-

WORDS TO KNOW

Amalgam: A mixture of mercury, silver, and other metals used to make fillings for cavities.

Caries: The medical term for tooth decay.

Cavity: A hole or weak spot in tooth enamel caused by decay.

Dentin: The middle layer of a tooth.

Enamel: The hard, outermost layer of a tooth.

Fluoride: A chemical compound that is effective in preventing tooth decay.

Plaque: A thin, sticky film composed of sugars, food, and bacteria that covers teeth.

Pulp: The soft, innermost layer of a tooth.

Sealant: A thin plastic substance that is painted on teeth to prevent cavities from developing.

Magnigification of dental plaque, which causes tooth decay. (© Hossler, Ph.D. Reproduced by permission of Custom Medical Stock Photo.)

face. The sugar often comes from sweet foods such as sugar or honey. But it can also come from starchy foods such as bread and rice. When a starch breaks down in the mouth, it forms sugar. Bacteria that live on the surface of a tooth eat sugar. When they do so they change the sugar into an acid called lactic acid.

Healthy tooth enamel may be able to resist this acid. But tooth enamel often has tiny holes and weak spots. Lactic acid can soak into these holes and dissolve the minerals of which enamel is made. Over time, the hole may get larger and larger. If the hole penetrates into the next tooth layer, called the dentin, the tooth becomes sensitive to touch and temperature. Decay can even penetrate to the center of the tooth, the pulp. In that case, the inner tooth may become inflamed and begin to ache.

SYMPTOMS

The signs of tooth decay are usually obvious. A tooth may be sensitive to the touch, to hot or cold temperatures, or to very sweet foods. Or it may simply start to ache. A tooth that starts hurting usually has something wrong with it.

DIAGNOSIS

Tooth decay is often discovered during regular dental checkups. Many adults have a routine dental checkup every six months. During these checkups, a dentist looks at and probes the patient's teeth. If there is tooth decay, it is usually easy for the dentist to find.

Some cases of tooth decay are harder to detect. They may occur between or on the back of teeth. In such cases, they are diagnosed by taking an X ray of the patient's mouth. Decay shows up as a dark spot on the X-ray film.

Tooth decay in very young children is often not diagnosed. Parents may not think it necessary to take a young child to the dentist and decay may be well advanced before it is discovered. For this reason, many dentists recommend having children one to two years of age examined for tooth decay.

TREATMENT

Tooth decay is usually treated with a filling. The dentist first removes all of the decayed material with a drill. The opening is then filled with some

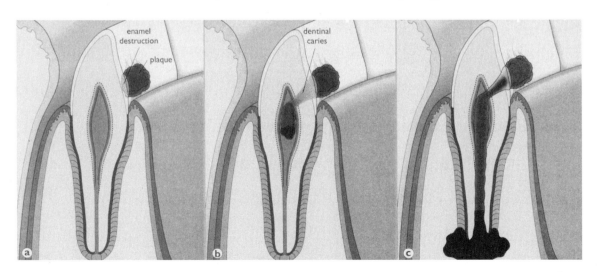

The development of dental cavities in three stages. (Reproduced by permission of Biophoto Associates/Science Source/Photo Researchers, Inc.)

long-lasting material. Two common materials are mercury amalgam (pronounced uh-MAL-gum) and composite resin. A mercury amalgam consists of a mixture of metals that is strong and resistant to wear. A composite resin is a sturdy, plastic-like material.

Additional treatment may be necessary if decay has reached the pulp of the tooth. In that case, the center part of the tooth may also have to be removed. This procedure is called a root canal. The decayed material is taken out and replaced with a metal pin. The tooth is then covered with an artificial coating called a crown.

PROGNOSIS

The sooner tooth decay is treated, the less of a problem it is. Without treatment, decay attacks more and more of a tooth, which may make it necessary for a root canal. In extreme cases, a tooth may need to be removed.

PREVENTION

It is easier and less expensive to prevent tooth decay than to treat it. The four major steps in preventing tooth decay are: proper oral (mouth) hygiene; fluoride treatments; use of sealants; and attention to diet.

Oral Hygiene

The three steps in proper oral hygiene are brushing, flossing, and regular checkups. Dentists recommend brushing the teeth at least twice a day, after meals and snacks if possible. Regular brushing keeps plaque and bacteria from collecting on teeth.

THE FIRST DENTAL DRILLS

The first powered dental drill was invented by George Washington's dentist, John Greenwood (1760–1819). The drill was operated using the foot-treadle (pedal) from Greenwood's mother's spinning wheel. Greenwood's son continued to use the drill, but other dentists did not adopt the idea. Instead, they continued to use small picks to clean the decay from teeth.

The first dental drill operated by a motor was invented in 1864 by Englishman George F. Harrington. Harrington's drill was powered by a tightly-wound spring, like the spring in a clock. Only four years later, an American inventor, George F. Green, redesigned the drill. His model used the power of compressed air.

The dental drill is still an essential part of every dentist's equipment. However, today's drills are much more advanced than those of Harrington and Green. The finest drills operate at a speed of up to 400,000 revolutions per minute. By comparison, the earliest commercial drills were rather slow and ran at no more than about 600 to 800 revolutions per minute.

Flossing removes food particles and plaque from between teeth and other areas not reached by a toothbrush. Regular visits to the dentist make it possible to catch tooth decay before it becomes too serious.

Fluoride Treatments

Fluorides are chemicals that help reduce tooth decay by combining with minerals in the teeth to form a hard, tough surface. Bones and teeth all contain fluorides naturally. Using extra fluoride increases the natural strength of tooth enamel. Some communities add fluorides to their water supplies. People in those communities get the fluoride they need from their drinking water. Many kinds of toothpaste and mouthwash also contain fluoride. In areas where fluoride is not added to the public water supply, it can be obtained from these sources. Fluoride treatments are also available from dentists. The fluorides can be brushed directly on tooth surfaces.

Fluorides are especially important for young children's dental health. The fluorides become part of new teeth as they develop and grow and become harder and more resistant to bacterial acids.

Sealants

A sealant is a thin, plastic material used to cover tooth surfaces. It protects enamel from attack by bacterial acids. Sealants are especially helpful on irregular surfaces of the teeth. They prevent food and plaque from getting trapped on these surfaces.

Sealants are usually clear or tooth-colored. They do not affect the appearance of a person's teeth and may last as long as ten years. Some dentists recommend the application of sealants as soon as a child's permanent teeth appear, in order to protect the teeth from ever becoming decayed.

Diet

Diet is an important factor in maintaining good oral health. People whose diet includes large amounts of sugar and starch are likely to have more tooth decay. Foods that stick to the teeth can also be a problem because they help bacteria stay on tooth surfaces longer.

FOR MORE INFORMATION

Organizations

American Dental Association. 211 East Chicago Avenue, Chicago, IL 60611. (312) 440-2500. http://www.ada.org.

American Dental Hygienists' Association. 444 North Michigan Avenue, Chicago, IL 60611. (800) 847-6718.

National Institute of Dental Research. 31 Center Drive, MSC 2190, Building 31, Room 5B49, Bethesda, MD 20892-2190.

TOURETTE SYNDROME

DEFINITION

Tourette syndrome (TS; pronounced ter-ET sin-drohm) is an inherited disorder of the nervous system. It is named after the French physician George Gilles de la Tourette who first described the condition more than a century ago. The condition usually appears before the age of eighteen. Patients develop a pattern of motor tics. A motor (muscular) tic is a repeated, jerky action, such as twisting one's head from side to side. The action has no functional purpose and can occur in any part of the body.

Patients also develop vocal tics. Vocal tics include loud grunts or barking noises. They may also include words or short phrases. In most cases, the tics come and go, and are replaced by different types of sounds and movements. As the patient grows older, the tics may become quite complex.

DESCRIPTION

Motor tics usually occur in bouts that take place several times a day. The tics may make it difficult for a patient to perform simple everyday tasks such as tying one's shoelaces. More complex tasks, such as driving a car, are even more difficult.

Vocal tics can be the source of serious social problems. Some TS patients feel an irresistible urge to shout swear words or offensive racial terms. The patient finds it nearly impossible to control these urges. Some people find it hard to be in the company of a TS patient for this reason. Family members and friends often learn to adjust to these vocal tics. But TS patients usually live in fear of shocking other people or embarrassing themselves. They may withdraw from contact with other people.

The tics of TS are often said to be involuntary. That explanation means that a person has no control over the tic. But that description is not exactly correct. The patient is often able to control a tic for several hours at a time. But that control does not last forever. Eventually the tic is allowed to come out. When it does, it is stronger and longer lasting than usual. Tics often become worse when a patient is under stress but are usually less of a problem during sleep.

WORDS TO KNOW

Biofeedback: The process of providing a person with information on some body function, such as blood pressure, so that it can be controlled to some extent.

Compulsion: A very strong urge to do or say something that usually cannot be resisted for long.

Dyslexia: Difficulty in reading, spelling, and/or writing words.

Genetic disorder: A medical problem caused by one or more defective genes. Genes are passed from one generation to another.

Tic: A muscular contraction or vocal sound over which a patient has very little control.

Some TS symptoms are similar to those of some mental disorders. For example, patients may seem grouchy and depressed. They may tend to think the same thoughts over and over again. This behavior is a kind of mental tic known as obsession. The exact relationship between TS and mental disorders such as obsessive-compulsive disorder (see obsessive-compulsive disorder entry) is still not well understood.

CAUSES

Tourette syndrome is a genetic disorder. That is, the chance of having TS is greatly increased if some other family member also has the condition. If one parent has TS, his or her children have a higher than normal chance of developing the disorder. There is about a 50 percent chance that the child of a TS patient will inherit the TS gene. Male children with the TS gene are three to four times more likely to develop symptoms than are female children with the gene. However, only about 10 percent of those who inherit the TS gene develop symptoms that require medical attention.

SYMPTOMS

Patients with TS can exhibit a range of symptoms. Most patients will have some but not all of the symptoms. Motor tics and obsessive thoughts are the most common symptoms. Compulsive behavior is also common among TS patients. A compulsive behavior is an action performed over and over again for no apparent reason. Constant hand washing is an example of compulsive behavior.

Patients with TS may have other mental disorders. For example, they may have trouble controlling their impulses, or they may talk in their sleep or awaken frequently. Many TS patients also have the learning disorder known as dyslexia (see dyslexia entry).

The tics associated with TS can be simple or complex. A simple tic involves a sudden, brief movement of a single group of muscles. It is generally repeated several times. A complex tic consists of a repeated pattern of movements that can involve several muscle groups, usually in the same order. An example of a complex tic might be a side-to-side head movement followed by eye blinking followed by opening the mouth then stretching the neck.

Vocal tics can consist of sounds and noises that have no meaning. Or they can involve the use of words and phrases repeated over and over again. Tics tend to get better and worse in cycles. Patients often develop new tics as they grow older. The symptoms of TS may get better for weeks or months, only to become worse later.

Some examples of tics associated with TS include the following:

- Simple motor tics: Blinking the eyes, pouting the lips, shaking or jerking the head, shrugging the shoulders, grimacing (making faces), sudden kicking movements, snapping the jaws, and clicking the teeth.
- Complex motor tics: Jumping up and down, touching parts of the body or certain objects, smelling things over and over again, stamping the feet, twirling about, throwing or arranging objects, head-banging, writing the same letter repeatedly, and making obscene gestures.
- Simple vocal tics: Clearing the throat, coughing, snorting, barking, grunting, clicking the tongue, whistling, hissing, and making sucking sounds.
- Complex vocal tics: Repeating phrases such as "Oh boy," "all right," or "what's that?"; saying dirty words or offensive racial expressions; speaking very rapidly or loudly, and repeating whole sentences over and over.

DIAGNOSIS

There are no specific tests for TS. However, motor and vocal tics are usually clear symptoms of the condition. A medical history is usually taken to find out if other family members have the condition. The behaviors characteristic of TS must be present for at least a year and should begin before the age of eighteen to justify a diagnosis of Tourette syndrome.

Diagnosis can sometimes be difficult. Many patients learn to hold back their tics when others are around. Family members, school teachers and nurses, and even doctors may not have the chance to observe tics. In some cases, diagnosis is not made until the patient learns to trust a doctor enough to let him or her see the symptoms of TS.

In some cases, tests are conducted to rule out other mental disorders. For example, blood tests may indicate whether or not muscular diseases are present. Electroencephalograms (EEG; pronounced ih-LEK-tro-in-SEH-fuh-lo-gram) may show the presence of brain disorders that have symptoms similar to those of TS.

TREATMENT

In a majority of cases, patients with TS learn to live with and adapt to their condition. They do not require medication in order to live a reasonably normal life. In serious cases, a drug used to treat severe mental disorders can be used. Haloperidol (pronounced hal-oh-PER-uh-dol, trade name Haldol) or pimozide (pronounced PIM-uh-zide, trade name Orap) are the drugs usually chosen for treatment. They are given at first in low doses and then increased until tics begin to improve.

The drug clonidine (pronounced KLON-uh-deen) is sometimes used with TS patients also. The drug was developed originally to treat high blood pressure. But it may also help relieve the motor tics associated with TS. It usually does not work as well with vocal tics. The drug helps children with TS to focus their attention on tasks. It also makes many patients less frightened of their own symptoms.

Medication is not always the best form of treatment. In many cases, tics often get better by themselves. The best treatment for a patient may a calm, comfortable atmosphere. Children who have TS often do quite well in a regular classroom. If they do require medication, the dose should be monitored carefully. It should be reduced as soon and as much as possible when symptoms begin to get better. Children with severe symptoms may require special classrooms, a private place to study, or individual tutoring.

Alternative Treatment

Counseling will not help cure a person's tics. But it may help the patient understand the nature of his or her condition and how to deal with it. Like any ongoing childhood illness, TS can place great strain on a family. Family counseling can help the TS child, parents, and brothers and sisters better understand the medical condition. Family members can be taught how to be helpful without being over-protective.

Relaxation techniques may reduce the number and severity of tics. Yoga and biofeedback are two such techniques. Homeopathic practitioners believe that patients with TS can be helped with a healthy, well-balanced diet.

PROGNOSIS

There is no cure for Tourette syndrome. However, many patients improve as they grow older and often reach the point where they can do without drugs. A few patients recover completely after their teenage years. Others learn to live with their condition.

TOURETTE SYNDROME DOES NOT AFFECT ONE'S INTELLIGENCE OR THINKING ABILITIES.

TS does not affect one's intelligence or thinking abilities. The most serious difficulty can sometimes be the social problems associated with TS. Patients may become depressed and withdrawn because of embarrassment over their symptoms.

PREVENTION

The only way to prevent Tourette syndrome is with family planning. A parent who has TS is likely to pass the condition to his or her own children.

Parents may decide to take this information into consideration when deciding whether or not to have children.

FOR MORE INFORMATION

Books

Eisenreich, Jim. *Children With Tourette Syndrome: A Parent's Guide.* Bethesda, MD: Woodbine House, 1992.

Shimberg, Elaine Fantle, and Oliver Sacks. *Living With Tourette Syndrome.* New York: Fireside, 1995.

Organizations

Tourette Syndrome Association. 42-40 Bell Boulevard, Bayside, NY 11361-2820. (718) 224-2999. http://neuro-www2.mgh.harvard.edu/tsa/tsamain.nclk.

Web sites

Guide to the Diagnosis and Treatment of Tourette Syndrome. Internet Mental Health. [Online] http://www.mentalhealth.com (accessed on October 27, 1999).

TOXIC SHOCK SYNDROME

DEFINITION

Toxic shock syndrome (TSS) is an uncommon, but potentially serious, illness. It almost always occurs in women using super-absorbent tampons during menstruation, but researchers are still not entirely clear what the connection is between this kind of tampon and TSS.

DESCRIPTION

Toxic shock syndrome first came to public attention in the 1970s when thousands of young women began to go to emergency rooms with a common set of symptoms. Those symptoms included high fever, vomiting, peeling skin, low blood pressure, diarrhea, and a rash resembling sunburn. Most of these women had one thing in common: they were all menstruating. And the majority were using a new type of tampon called a super-absorbent tampon.

The epidemic reached its peak between 1980 to 1984. During that period, about fifteen thousand people a year were diagnosed with TSS. About 15 percent of those who got the disease died of it.

Doctors were not certain what the connection was between TSS and super-absorbent tampons, but it was obvious that some connection existed. Tampon manufacturers were encouraged to discontinue the product and when the manufacturers did, the number of TSS cases began to fall dramatically. Since 1998, only about 5,000 cases of TSS are diagnosed annually. The death rate has fallen to about 5 percent.

For many years, TSS has been thought of as a woman's disease because of the connection between TSS and tampons. And while TSS is largely a disease that affects menstruating women under the age of thirty, individuals of either sex, any age, and any race or ethnic group can get disease.

Streptococcal Toxic Shock Syndrome (STSS)

The form of toxic shock syndrome first seen in the 1970s is caused by a group of bacteria known as *Staphylococcus aureus* (pronounced STAFF-uh-loh-kock-us AW-ree-us). In 1987 a new form of TSS was discovered that is caused by a different bacterium that belongs to the *Streptococcus* (pronounced strep-tuh-KOK-us) family.

CAUSES

The *Staphylococcus* bacterium that causes toxic shock syndrome is found in the nose and mouth and, less often, the vagina. The bacterium releases a toxin (poison) that can get into the bloodstream. The toxin can cause an infection that is potentially fatal.

Researchers are still not certain as to how tampons promote the growth of *Staphylococcus* bacteria. One theory is that the tampons trap oxygen, which bacteria need to survive. Oxygen normally is not present in the vagina in large amounts. Another theory is that tampons provide a warm, moist environment that encourages the growth of bacteria. Yet another theory places the blame for TSS on the material of which the tampons were made. This theory suggests that the material irritated the vaginal lining. Sores on the vagina may have made it easier for bacterial toxins to get into the bloodstream.

SYMPTOMS

Toxic shock syndrome begins suddenly with a fever of 102° F (38°C) or more. Other symptoms include vomiting, a watery diarrhea, headache, and a sunburn-like rash. Blood pres-

WORDS TO KNOW

Shock: A sudden drop in blood supply and oxygen provided to the body's tissues.

Staphylococcus: A class of bacteria found on human skin and mucous membranes that can cause a variety of infectious diseases.

Streptococcus: A class of bacteria that causes a wide variety of infections.

Tampon: A cloth pad worn in the vagina to absorb fluids released during menstruation.

sure may drop quickly. When this happens, the patient may become confused or go into shock. The kidneys may fail. Later, the skin on hands and feet may peel.

Streptococcal toxic shock syndrome (STSS) is characterized by fever, dizziness, breathing problems, and a weak, rapid pulse rate. The patient's blood pressure drops suddenly and dramatically.

DIAGNOSIS

Any woman who is wearing a tampon and experiences the described symptoms should remove the tampon at once seek medical advice.

Toxic shock syndrome first came to public attention in the 1970s when thousands of young women began to go to emergency rooms with a common set of symptoms. The majority of the women were using a new type of tampon called a super-absorbent tampon. (Reproduced by permission of AP/Wide World Photos)

In diagnosing TSS, the first step taken by a doctor may be ruling out other diseases. For example, an examination of the vagina may be needed to rule out sexually transmitted diseases (see sexually transmitted diseases entry). Blood tests or a vaginal smear can then determine the presence of the bacteria that cause either TSS or STSS. In a vaginal smear, a small amount of vaginal fluids is removed with a cotton swab. The fluid can then be examined under a microscope to determine if the bacteria that cause TSS and STSS are present.

TREATMENT

Both TSS and STSS are bacterial infections. They can both be treated, therefore, with antibiotics, drugs that fight bacteria. The vagina may also be cleaned to remove bacteria that cause the two diseases.

PROGNOSIS

When treated promptly and correctly, both TSS and STSS can be cured. TSS tends to recur within a period of about six months. The bacteria that cause the two diseases can also spread to other parts of the body and can produce complications in the liver, kidneys, lungs, and other organs. Untreated toxic shock syndrome can be fatal.

PREVENTION

Recommendations for preventing toxic shock syndrome usually involve instructions about the use of tampons. Experts recommend that women select products with the lowest possible absorbency. They also suggest that tampons be worn only during the day and that they be changed every four to six hours. Above all, women should wash their hands before inserting a tampon. Anyone who has had TSS even once should not use tampons again.

FOR MORE INFORMATION

Books

Barrett, Laurie. *The Coming Plague.* New York: Penguin Books, 1994.

Starr, Carolina V. *Toxic Shock Syndrome.* San Francisco, CA: Permeable Press, 1996.

Turkington Carol A. *Infectious Disease A to Z.* New York: Facts on File, 1998.

TUBERCULOSIS

DEFINITION

Tuberculosis (pronounced too-BUR-kyoo-LOH-siss), or TB, is a contagious disease of the lungs that can spread to other parts of the body and may be fatal. TB is caused by a microorganism known as the tubercle bacillus, or *Mycobacterium tuberculosis*. The disease can now be treated, cured, and prevented. However, scientists have never come closing to wiping it out and TB remains one of the most serious diseases worldwide.

DESCRIPTION

Some parts of the population are at higher risk of getting TB than others. For instance, tuberculosis is more common among elderly people. Typically, more than one-fourth of the TB cases reported in the United States occur among people above age sixty-five.

Elderly people are especially vulnerable for a number of reasons. First, the disease can take years to become active, so an older person may have gotten the disease earlier in life and only discovered it after it became active. Second, people who live in nursing homes and similar facilities are often in close contact with each other and the disease can spread more easily in such conditions. Third, the body's immune system becomes weaker as a person grows older and older people may find it more difficult to hold off an attack of the tubercle bacillus. The immune system is the body's network system for fighting off disease and infection.

Race also can be a factor in determining the risk of getting tuberculosis. TB occurs most commonly among African Americans. Other minorities are also at higher risk. Currently about two-thirds of all TB cases in the United States affect African Americans, Hispanics, Asians, and people from the Pacific Islands. Another one-fourth of cases in the United States affect people born outside the country.

People who are infected with the human immunodeficiency virus (HIV) are also at high risk for tuberculosis (see AIDS entry). HIV can damage a person's immune system, making it difficult for the body to fight off the TB bacterium. People who abuse alcohol and illegal drugs are also at high risk for the disease.

CAUSES

The most common method by which TB is transmitted is coughing or sneezing. When a person coughs or sneezes, he or she releases a fine mist of water droplets. If the person carries the tubercle bacillus, those droplets may contain thousands of the bacteria. A person nearby may inhale those water droplets and the bacteria they contain. The bacteria can then travel to that person's respiratory system and cause a new infection.

About a third of the people standing close to a person with TB are likely to develop the disease. Tuberculosis is not transmitted by contact with a person's clothing, bed linens, or dishes and cooking utensils. A fetus may become infected, however, by taking in bacilli from the mother.

Progression

The tubercle bacilli a person inhales may or may not cause tuberculosis. The human immune system has a variety of ways to capture and kill these bacteria. If the immune system is successful in doing so, the person will not become ill with TB.

Inhaled bacilli, however, may survive the immune system. They may travel throughout the body to organs other than the lungs. In some cases, the bacilli remain active enough to cause tuberculosis. In about 5 percent of all cases, a person develops tuberculosis within twelve to twenty-four months of being exposed to TB bacteria.

By contrast, less than 10 percent of all people who inhale the tubercle bacillus actually become ill. The rest develop no symptoms of the disease and have negative X rays for the disease. In such cases, the disease is said to be inactive. The bacilli remain alive in cells, but they are not active enough to actually cause disease. They may become more active later in life, however.

WORDS TO KNOW

Bacillus Calmette-Guérin (BCG): A vaccine made from weakened mycobacterium that infects cattle. It is used to protect humans against pulmonary tuberculosis and its complications.

Extrapulmonary: Outside of the lungs.

Lesion: Any change in the structure or appearance of a part of the body as the result of an injury or infection.

Mantoux test: Another name for the PPD test, which is used to determine whether a person has been infected with the tuberculosis bacterium.

Miliary tuberculosis: A form of tuberculosis in which the bacillus spreads throughout the body producing many thousands of tubercular lesions.

Mycobacteria: A group of bacteria that includes *Mycobacterium tuberculosis*, the bacterium that causes tuberculosis.

Pericardium: the membrane surrounding the heart.

Pulmonary: Relating to the lungs.

Purified protein derivative (PPD): A substance injected beneath the skin to see whether a person presently has or has ever had the tubercle bacillus.

Sputum: Secretions produced inside an infected lung. When the sputum is coughed up it can be studied to determine what kinds of infection are present in the lung.

Vaccine: A substance that causes the body's immune system to build up resistance to a particular disease.

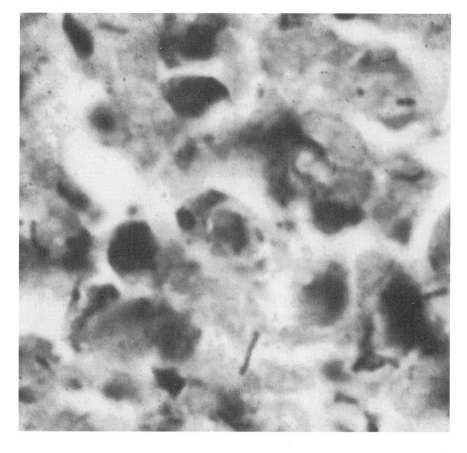

Tuberculosis is caused by a microorganism known as the tubercle bacillus, or *Mycobacterium tuberculosis.* (© LeBeau. Reproduced by permission of Custom Medical Stock Photo.)

In such cases, a person may become ill with tuberculosis long after being exposed to the TB bacteria.

Scientists believe that anywhere from ten to fifteen million Americans are carrying inactive tubercle bacilli in their bodies.

SYMPTOMS

Cases of tuberculosis are often classified as to whether they occur in the lung (pulmonary tuberculosis) or elsewhere in the body (extrapulmonary tuberculosis). Pulmonary tuberculosis is often confused with other diseases of the respiratory system. A person with TB may feel slightly sick or develop a mild cough. The person may also cough up small amounts of greenish or yellow sputum in the morning; the sputum can sometimes contain blood.

Other symptoms include a low-grade fever, a loss of interest in food, mild chest pain, difficulty in breathing, and night sweats. If the TB bacilli travel from the lungs to the lymph nodes, which help fight off illness, other symptoms, such as skin infections, may develop. More serious symptoms can also develop, including severe weight loss. Modern antibiotics, however, can prevent patients from reaching that stage of the disease.

Extrapulmonary Tuberculosis

Some of the tissues and organs in which extrapulmonary tuberculosis may appear are the following:

- **Bones.** TB is particularly likely to infect the spine and the ends of the long bones. Children are especially susceptible to spinal tuberculosis. If the disease is not treated, it may cause collapse of the vertebrae and paralysis in one or both legs.
- **Kidneys.** The kidneys are another common location for extrapulmonary tuberculosis. Although there are few signs of TB kidney infections, the disease may spread to the bladder, the prostate gland (in men), and other nearby organs and tissues.
- **Female reproductive organs.** In women, TB bacilli may spread to the ovaries and the peritoneum (pronounced per-i-tuh-NEE-uhm), the membrane lining the abdominal cavity.

THE FIGHT AGAINST TUBERCULOSIS THEN AND NOW

In the mid-seventeenth and eighteenth centuries, many countries underwent an Industrial Revolution. Because of inventions such as the steam engine, cities saw an increase of factory and industrial jobs, and more and more people moved from farms in the country to work in the city. Once there, workers often lived in very close contact with relatives and neighbors. Under those crowded and unsanitary conditions, tuberculosis was able to spread easily among the population.

Before scientists knew what caused tuberculosis, the disease was commonly referred to as consumption.

Until recently, there was no way of treating the disease. Instead, people with "consumption" were isolated in private hospitals or sanitariums. The purpose of isolation was to prevent the disease from spreading to uninfected people. Because of this practice, the study of tuberculosis also became separated from other fields of medicines. Entire organizations were created to study the disease, its effects on patients, and its impact on society as a whole.

In 1885 the German microbiologist Robert Koch discovered the tubercle bacillus and showed that this microorganism was responsible for tuberculosis. At the time, TB was responsible for one out of every seven deaths that occurred in Europe.

At the turn of the twentieth century, more than 80 percent of all Americans had been infected with TB before the age of twenty. Most of these people did not become ill since their bodies were able to fight off the disease. However, tuberculosis was still the most common cause of death among Americans. Even as late as 1938 there were more than seven hundred TB hospitals in the United States.

The first step in the conquest of TB occurred with the discovery of streptomycin in the early 1940s. Streptomycin is an antibiotic that kills the tubercle bacillus. Eventually, a number of other anti-

---

- **Abdominal cavity.** Peritonitis (pronounced per-i-tuh-NIE-tiss), infection of the peritoneum, produces symptoms similar to those of stomach cramps and appendicitis (see appendicitis entry).
- **Joints.** Infection of the joints results in a form of arthritis (see arthritis entry) that most commonly affects the hips and knees. Less commonly, the wrist, hand, and elbow joints may become painful and inflamed.
- **Meninges** (pronounced mu-NIHN-jeez). The meninges are tissues that cover the brain and the spinal cord. Infection of the meninges by the TB bacillus causes tubercular meningitis (see meningitis entry). This condition is most common among children, but most dangerous among the elderly. Symptoms of tubercular meningitis include headaches and drowsiness. If left untreated, a person with tubercular meningitis may lose consciousness and suffer permanent brain damage.
- **Skin, intestines, adrenal glands, and blood vessels.** The TB bacterium can infect all of these body parts. One serious result can occur when the body's main artery, the aorta, becomes infected. The infection may cause the aorta to rupture, resulting in the person's death. Infection of the pericardium, the membrane surrounding the heart, can cause pericarditis (pronounced per-i-kar-DIE-tiss) which interferes with the heart's ability to pump blood.
- **Miliary tuberculosis.** Miliary tuberculosis occurs when very large numbers of tubercle bacilli spread throughout the body. Huge numbers of tiny

tuberculosis drugs were developed and progress was made in overcoming the disease.

By 1985 a conference was held to develop plans to eliminate tuberculosis forever. The number of cases of TB had been dropping for many years and many experts thought that TB was no longer going to be a serious disease. Then, in the late 1980s, the number of TB cases began to rise, both in the United States and around the world. Why did this change come about? At least five factors are thought to play a role in the return of TB as a major health problem:

- Education. Efforts to educate people about the disease may have lessened as the perceived threat of TB decreased.

- AIDS/HIV epidemic. As HIV weakens a person's immune system, a patient can become more prone to developing infectious diseases, such as tuberculosis.

- Living conditions. People who are poor, or homeless, or who live in crowded and unsanitary conditions may also develop weakened immune systems, or increase their chances of coming in contact with the disease. Drug users often have weakened immune systems as well. As the number of people in these categories increases, so does the rate of tuberculosis.

- Population movement. The increased movement of people across national boundaries is another factor. When people take vacations, conduct business, or move to new countries, they may take TB with them.

- Drug Resistance. TB bacteria have become resistant to many of the drugs once used to treat the disease.

Experts estimate that eight to ten million new cases of tuberculosis develop worldwide every year. The disease is thought to be responsible for about three million deaths annually. While there are various ways to fight the disease, if root problems, such as homelessness, poverty, drug use, and drug resistance are not solved, tuberculosis may once again become a major health problem.

lesions (pronounced LEE-zhuns) develop throughout the body causing severe anemia, weakness, weight loss, and wasting. Lesions are any change in the structure or appearance of a part of the body as the result of an injury or infection.

DIAGNOSIS

The first sign of tuberculosis may be the presence of one or more of the symptoms described. For example, someone who experiences persistent cold-like systems might seek medical advice. In such cases, a medical worker can take samples of a person's sputum. The sputum can then be cultured (grown and studied) to look for tubercle bacilli. Standard chemical tests are available for the detection of these bacilli.

Body fluids other than sputum can also be collected and cultured. For example, studies of the urine will indicate whether the kidneys or bladder have been infected.

Perhaps the most common warning sign for tuberculosis is an abnormal chest X ray. The X ray of a person with pulmonary tuberculosis will show numerous white, irregular areas against a dark background and/or enlarged lymph nodes. Chest X rays are recommended for anyone who has close contact with a TB patient. For example, health care workers who have contact with people at risk for the disease should have regular chest X rays.

The most common method for diagnosing TB has traditionally been a tuberculin skin test. Tuberculin consists of antigens, substances produced by an *M. tuberculosis* culture. In a tuberculin skin test, these antigens are injected beneath the skin. If TB bacteria are present, the injection becomes hard, swollen, and red within one to three days. This change is generally a good indication that infection has occurred.

Today, skin tests generally use a substance called purified protein derivative (PPD). The PPD test, also called the Mantoux test, tends to provide more accurate results than the traditional tuberculin test. However, both false positives and false negatives do occur. A false positive is a test that suggests infection has occurred when it really has not. A false negative is a test that shows that no infection has occurred when, in fact, it actually has.

TREATMENT

In the past, treatment of tuberculosis was primarily supportive. Patients were kept in isolation, away from the healthy population. They were encouraged to rest and to eat well. If these measures failed, surgery was used. Today, surgical procedures are used much less often. Instead, drug therapy has become the primary means of treatment. Patients with TB can now safely rest at home; they pose no threat to other members of the household.

Drug Therapy

Drugs provide the most effective treatment for TB patients. Three principles govern the use of drug treatment for tuberculosis:

- First, the number of bacilli must be lowered as quickly as possible. By so doing, the risk of transmitting the disease to other people is reduced.
- Second, efforts must be made to prevent the development of drug resistance. If a person develops a resistance to a drug, it will no longer be helpful in curing the disease. As a result, most patients are given a combination of two or three different drugs at first.
- Third, drug treatment must be continued to prevent reoccurrence of the disease.

Five drugs are used today to treat tuberculosis. They are isoniazid (also known as INH; pronounced eye-suh-NY-uh-zid, trade names Laniazid, Nydrazid); rifampin (pronounced ry-FAM-puhn, trade names Rifadin, Rimactane); pyrazinamide (pronounced pir-uh-ZIN-uh-mide, trade name Tebrazid); streptomycin (pronounced strep-tuh-MYS-uhn); and ethambutol (pronounced eth-AM-byoo-tol, trade name Myambutol). The first three drugs are often combined into a single capsule so that patients have fewer pills to take.

Surgery

Surgery is sometimes used to treat tuberculosis when medication is not effective. One form of surgery involves the introduction of air into the chest. This procedure causes the lung to collapse. In a second procedure, one or more ribs may be removed. A third procedure involves the removal of all or part of a diseased lung. Other forms of surgery may be used in cases of extrapulmonary tuberculosis.

PROGNOSIS

The prognosis for recovery from TB is good for most patients. The key to success is early diagnosis of the disease followed by a careful program of medication. The most serious form of tuberculosis, miliary tuberculosis, is still fatal in many cases, but it is seldom seen in developed countries today.

PREVENTION

Probably the most important form of prevention is to reduce the overcrowded and unsanitary conditions in which many people live. This action reduces the risk of transmitting TB from infected to uninfected people.

Vaccinations

The Bacillus Calmette-Guérin vaccine (BCG) is available for use against tuberculosis. A vaccine is a substance that causes the body's immune system to build up resistance to a particular disease. BCG is made from a type of mycobacterium that infects cattle. When injected into humans, it stimulates the immune system against *M. tuberculosis*. The vaccine, however, is more effective in some groups of people than in others. Scientists are conducting studies to better understand why the vaccine is not as effective in some parts of the population.

Preventative Use of Isoniazid

Isoniazid can be used to prevent the development of TB as well as to treat it. There is no point in giving the drug to everyone, however, since most people never come into contact with someone who has tuberculosis, so their risk of infection is small. However, some people encounter TB carriers often. These people can benefit from taking isoniazid on a regular basis. The treatment involves receiving a dose of isoniazid once every six to twelve months.

Among the groups that should consider the use of isoniazid as a preventative against TB are: health care workers who have contact with TB patients; people who are HIV positive; intravenous drug users; anyone who has had positive PPD results and abnormal chest X rays in the past; people with depressed immune systems; and members of high-risk groups who have had positive PPD tests.

FOR MORE INFORMATION

Books

Hyde, Margaret O. *Know About Tuberculosis*. New York: Walker & Company, 1994.

Landau, Elaine. *Tuberculosis*. New York: Franklin Watts, Inc., 1995.

Silverstein, Alvin, Virginia Silverstein, and Robert Silverstein. *Tuberculosis*. Hillside, NJ: Enslow Publishers, Inc., 1994.

Organizations

National Institute of Allergy and Infectious Diseases. Building 31, Room 7A-50, 31 Center Drive, MSC 2520, Bethesda, MD 20892–2520. http://www.niaid.nih.gov.

ULCERATIVE COLITIS

DEFINITION

Ulcerative colitis (pronounced UHL-suh-RATE-ihv kuh-LY-tiss) is an inflammation of the large intestine that causes swelling, ulcerations (open sores), and loss of function in the large intestine.

DESCRIPTION

Ulcerative colitis is a form of inflammatory bowel disease (IBD). The term inflammatory bowel disease refers to a large group of disorders that affect the gastrointestinal (pronounced gas-troh-ihn-TESS-tuh-nuhl) system. Also known as the digestive system, the gastrointestinal (GI) system includes the stomach, small intestine, and large intestine.

Inflammation is a process that occurs when the body's immune system begins to fight off foreign invaders, such as viruses, bacteria, and fungi. The immune system is a network of organs, tissues, cells, and chemicals designed to kill invading organisms. Some of the chemicals produced by the immune system irritate the body's own tissues. They cause heat, redness, swelling, and loss of function. These changes are all characteristic of inflamed tissue.

In ulcerative colitis, inflammation occurs in the lining of the large intestine and the rectum. In rare cases, it may extend into the small intestine. In most cases, however, the small intestine remains normal.

Ulcerative colitis is one of two common forms of IBD. The other form is called Crohn's disease (see Crohn's disease entry). The major difference between the two diseases is that Crohn's disease may occur in both large and small intestines while ulcerative colitis is usually found only in the large intestine and rectum. Another difference is the damage done to tissues. Ulcerative colitis occurs only in the lining of the intestine while the damage caused by Crohn's disease can extend to all layers of the intestinal wall.

The inflammation associated with ulcerative colitis can eventually cause portions of the intestinal lining to peel off, exposing open pits, or ulcerations, which can easily become infected.

Ulcerative colitis occurs in all age groups and affects men and women equally. The most common age of diagnosis is between fifteen and thirty-five years of age.

CAUSES

No one knows for sure what causes inflammatory bowel disease. A number of theories have been developed to explain the condition. Some researchers believe that the disorder is caused by some organism, such as a bacterium or virus. No such organism has been found, however. Other researchers think the body's immune system becomes confused and begins to attack the body's own cells as though they were foreign invaders that needed to be killed.

SYMPTOMS

The first symptoms of ulcerative colitis are abdominal pain and cramping. The patient is likely to feel an urgent need to have a bowel movement. Blood and pus may appear in the stool. Some patients experience diarrhea,

WORDS TO KNOW

Colonoscopy: A procedure in which a long, thin tube is inserted through a patient's rectum into the colon to permit examination of the inner walls of the colon.

Crohn's disease: A form of inflammatory bowel disease that affects the large and small intestine.

Inflammation: A series of events that may result from the immune system's attempt to fight off foreign invaders. Inflammation involves heat, redness, swelling, and loss of function in the part of the body that is affected.

Inflammatory bowel disease: A group of disorders that affect the gastrointestinal (digestive) system.

Intestinal perforation: A hole in the lining of the intestine, which allows partially digested foods to leak into the abdominal cavity.

Sulfasalazine: A drug commonly used to treat inflammatory bowel diseases, consisting of an aspirin-like part to reduce inflammation and an antibiotic part to fight bacteria.

Toxic dilation of the colon: An expansion of the colon that may be caused by inflammation due to ulcerative colitis.

Ulcer: An open sore.

fever, and weight loss. If the diarrhea continues, signs of dehydration may appear. Dehydration occurs when the body loses water too rapidly. It results in low blood pressure, fast heart rate, and dizziness.

There are three serious complications of ulcerative colitis: intestinal perforation, toxic dilation of the colon, and colon cancer (see colon cancer entry).

Intestinal perforation is a life-threatening condition. It develops when a hole forms in the intestinal wall, which is caused by long-standing inflammation of the intestinal lining. First, an ulcer forms. Then the ulcer expands and breaks through the intestinal wall. The danger arises because contents of the intestine may spill out into the abdomen. These contents contain bacteria that can cause massive infection. The infection can quickly become so severe that it causes death. An infection of this kind is called peritonitis (pronounced per-i-tuh-NIE-tiss).

Toxic dilation of the colon refers to a significant increase in the size of the intestine. Inflammation is thought to cause intestinal muscles to relax. As they relax, the intestine gets larger and larger. Stretching of the intestinal walls

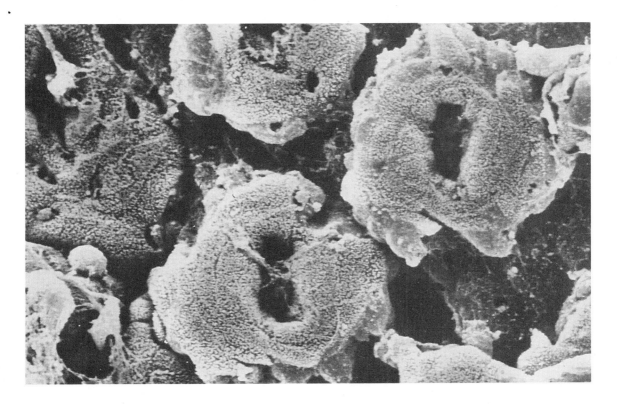

A magnified image of a human colon with ulcerative colitis. (© 1995 Professors P.M. Motta and F.M. Magliocca/Science Photo Library. Reproduced by permission of Custom Medical Stock Photo.)

causes them to become thinner. At some point, the intestinal lining may break. When this happens, peritonitis may result.

Colon cancer occurs when cells in the intestinal lining begin to grow uncontrollably. The cells may form tumors that can interfere with normal body functions or spread to other parts of the body. The risk of colon cancer increases in the years after ulcerative colitis is diagnosed. Ten years after diagnosis, the risk for colon cancer is less than 1 percent. After fifteen years, however, the risk increases to about 10 percent. After twenty and twenty-five years, the risk increases to about 23 percent and 42 percent, respectively.

DIAGNOSIS

A doctor may suspect a patient has ulcerative colitis if the patient has the symptoms described. Examination of the stool may reveal the presence of blood and pus. Pus consists largely of white blood cells. The presence of white blood cells suggests an infection somewhere in the body.

The usual method used to confirm a diagnosis of ulcerative colitis is colonoscopy (pronounced KO-lon-OSS-kuh-pee). Colonoscopy is a procedure that involves inserting a long, thin tube into a patient's rectum. The tube is then pushed upward into the colon. The tube may have a light, a camera, and a small knife attached at the end. The light and camera allow the doctor to examine the walls of the large intestine. The knife makes it possible to remove a small sample of tissue, which can then be studied under a microscope. The appearance of white blood cells in the tissue may confirm the presence of ulcerative colitis.

TREATMENT

The first step in treating ulcerative colitis is to reduce inflammation. A drug known as sulfasalazine (pronounced SULL-fuh-SAL-uh-zeen) is used for this purpose. Sulfasalazine consists of two parts. One part is a form of salicylic acid, the major component of aspirin. The salicylic acid compound helps reduce inflammation. The second part of sulfasalazine is an antibiotic. The antibiotic kills any harmful bacteria that may be present in the intestine.

Complications caused by ulcerative colitis may require other treatments. For example, a patient with toxic dilation of the colon may require hospitalization. The patient may be given

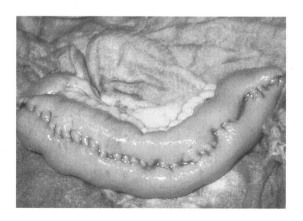

A specimen of a colon with ulcerative colitis. (Reproduced by permission of Photo Researchers, Inc.)

steroids and antibiotics intravenously (through a needle in the vein). Steroids are a powerful anti-inflammatory medication. In the most severe cases, surgery may be required to remove the colon.

Colon cancer is treated in much the same way as other forms of cancer: with surgery, radiation treatments, or chemotherapy.

Alternative Treatment

There are natural remedies that may help reduce inflammation associated with ulcerative colitis. Omega-3 fatty acids, which are found in fish oil and flaxseed, are available in pill form or as enemas.

PROGNOSIS

The prognosis for ulcerative colitis depends on how severe the first attack is. About 10 percent of all patients die if the first attack comes on suddenly and is quite severe. Prognosis is especially poor for patients over the age of sixty. Among these patients, a severe initial attack is fatal in more than 25 percent of cases.

Mild cases of the disorder can usually be treated quite successfully. However, the disease can reappear after it has been inactive for a period of time. Overall, about 20 to 25 percent of all patients eventually require removal of the colon. This procedure is very successful, however, and generally results in a complete cure of the disease.

PREVENTION

There are no known methods of preventing ulcerative colitis.

FOR MORE INFORMATION

Books

Long, James W. *The Essential Guide to Chronic Illness*. New York: Harper-Perennial, 1997.

Saibil, Fred. *Crohn's Disease and Ulcerative Colitis*. Buffalo, NY: Firefly Books, 1997.

Thompson, W. Grant. *The Angry Gut: Coping With Colitis and Crohn's Disease*. New York: Plenum Press, 1993.

Organizations

Crohn's & Colitis Foundation of America, Inc. 386 Park Avenue South, 17th Floor, New York, NY 10016–8804. (800) 932–2423.

ULCERS

DEFINITION

An ulcer is any break in the skin or in a mucous membrane. Mucous membrane is a thin tissue that lines the interior surface of body openings. The term ulcer is used most commonly to refer to ulcers that occur in the upper part of the digestive system, such as peptic ulcers. At one time, doctors believed that ulcers were caused by too much stress. However, it is now known that bacterial infection accounts for more than three-quarters of all peptic ulcers.

DESCRIPTION

Experts estimate that about 2 percent of the adult population in the United States have active ulcers and that about 10 percent of all adults will have an ulcer at some point in their lives. Males have about three times as many ulcers as females.

Ulcers are sometimes classified according to the part of the digestive system in which they occur. Gastric ulcers occur in the stomach. Duodenal ulcers occur in the duodenum. The duodenum (pronounced doo-uh-DEE-nuhm) is the upper part of the small intestine, adjacent to the stomach.

A peptic ulcer is one that occurs in the upper digestive tract, in which the break in the mucous membrane is exposed to gastric acidic secretion. About 80 percent of all peptic ulcers occur in the duodenum. They are most common among males between the ages of twenty and forty-five. Gastric ulcers account for about 16 percent of all peptic ulcers and are most common in males between the ages of fifty-five and seventy.

WORDS TO KNOW

Duodenum: The upper part of the small intestine, joined to the lower part of the stomach.

Endoscope: An instrument consisting of a long, narrow tube that can be inserted down the patient's throat to study the health of the patient's digestive system.

Helicobacter pylori: A bacterium that lives in mucous membrane and is responsible for the development of ulcers.

Nonsteroidal anti-inflammatory drugs (NSAIDs): A group of drugs used to treat pain and fever, including aspirin, ibuprofen, and acetaminophen.

Peptic ulcer: A general name referring to ulcers in any part of the digestive system.

CAUSES

There are three major causes of peptic ulcers: infection, certain types of medications, and other medical problems that cause the release of too much stomach juices.

Helicobacter pylori is a bacterium that lives in mucous membranes in the digestive system. It causes about 95 percent of all duodenal ulcers and 70 percent of all gastric ulcers.

The use of nonsteroidal anti-inflammatory drugs (NSAIDS) also tends to cause ulcers. Nonsteroidal anti-inflammatory drugs are painkillers. People use these drugs for headaches, sore muscles, menstrual cramps, and similar complaints. Some common NSAIDS are aspirin, ibuprofen (pronounced i-byoo-PRO-fuhn, trade names Advil, Motrin), and acetaminophen (pronounced uh-see-tuh-MIN-uh-fuhn, trade name Tylenol). People who use NSAIDS on a regular basis are forty times more likely to get ulcers than those who do not. Aspirin is the NSAID most likely to cause ulcers. Aspirin should not be given to children because of the risk of Reye's syndrome (see Reye's syndrome entry).

Some medical problems can increase the risk of ulcers. For example, Zollinger-Ellison syndrome causes an unusually large release of digestive juices in the stomach and this excess secretion can create ulcers.

Other factors may also increase a person's risk for ulcers. For example, smokers are more likely to develop an ulcer and are also more likely to die from the complications of an ulcer. People with blood type A are more likely to have gastric ulcers, while those with type O are more likely to develop duodenal ulcers.

Scientists are still debating the role of stress in the formation of ulcers. Stress is no longer regarded as a primary cause of the disorder. But some specialists think that it may be a contributing factor.

SYMPTOMS

The symptoms of gastric ulcers include feelings of indigestion and heartburn, weight loss, and repeated cases of bleeding in the stomach. Ulcer pain is sometimes described as gnawing, dull, aching, or similar to hunger pangs. Patients may experience nausea or appetite loss. In many cases, ulcer pain comes and goes over long periods of time.

The primary symptoms of duodenal ulcers include heartburn, stomach pain, weight gain, and a burning feeling at the back of the throat. A patient is most likely to feel discomfort two to four hours after meals.

About 20 percent of all people with peptic ulcers experience no symptoms. This form of the condition is called painless or silent ulcers. Between 10 to 20 percent of all peptic ulcer patients develop complications at some time in their illness. All of these complications can be very serious. In many cases, complications appear without any other signs of an ulcer. Some common complications include:

- **Hemorrhage.** Bleeding is the most common complication of ulcers. If bleeding continues, a patient may become anemic. Anemia (see anemias entry) is a condition that develops when a person does not have enough red blood cells. It can lead to extreme tiredness, weight loss, and, in the worst cases, death. About 6 to 10 percent of all patients with a bleeding ulcer die of the problem.

- **Perforation.** A perforation is a hole in the wall of the stomach or intestine. The hole allows stomach fluids to leak out into the abdominal cavity. These fluids are very acidic and can cause serious damage to body tissues. The signs of perforation include severe pain, fever, and tenderness of the abdomen. About 5 percent of patients with a perforated ulcer die of the condition.
- **Penetration.** Penetration occurs when an ulcer spreads to some organ adjacent to the digestive system. It may affect the liver or pancreas, for example. Signs of penetration include severe pain that spreads to the lower back.
- **Obstruction.** Over time, ulcers can form scar tissue. In some cases, this scar tissue can block the opening between the stomach and the duodenum. Food is not able to move all the way through the digestive system. The most common symptom of an obstruction is vomiting. The vomiting is caused by undigested food expelled from the stomach. Obstruction occurs in about 2 percent of all ulcer patients.

DIAGNOSIS

The first indication of an ulcer is likely to be a patient's complaint about one or more of the described symptoms. When a patient visits a physician for diagnosis, a physical examination alone is not enough. A doctor will look for certain factors in the patient's history that may suggest the presence of an ulcer. These factors include:

- If the patient is male
- Age over forty-five
- Recent weight loss, bleeding, repeated episodes of vomiting, back pain, or anemia
- History of using aspirin or other NSAIDs
- History of heavy smoking
- Family history of ulcers or stomach cancer

Endoscopy (pronounced en-DOS-kuh-pee) is one of the best ways to diagnose an ulcer. An endoscope consists of a long, narrow tube that can be inserted down the patient's throat. The tube contains a light and a tiny camera at one end. The doctor can actually look at the interior walls of the stomach and duodenum. If necessary, tiny scissors may also be attached to the endoscope. The scissors can be used to cut off a small sample of mucous membrane, which can be examined for the presence of stomach cancer. About 5 percent of ulcers develop into stomach cancer.

Imaging techniques can also be used to diagnose ulcers. These techniques are not as reliable as endoscopy but they are more comfortable for the patient. Imaging requires the patient to drink a fluid containing a substance that is opaque, or nontransparent, to X rays. An X-ray photograph is then taken of the patient's digestive system. The opaque substance appears as a white patch on the photograph and shows any abnormal structures, such as an ulcer, that may be present.

Blood tests are usually not very helpful in diagnosing ulcers. However, they may indicate when a patient has become anemic because of a bleeding ulcer.

The most important laboratory tests to perform are those that detect the *Helicobacter pylori* bacterium. One such test is a breath test. A patient is given a drink containing a radioactive substance that the bacterium will react with if it is present. The patient is then asked to breathe into a mechanism that determines whether the patient's breath is radioactive. If it is, that means the bacterium is present. This kind of test is important since the vast majority of people with ulcers are infected with *Helicobacter pylori*.

TREATMENT

Many symptoms of ulcers can be treated with over-the-counter medications. These medications may relieve the pain, nausea, and general discomfort caused by ulcers. However, they do not cure the disorder.

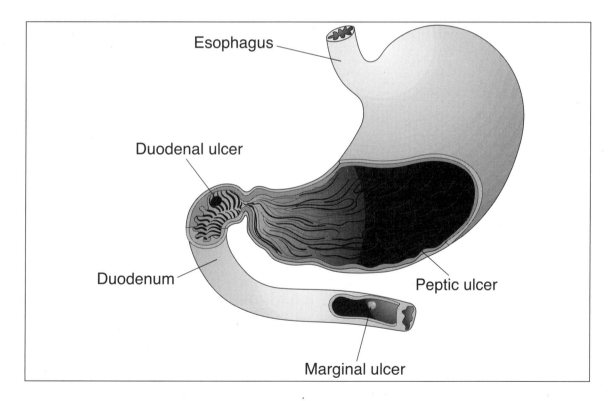

Illustration of the stomach with peptic ulcers. A peptic ulcer is one that occurs in the upper digestive tract. (Reproduced by permission of Electronic Illustrators, Inc.)

Two other types of medications are designed to reduce the symptoms of ulcers. Antisecretory drugs are drugs that reduce the amount of acid produced in the stomach. Acid attacks mucous membranes and can produce ulcers, so by lowering the amount of stomach acid released, the risk of ulcer formation can be reduced.

Protective drugs are also used to treat ulcers. A protective drug is a substance that forms a thin lining over mucous membranes, which protects the mucous membranes from attack by stomach acid.

Surgery is generally not used to treat ulcers. However, some of the complications caused by ulcers may require surgery. For example, doctors may cut the vagus nerve to the stomach. The vagus nerve (pronounced VAY-guhss) controls the release of stomach acid. After the cut, less stomach acid will be released, thus reducing the risk of ulcer formation.

One direct method for treating ulcers is to kill the bacteria that is responsible for most the vast majority of deaths caused by ulcers. Unless these bacteria are eliminated from the digestive system, ulcers will come back again and again. The drug used to kill *Helicobacter pylori* is the antibiotic tetracycline (pronounced tet-ruh-SI-kleen).

Alternative Treatment

Herbalists believe that a variety of natural products can help heal ulcers. For example, they recommend raw cabbage juice to help heal an ulcer. Some herbs that may soothe the symptoms of ulcers include plantain, marsh mallow, slippery elm, geranium, and goldenseal. Nutrition experts recommend taking certain vitamins and minerals, including vitamins A, C, and E, and the minerals zinc and selenium.

PROGNOSIS

The prognosis for recovery from ulcers is good for most patients. Nearly all ulcers respond to the medications now used to treat them. The rate of recurrence of ulcers can be cut to 5 percent through the elimination of the *Helicobacter pylori* bacterium.

PREVENTION

Methods for preventing ulcers include the following:

- Elimination of the *Helicobacter pylori* bacterium
- Avoiding unnecessary use of aspirin and other NSAIDs
- Giving up smoking
- Cutting down on alcohol, tea, coffee, sodas, and other products that contain caffeine

FOR MORE INFORMATION

Books

Ostrov, Rikki. *Ulcers: A Guide to Diagnosis, Treatment and Prevention.* Thorsons Publications, 1996.

Thompson, W. Grant. *The Ulcer Story: The Authoritative Guide to Ulcers, Dyspepsia, and Heartburn.* New York: Plenum Press. 1996.

Organizations

American College of Gastroenterology. 4900-B South 31st Street, Arlington, VA 22206-1656. (703) 820-7400.

American Gastroenterological Association. 7910 Woodmont Avenue, #914, Bethesda, MD 20814. (800) 668-5237. http://www.gastro.org.

International Foundation for Functional Gastrointestinal Disorders. PO Box 17864, Milwaukee, WI 53217. (888) 964-2001.

VISION DISORDERS

DEFINITION

Vision disorders are conditions caused by the eye's inability to properly focus light rays. Three major types of vision disorder are hyperopia (pronounced HY-puh-ROH-pee-uh), or farsightedness; myopia (pronounced my-OH-pee-a) or nearsightedness; and astigmatism, which causes the eye to form a blurred image of an object.

DESCRIPTION

Light that strikes the eyeball first passes through the cornea. The cornea is the tough, transparent covering at the front of the eye. It is shaped like a dome, with the top of the dome facing outward. Light then passes through the lens. The lens is located just inside the eyeball, behind the cornea. The lens has a double-convex shape. That is, it bulges outward in the middle.

The cornea and lens bend light as light waves pass through them. This process is known as refraction. In a normal eye, the light waves are brought to focus on the retina. The retina is a thin membrane at the back of the eye. Light waves cause chemical changes in the retina. These chemical changes set off a signal that passes through the optic nerve to the brain. The brain reads that signal as a visual image.

Muscles in the front of the eye can change the shape of the lens. These muscles adjust the lens shape to see objects close at hand or far away. This process is known as accommodation.

Visual disorders develop when the cornea and/or the lens do not properly focus light waves. The light waves do not come to a focus (that is, they do not all reach the same point) on the retina. They may come to a focus in front of the retina or behind the retina.

When light waves come to a focus in front of the retina, the person has myopia, or nearsightedness. People who are nearsighted can see objects close at hand, but they cannot see objects far away clearly. When light waves come to a focus behind the retina, the person has hyperopia, or farsightedness. People who are farsighted (hyperopic) can see objects far away but cannot clearly see objects close at hand.

In healthy eyes the cornea has a smooth, regular shape. Some people have corneas with an ellipsoidal shape, like a football or a squashed baseball. Such corneas scatter light waves across the retina, causing objects to appear as blurred images. This condition is called astigmatism.

CAUSES

Most vision disorders are thought to be inherited. That is, the disorders are passed down from one generation to the next. Most babies are born slightly hyperopic. However, this pattern changes as they grow older. In most cases, children develop normal vision. They may, however, become more hyperopic, or they may develop myopia.

WORDS TO KNOW

Accommodation: The ability of the lens to change its shape in order to focus light waves from distant or near objects.

Astigmatism: A condition in which light from a single point fails to focus on a single point of the retina. The condition causes the patient to see a blurred image.

Cornea: The clear, dome-shaped outer covering of the front of the eye.

Diopter: The unit of measure used for the refractive (light bending) power of a lens.

Hyperopia: Farsightedness. A condition in which vision is better for distant objects than for close ones.

Lens: In the eye, a transparent, elastic, curved structure that helps focus light on the retina.

Myopia: Nearsightedness. A condition in which far away objects appear fuzzy, because light from a distance doesn't focus properly on the retina.

Optic nerve: A bundle of nerve fibers that carries visual signals from the retina to the brain.

Radial keratotomy (RK): A surgical procedure in which the shape of the cornea is changed in order to correct myopia.

Refraction: The bending of light waves as they pass through a dense substance, such as water, glass, or plastic.

Retina: A membrane at the back of the eye that is sensitive to light and that converts light waves into signals sent to the brain by way of the optic nerve.

Some eyecare specialists argue that vision disorders may be caused by a number of factors. For example, they think that factors in the environment, such as work conditions, stress, and eye strain, can contribute to the development of vision disorders.

The development of astigmatism has been attributed to a number of factors. For example, people with allergies often rub their eyes repeatedly. This constant rubbing may cause damage to the cornea. Diabetes (see diabetes mellitus entry) is also known to change the shape of the cornea over time.

SYMPTOMS

The primary symptom of any vision disorder is the inability to see objects clearly. Objects near by or far away will seem blurry to a person with farsightedness or nearsightedness. Objects at almost any distance will seem blurry to a person with astigmatism.

Blurry vision may lead to other problems. People who have trouble seeing clearly may begin to squint in order to see better. Constant squinting can lead to discomfort, headaches, and eyestrain.

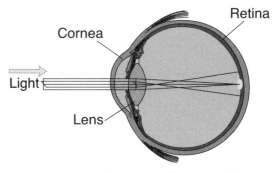

Horizontal line out of focus

DIAGNOSIS

Vision disorders are sometimes difficult to diagnose. Many people with vision disorders are not aware of their problem. They have often grown up seeing the world slightly out of focus and their view of objects may seem perfectly normal.

As a result, many vision problems are detected by others. For example, school teachers may realize that a pupil is unable to read the blackboard. Or a parent may notice that a child is constantly squinting while trying to read. In such cases, the individual is referred to an eye specialist for examination.

Many tests are available for detecting vision disorders. The most common tests involve the use of the familiar eye chart. The eye chart contains rows of letters of decreasing size going from

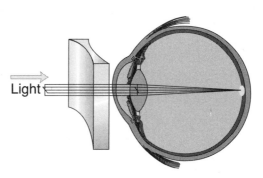

Astigmatism corrected by lens

Astigmatism is a condition in which light from a single point fails to focus on a single point of the retina. The condition causes the patient to see a blurred image. (Reproduced by permission of Electronic Illustrators Group)

top to bottom. The patient is asked to read each row on the chart. The last row the patient is able to read tells how accurate is his or her vision.

The results of an eye chart test are usually indicated by a pair of numbers, such as 20/50. These numbers show how well a person can see an object compared to a person with normal eyesight. A person with 20/50 vision can see at 20 feet from an eye chart what a person with normal vision can see at 50 feet from the chart.

Vision disorders are measured by having a patient look through various lenses at an eye chart. The lens are changed until the patient is able to see the letters on the chart clearly. The degree of error in the patient's eye is determined by the lens needed to produce perfect vision. This degree of error is measured in units called diopters (abbreviated: D). The prescription a doctor writes for glasses will indicate the shape of the lens (the diopter measurements) needed to provide perfect vision.

A simple test for astigmatism consists of a dial containing lines that radiate outward from the center. A person with astigmatism will be able to see some lines more clearly than other lines.

Doctors may also use direct tests on the eye. For example, a device known as a corneal topographer can be used to measure the shape of the cornea and determine whether the shape is correct or not. Doctors can also shine a light directly at the retina in a person's eye to look for any damage.

TREATMENT

Traditionally, the usual treatment for vision disorders has been fitting the patient with eyeglasses. Eyeglasses consist of glass or plastic lenses set in a

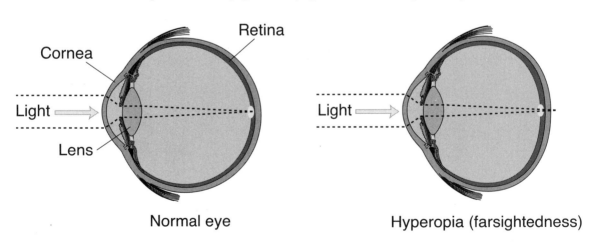

Normal eye

Hyperopia (farsightedness)

Hyperopia or farsightedness is a condition in which vision is better for distant objects than for close objects. (Reproduced by permission of Electronic Illustrators Group)

frame. These corrective lenses compensate (make up) for any errors in the patient's cornea and lens. If the patient's lens is too flat, for example, the lenses in the eyeglasses will be more round. Hyperopia, myopia, and astigmatism can all be treated very effectively, easily, and inexpensively with eyeglasses.

Some patients prefer to use contact lenses instead of eyeglasses. The principle behind contact lenses is the same as that behind eyeglasses. In the case of contact lenses, however, the corrective lens is placed directly on the eye.

Many vision disorders can now be treated surgically. An example is radial keratotomy (RK). Radial keratotomy (pronounced RAY-dee-uhl KARE-uh-TOT-uh-mee) is now a common procedure for the treatment of myopia. In RK, a doctor makes very small incisions (cuts) in the cornea to change its shape. The goal is to produce a cornea that has exactly the right shape to produce normal vision.

Traditional RK surgery is done with a very small diamond-tipped blade. Another approach now being studied involves the use of a laser beam to make the necessary incision. By 1999 this procedure had not yet received government approval in the United States for general use.

A form of RK surgery with lasers has been approved for treatment of astigmatism. The procedure is still quite new, however, and a patient should consider the risk carefully before choosing RK surgery.

PROGNOSIS

Most cases of vision disorder can be treated successfully with eyeglasses or contact lenses. Surgical procedures are often successful, as well. However,

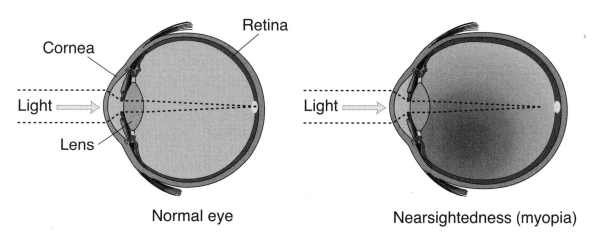

Myopia or nearsightedness is a condition in which vision is better for near objects than for distant objects. (Reproduced by permission of Electronic Illustrators Group)

many of surgical procedures are still in the early stages of development and carry considerably more risk than the use of eyeglasses or contact lenses.

PREVENTION

All forms of vision disorder are regarded as genetic. To the extent that is true, there is nothing a person can do to avoid vision problems. However, some experts believe that environmental factors may determine whether or not vision disorders develop. They suggest that maintaining good nutrition, reading and working in good light, and wearing corrective lenses as prescribed can reduce the risk of eye problems.

Regular eye examinations are also important. Eye characteristics change over time, so new corrective lenses may be needed occasionally. Also, eye examinations detect other types of eye disorders, such as glaucoma (see glaucoma entry), that are more serious than vision disorders.

See also: Color blindness.

FOR MORE INFORMATION

Books

Rosanes-Berrett, Marilyn B. *Do You Really Need Eyeglasses?* Barrytown, NY: Station Hill Press, 1990.

Zinn, Walter J., and Herbert Solomon. *Complete Guide to Eyecare, Eyeglasses, and Contact Lenses.* Hollywood, FL: Lifetime, 1996.

Periodicals

"Insight on Eyesight: Seven Vision Myths: Blind Spots about Vision Can Cause Needless Worry, Wasted Effort, and Unnecessary Treatment." *Consumer Reports on Health* (April 1997): p. 42.

Organizations

American Academy of Ophthalmology. PO Box 7424, San Francisco, CA 94120–7424. (800) 222–EYES. http://www.eyenet.org.

American Optometric Association. 243 North Lindbergh Boulevard, St. Louis, MO, 63141. (314) 991–4100. http://www.aoanet.org.

International Myopia Prevention Association. RD No. 5, Box 171, Ligonier, PA 15658. (412) 238-2101.

Myopia International Research Foundation. 1265 Broadway, Room 608, New York, NY 10001. (212) 684-2777.

National Eye Institute. 2020 Vision Place, Bethesda, MD 20892–3655. (301) 496-5248. http://www.nei.nih.gov.

Web sites

The Refractive Surgery Patient Resource Center. [Online] http://www.eyeinfo. com (accessed on November 1, 1999).

WARTS

DEFINITION

Warts are small, benign (harmless) growths caused by a viral infection. They occur on the skin or the mucous membrane. The mucous membrane is tissue that lines the nose, throat, digestive tract, and other body openings. The viruses that cause warts are members of the human papilloma virus (HPV) family. Warts can be transmitted from one person to another and they can travel from one part of the body to another.

DESCRIPTION

Warts occur most commonly among children, young adults, and women. They are a problem for 7 to 10 percent of the population. Warts are caused by nearly sixty different kinds of HPV. Each type prefers a certain part of the body. For example, some types of HPV produce warts on the skin, others cause warts inside the mouth, and still others produce warts on the genital and rectal areas.

Viruses enter the body through the skin or mucous membrane. They usually do not produce symptoms for one to eight months after entering the body. When warts appear, they are usually skin-colored and feel rough to the touch, but they can also be dark, flat, and smooth.

People differ in their sensitivity to HPV. Some individuals get warts over and over again. Others seldom or never get them. The virus is able to penetrate the body more easily if the skin has been damaged. For example, children who bite their nails may damage their skin in the process, which makes it easier for the virus to enter the body and cause warts. People with weakened immune systems are especially sensitive to HPV and wart infections.

CAUSES

The most common types of warts include:

- Common hand warts
- Foot warts
- Flat warts
- Genital warts

Hand Warts

Common hand warts grow around the nails, on the fingers, and on the backs of hands. They appear most often where the skin is broken.

Foot Warts

Foot warts are also called plantar warts. Plantar warts usually occur on the ball of the foot, the heel and the bottom of the toes. The skin in these areas is subject to weight, pressure, and irritation and has a tendency to crack or break open, providing an opening for the virus. Foot warts usually do not stick up above the skin.

People of all age groups can get plantar warts. But they are most common among adolescents between the ages of twelve and sixteen. The virus can be picked up in locker rooms, swimming pools, or by walking barefooted on dirty surfaces. People with diabetes mellitus (see diabetes mellitus entry) are very likely to develop plantar warts. The warts develop in areas where sores did not heal properly.

Flat Warts

Flat warts are smaller and smoother than other kinds of warts and tend to grow in large numbers. Although they can appear anywhere on the body, flat warts appear most often on the legs of women and the faces of children and young adult males.

WORDS TO KNOW

Cryosurgery: The use of liquid nitrogen for the purpose of removing diseased tissue.

Human papilloma virus (HPV): A family of viruses that cause hand, foot, flat, and genital warts.

Genital Warts

Genital warts are a type of sexually transmitted disease (STD). A sexually transmitted disease (see sexually transmitted diseases entry) is a condition that is passed from one person to another during sexual activity. The forms of HPV that cause genital warts are very contagious. A person who has sexual contact with someone

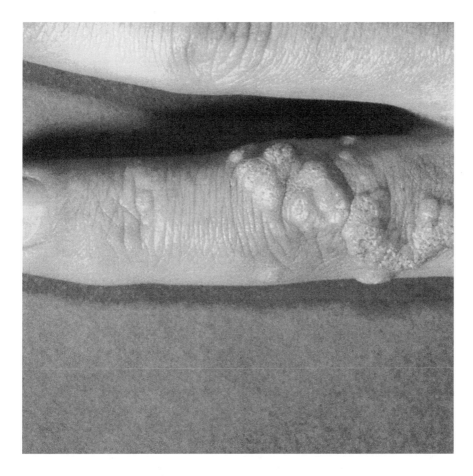

Common hand warts grow around the nails, on the fingers, and on the backs of hands. (Reproduced by permission of Custom Medical Stock Photo)

infected with HPV is very likely to contract the disease. Experts estimate that two-thirds of these people will develop genital warts within three months of contact. As a result, about one million new cases of genital warts are diagnosed each year in the United States.

SYMPTOMS

While it is very easy to recognize the presence of warts, depending on the area of the body that is infected, the symptoms may vary. For instance, if left untreated, plantar warts can grow to a size of one inch or more. They can spread out and form clusters of warts that can become painful at times. They cause the most discomfort when they occur on parts of the foot where pressure occurs, such as the heel or ball of the foot. Some people say they feel as if they have a stone in their shoe all the time.

Genital warts are usually small flat bumps. They may also be thin and tall. They are mostly soft, and not scaly, like other kinds of warts. In women, genital warts usually appear within the vagina, on the cervix, and around the anus or within the rectum. In men, the warts usually appear on the tip of the penis, on the scrotum, or around the anus. Genital warts can also develop in the mouth of a person who has had oral sexual contact with an infected person.

DIAGNOSIS

The distinctive appearance of warts makes them fairly easy to diagnose. Patients with genital warts should seek medical attention. A doctor can confirm the presence of genital warts with a simple visual examination.

TREATMENT

Many over-the-counter wart treatments are available that remove hand and foot warts. These products are usually in the form of lotions, ointments or plasters. They work by removing the skin affected by a wart virus. After treatment, the skin and wart simply drop off. These products must be used with care, however. The chemicals they contain are quite strong and can affect healthy skin as well as infected skin. People with diabetes or heart conditions should not use these products.

Non-prescription drugs are also available for the treatment of flat warts. These products cause the skin to become saturated with water. Over time, the skin layer peels off, taking the wart virus with it. Flat wart remedies can take as long as three months to work, depending on the size and depth of the wart.

Moist patches are often the easiest and most effective products to use. They are placed on a wart for forty-eight hours. Then they are replaced with a new patch. In some cases, the patch may irritate the skin. In that case, the person should switch to a milder medication or stop treatment for a while.

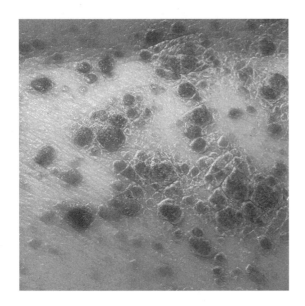

Flat warts are smaller and smoother than other kinds of warts and tend to grow in large numbers. (Reproduced by permission of Custom Medical Stock Photo)

Professional Treatment

A doctor should be consulted if home remedies do not work within a month. Doctors have many methods available for removing warts. One method involves the use of chemicals stronger than those found in non-prescription drugs. The use of these chemicals is often effective, but they may produce some burning and discomfort for a few days.

A second method of wart removal is cryosurgery (pronounced KRY-oh-SUR-juh-ree). Cryosurgery is the process by which tissue is frozen with liquid nitrogen, which has a temperature of about $-330°$ F ($-200°$ C). This process freezes the tissue very quickly and the frozen tissue can then simply be removed. Healing of the frozen area usually occurs quickly.

Another method of wart removal is electrocautery in which an electric needle is used to burn the wart. The tissue around the wart is killed and can be peeled off, taking the wart with it. Laser surgery works in a similar way. A laser beam is aimed at the wart and the heat of the laser kills the skin around the wart, and the skin and wart simply fall off.

Genital warts are very difficult to treat. Any of the described methods can be used. But the first round of treatment may not be very effective. Although it may be possible to remove the warts, the virus that causes the warts may continue to survive under the skin and can produce new warts at a later time.

Plantar warts are also very resistant to treatment. The use of chemicals can be successful if the warts are diagnosed early. However, the treatment may take many months. In the most serious cases, surgical removal of the warts may be necessary.

Alternative Treatment

A number of alternative approaches have been recommended for the treatment of warts. The scientific justification for some of these treatments is inconclusive. The suggestions listed should not be used for genital warts, which should be treated by a doctor.

For the treatment of common or plantar warts, alternative practitioners recommend the following remedies:

- Apply a paste made of vitamin C powder to the wart for one to two weeks.
- Place a crushed or sliced clove of garlic over the wart for seven consecutive nights while sleeping.
- Soak the wart in water. Then make scratches in the wart with a sterile needle. Apply drops of thuja dissolved in alcohol to the wart. Repeat several times a day for one to two weeks.
- Tape a piece of banana peel on the wart over night, with the inner side of the peel touching the skin. Repeat nightly for one to two weeks.

Strengthening one's immune system is an objective of some forms of alternative treatment. A stronger immune system may be able to fight off the viruses that cause warts. A well-balanced diet rich in vitamins A, C, and E may help strengthen the immune system. Avoiding stress is thought to be another way of strengthening the immune system.

PROGNOSIS

Even if warts are removed, the viruses that cause them may remain in the body and the warts may reappear at a later time. This problem is especially common in cases of genital warts. In addition, genital warts can cause other problems. The human papilloma virus can also cause infections of the cervix. Women who have had genital warts should see their doctor regularly and should have a pap smear every six months. A pap smear is a test for cervical cancer.

Plantar warts are difficult to treat because of the weight placed on feet. The goal of treatment is to destroy the plantar wart and the virus without damaging healthy skin but the treatment can often cause pain until the foot heals completely.

PREVENTION

Using condoms during sexual activity can prevent genital warts. Condoms do not offer protection against areas that are not covered, however, such as the upper thighs. Plantar warts may be prevented by practicing good foot care. Good foot care involves keeping feet clean and dry, changing socks daily, and taking note of growths on the skin or changes in skin appearance.

FOR MORE INFORMATION

Books

The Editors of Time-Life Books. *The Medical Advisor: The Complete Guide to Alternative and Conventional Treatments.* Alexandria, VA: Time-Life Books, 1997.

Stupik, Ramona. *AMA Complete Guide to Women's Health.* New York: Random House, 1996.

Periodicals

Siwek, J. "Warts on the Hands." *Washington Post Health* (April 19, 1995): p. 15.

"What to Do about Warts." *Consumer Reports on Health* (July 1997): pp. 81-82.

Organizations

American Academy of Dermatology. P.O. Box 4014, 930 North Meacham Road, Schaumburg, IL 60168-5014. (847) 330-2300. http://www.aad.org.

American Podiatric Medical Association. 9312 Old Georgetown Road, Bethesda, MD 20814-1698. (301) 571-9200. http://www.apma.org.

WHIPLASH

DEFINITION

Whiplash is an injury that occurs when the neck and head experience a sudden, sharp motion. The injury often affects the bones, muscles, nerves, and tendons of the neck.

DESCRIPTION

About one million whiplash injuries occur in the United States every year. Most occur during car accidents or sporting events. In such cases, an unexpected force jerks the head backward and then, almost immediately, forward causing the bones of the neck to snap out of position. Nerves in the neck may be pinched, resulting in damage to or destruction of certain body parts.

Poor driving habits can increase the risk of whiplash injury. A person who is tired, tense, or under the influence of alcohol may drive carelessly. Bad weather conditions can also increase the chance of an accident. Finally, the medical condition known as osteoarthritis (pronounced AHS-tee-oh-arr-THRY-tiss), which weakens the joint cartilage, increases the risk of whiplash injury (see arthritis entry).

CAUSES

Whiplash is likely to occur when a person's muscles are either too tight or too lose. In such cases, the chance of damage to the neck is especially high.

SYMPTOMS

The symptoms of whiplash may occur immediately after an accident. Or they may not develop for hours, days, or weeks after an injury. Some symptoms of whiplash are the following:

- Pain or stiffness in the neck, jaw, shoulders, or arms
- Dizziness
- Headache
- Loss of feeling in an arm or hand
- Nausea and vomiting

Less common symptoms include vision problems and feelings of depression.

DIAGNOSIS

Whiplash injuries are often difficult to diagnose. X rays and other imaging techniques may not reveal any damage to bones or muscles. Diagnosis is usually based, instead, on other techniques, such as observation of a patient's symptoms and a physical examination. Sometimes, further examination of the patient's nervous system may also be necessary.

TREATMENT

Whiplash is usually treated by one or more of three methods: medication, physical therapy, and supportive devices. Medication helps relieve pain and reduce inflammation. Physical therapy is used to realign the spine to relax pinched nerves and improve blood flow. Padded collars and other supportive devices hold the head and neck in position while they heal. In severe cases, cervical traction, may be used. Cervical traction involves a steady pull on the neck to keep it in the correct position as it heals.

Self-care

Some simple methods of self-care can often be used with whiplash injuries. For example, the injured area can be wrapped with ice for ten to twenty minutes every hour for the first day. After twenty-four hours, cold packs can be alternated with heat treatments. Letting a warm shower run on the neck and shoulders for ten to twenty minutes twice a day is recommended. Between showers, warm towels or a heat lamp can be used to warm and soothe the neck for ten to fifteen minutes several times a day.

Gentle massage and attention to one's posture can also be helpful. Sleeping without a pillow can promote healing. The use of a cervical collar, a device that holds the neck in place, or a small rolled towel under the chin can also provide support and prevent muscle fatigue.

THE USE OF SEATBELTS IS AN IMPORTANT FACTOR IN PREVENTING WHIPLASH INJURIES.

Self-care, however, is seldom sufficient for the treatment of whiplash injury. The patient should consult a family doctor, an orthopedic specialist, or a chiropractor after such an injury. Professional care is especially important if the injury results in pain, weakness, or numbness in the face or arms following an injury.

WORDS TO KNOW

Cervical traction: The process of using a mechanism to create a steady pull on the neck in order to keep it in the correct position while it heals.

Osteoarthritis: A type of arthritis that weakens the joint cartilage. It is most common among the elderly.

PROGNOSIS

With proper treatment, whiplash injuries can usually be cured in a week to a few months after injury occurs. In severe cases, numbness and weakness may last until recovery is complete.

PREVENTION

Whiplash injuries are less likely to occur when one is in good physical health. A proper diet and program of exercise help reduce stress and tension. The use of seatbelts is an important factor in preventing whiplash injuries. Careful, defensive driving techniques also can greatly reduce the risk of injury.

FOR MORE INFORMATION

Books

Ferrari, Robert. *The Whiplash Encyclopedia: The Facts and Myths of Whiplash.* Gaithersburg, MD: Aspen Publishers, Inc., 1999.

Melton, Michael R. *The Complete Guide to Whiplash.* Body Mind Publications, 1998.

WHOOPING COUGH

DEFINITION

Whooping cough is a highly contagious disease caused by bacteria. The disease is also known as pertussis (pronounced pur-TUSS-iss). The most prominent symptom of whooping cough is a distinctive, uncontrollable cough, followed by a sharp, high-pitched intake of air. This intake of air causes the characteristic "whoop" for which the disease is named.

DESCRIPTION

Whooping cough is caused by a bacterium called *Bortadella pertussis.* When inhaled, the bacterium attaches itself to cilia in the respiratory (breathing) tract. Cilia are tiny, hair-like projections on cells that beat back and forth constantly. This motion helps clear the respiratory system of bacteria, viruses, dead cells, and other material.

Bortadella pertussis interferes with the motion of cilia. The materials normally cleared away by cilia become lodged in the respiratory system and the cough that results is the body's way of attempting to rid the respiratory system of these materials.

Whooping cough exists everywhere in the world and can lead to a variety of diseases and complications, including death. Whooping cough can occur in people of all ages, but it is most serious when it strikes children under the age of two.

A person who has whooping cough at a young age becomes partially immune to the disease, which means that the person is less likely to have the same disease later in life.

CAUSES

Whooping cough is caused by bacteria entering a person's body. The bacteria are usually carried in droplets of water coughed into the air by an infected person. The incubation period for the disease is seven to fourteen days. The incubation period for a disease is the time between the start of the infection and the first appearance of symptoms. During this period, bacteria are multiplying in the respiratory tract.

SYMPTOMS

The second stage of whooping cough lasts about ten to fourteen days. During this period, the disease is often mistaken for a bad cold (see common cold entry). The patient has teary eyes, sneezing, fatigue, poor appetite, and a runny nose.

The third stage of the disease lasts two to four weeks. It is during this stage that the characteristic whooping cough begins. The cough is thought to be caused by inflammation of the respiratory system. The breathing tubes become narrowed, making it difficult for the person to get enough air to breathe normally. The effort to get air causes the gasping sound that accompanies the cough.

Severe exhaustion often occurs during the third stage of the disease. Patients can work so hard to get enough oxygen into their lungs that they become very tired. In children with whooping cough, the skin may begin to turn blue. The blue color indicates that the child's body is not getting enough oxygen.

WORDS TO KNOW

Bortadella pertussis: The bacterium that causes whooping cough.

Cilia: Tiny, hair-like projections on many cells that help keep the respiratory system clear of foreign materials.

Immunization: The process of injecting a material into a person's body that protects that person from catching a particular infectious disease later in life.

Throat culture: A sample of tissue taken from a person's throat for analysis. The culture is often taken by swiping a cotton swab across the back of the throat.

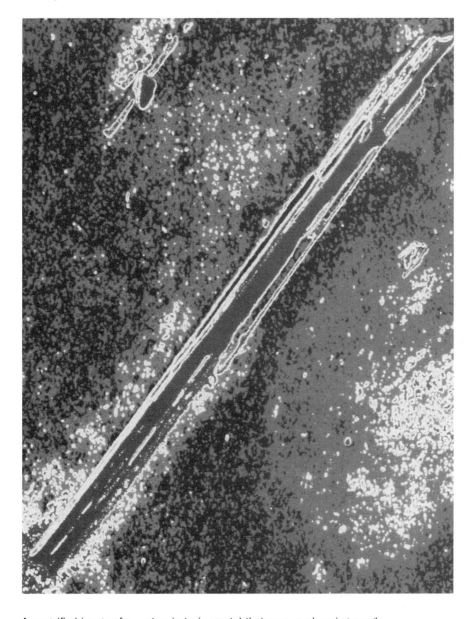

A magnified image of a pertussis toxin crystal that causes whooping cough.
(© 1992. Reproduced by permission of Custom Medical Stock Photo.)

Serious complications may also develop during this stage. For example, children may experience brain damage. Brain damage can occur because the brain is not getting enough oxygen, which causes brain cells to die. Also, the violent shaking caused by coughing can cause physical damage to the brain. An inadequate supply of oxygen to the brain can also cause seizures.

Another complication of whooping cough is hernias (see hernia entry). Hernias are abnormal protrusions (pushing out) of the intestine through the abdominal wall. The force of the coughs can cause the pressure needed to produce a hernia.

As the patient becomes weaker, he or she may become more subject to other bacterial infections of the lung, such as pneumonia (see pneumonia entry).

The final stage of whooping cough is recovery. This stage can last up to four weeks. Over this time, coughing may gradually become less intense as the patient gets better.

DIAGNOSIS

Whooping cough can be difficult to diagnose. Heavy coughing is characteristic of many diseases. For example, a heavy cold, a case of influenza (the flu; see influenza entry), or bronchitis (see bronchitis entry) all have symptoms similar to those of whooping cough.

A clear diagnosis can be made, however, by taking a throat culture. To do a throat culture, a doctor or nurse wipes a cotton swab across the back of the patient's mouth. The material collected is then studied under a microscope to determine if pertussis bacteria are present.

TREATMENT

Patients can be treated during the early stage of whooping cough with an antibiotic. The antibiotic usually used is erythromycin (pronounced i-rith-ruh-MY-sin). This treatment has limited value, however. The cilia are damaged early in the disease and once they are damaged, no drug can repair them. The cilia eventually grow back and begin to function normally. Until that happens, however, the patient will simply have to endure the symptoms of the disease.

There are ways, however, to make the patient more comfortable during the later stages of the disease. For example, liquids are recommended to keep the patient from becoming dehydrated. Rest is also suggested in order to reduce the amount and the intensity of the coughing.

PROGNOSIS

The vast majority of people who have whooping cough recover without further damage. Less than 1 percent of whooping cough cases end in death. Children are most likely to develop complications that lead to death. Common complications include pneumonia and extreme weight loss.

PREVENTION

Whooping cough can be prevented efficiently by immunization. Immunization is the process of injecting a person with a vaccine that prevents an infectious disease from occurring. A vaccine is a substance that causes the body immune system to build up resistance to a particular disease. The immunization shot given for whooping cough (pertussis) also contains vaccines for two other diseases, diphtheria and tetanus (see tetanus entry). The vaccine is sometimes called the DPT vaccine for the three diseases it helps protects against.

Medical experts recommend vaccinating all children for these diseases at the age of two months. The children are then protected for life. At one time, there was some concern about possible side effects from the DPT vaccine. Research has shown, however, that the vaccine is safe. In areas where it has not been used, there have been widespread epidemics of one or more of these diseases.

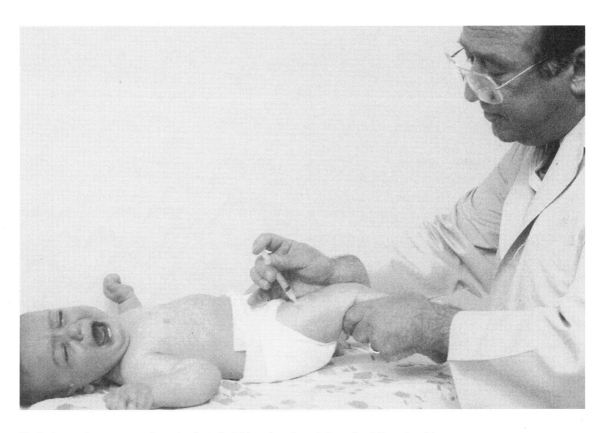

Medical experts recommend vaccinating all children for whooping cough at the age of two months. The children are then protected for life. (© 1991 CMSP. Reproduced by permission of Custom Medical Stock Photo.)

whooping cough

Books

Stoffman, Phyllis. *The Family Guide to Preventing and Treating 100 Infectious Diseases.* New York: John Wiley & Sons, 1995.

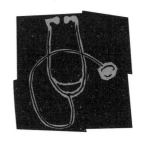

Where to Learn More

BOOKS

Abel, Ernest L. *America's 25 Top Killers*. Hillside, NJ: Enslow, 1991.

American Heart Association. *Living Well, Staying Well*. New York: American Heart Association and American Cancer Association, 1996.

Atkinson, David R., and Debbie Atkinson. *Hope Springs Eternal: Surviving a Chronic Disease*. Virginia Beach, VA: Are Press, 1999.

Bellenir, Karen, and Peter D. Dresser, eds. *Contagious and Non-contagious Infectious Diseases Sourcebook*. Detroit: Omnigraphics, Inc., 1996.

The Burton Goldberg Group. *Alternative Medicine: The Definitive Guide*. Puyallup, WA: Future Medicine Publishing, 1993.

Ciesielski, Paula F. *Major Chronic Diseases*. Guilford, CT: The Dushkin Publishing Group, 1992.

Daly, Stephen, ed. *Everything You Need to Know about Medical Treatments*. Springhouse, PA: Springhouse Corp., 1996.

Darling, David. *The Health Revolution: Surgery and Medicine in the Twenty-first Century*. Parsippany, NJ: Dillon Press, 1996.

Graham, Ian. *Fighting Disease*. Austin, TX: Raintree Steck-Vaughn, 1995.

Horn, Robert, III. *How Will They Know If I'm Dead? Transcending Disability and Terminal Illness*. Boca Raton, FL: Saint Lucie Press, 1996.

Hyde, Margaret O., and Elizabeth H. Forsyth, M.D. *The Disease Book: A Kid's Guide*. New York: Walker and Company, 1997.

Isler, Charlotte, R.N., and Alwyn T. Cohall, M.D. *The Watts Teen Health Dictionary.* New York: Franklin Watts, 1996.

The Johns Hopkins Medical Handbook: The 100 Major Medical Disorders of People over the Age of 50. *New York: Rebus, Inc., 1995.*

Long, James W. *The Essential Guide to Chronic Illness.* New York: Harper Perennial, 1997.

Roman, Peter. *Can You Get Warts from Touching Toads? Ask Dr. Pete.* New York: Julian Messner, 1986.

Shaw, Michael, ed. *Everything You Need to Know about Diseases.* Springhouse, PA: Springhouse Corp., 1996.

Stoffman, Phyllis. *The Family Guide to Preventing and Treating 100 Infectious Illnesses.* New York: John Wiley & Sons, 1995.

Weil, A. *Natural Health, Natural Medicine: A Comprehensive Manual for Wellness and Self-Care.* Boston: Houghton Mifflin, 1995.

WEB SITES

Centers for Disease Control and Prevention. http://www.cdc.gov

The Children's Health Center. http://www.mediconsult.com/mc/mcsite.nsf/conditionnav/kids~sectionintroduction

Healthfinder®. http://www.healthfinder.gov

InteliHealth: Home to Johns Hopkins Health Information. http://www.intelihealth.com

Mayo Clinic Health Oasis. http://mayohealth.org

National Institutes of Health. http://www.nih.gov

NOAH: New York Online Access to Health. http://www.noah.cuny.edu

WHO/OMS: World Health Organization. http://www.who.int

U.S. National Library of Medicine: Health Information. http://nlm.nih.gov/hinfo.html

ORGANIZATIONS

Centers for Disease Control and Prevention. 1600 Clifton Rd., NE, Atlanta, GA 30333. (404)639–3311. http://www.cdc.gov

National Institutes of Health (NIH). Bethesda, MD 20892. (301)496–1776. http:www.nih.gov

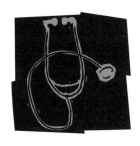

Index

Italic type indictes volume numbers; **boldface** type indicates entries and their page numbers; (ill.) indicates illustrations.

A

Abdominal hernia *2:* 393 (Ill.)
Abscesses *1:* 223
Absence seizure *2:* 289
ACE inhibitors *2:* 412
Acetaminophen *1:* 181
Acetylsalicylic acid *4:* 620
Acne *1:* 1-7, 4 (ill.)
Acupuncture *3:* 436 (Ill.)
Acutane *1:* 5
Acute retroviral syndrome *1:* 16
Acyclovir *1:* 181
Adaptive skills *3:* 515
ADD. *See* **Attention-deficit/hyperactivity disorder**
Addiction *1:* 7-14
Adenoid *2:* 272
ADHD. *See* **Attention-deficit/hyperactivity disorder**
Adult onset diabetes *2:* 252
AIDS *1:* 14-24
AIDS dementia complex *1:* 16
Alcoholic hepatitis *2:* 386
Alcoholism *1:* 25-31
Alendronate *3:* 558
Ali, Muhammad *1:* 207, *3:* 573 (ill.)
Allergens *1:* 32, 33, 78, 81 (ill.)
Allergies *1:* 32-39
Allergy flow chart *1:* 33 (ill.)
Allergy scratch test *1:* 36 (ill.)
Allergy shots *2:* 337
Alpha-blockers *2:* 412

Alpha-fetoprotein *2:* 263
ALS. *See* **Amyotrophic lateral sclerosis**
Alveoli *2:* 277
Alzheimer's disease *1:* 40-47
Amantadine hydrochloride *3:* 429
American Optical/Hardy, Rand, and Ritter Pseudoisochromatic Test *1:* 193
Amnesia *1:* 207
Amputation *2:* 317
Amyotrophic lateral sclerosis *1:* 48-53
Anaphylaxis *1:* 32, *2:* 334
Androgen *1:* 2
Anemias *1:* 53-61, 111, *4:* 670
Aneurysm. *See* **Cerebral aneurysm**
Angiography *1:* 88, 166
Angioplasty *2:* 361
Angiotensin converting enzyme (ACE) inhibitors *2:* 412
Ankylosing spondylitis *1:* 111
Anorexia Nervosa *1:* 61-67
Anti-androgen *1:* 2
Antibiotic *1:* 2
Antibodies *1:* 16, 32
Antibody *1:* 111
Anticholinergic drugs *3:* 576
Anticoagulants *2:* 359
Anticonvulsant medication *1:* 118
Antidepressants *1:* 104, 121, *2:* 248
Antigen *1:* 16, *2:* 385
Antihistamines *1:* 36
Anxiety disorders *3:* 551, 565
Aplastic anemia *1:* 56
Appendicitis *1:* 67-71, *1:* 69 (ill.)

Appendix *1:* 68
Appendix, inflamed *1:* 69 (ill.)
Appetite suppressant *3:* 543
Aqueous humor *2:* 324
Arenaviruses *2:* 379, 380
Aricept *1:* 45
Arsenic *4:* 661
Artemisinin *3:* 500
Arteriosclerosis *1:* 88, *2:* 406
Arthritis *1:* 71-78, 223, *2:* 406
Arthrography *4:* 745
Ascending infection *1:* 234
Asperger syndrome *1:* 104
Aspirin *2:* 348, *4:* 621
Asthma *1:* 32, 78-87
Astigmatism *4:* 794, 795 (ill.)
Ataxia *1:* 171
Atherosclerosis *1:* 87-94
Atherosclerosis flowchart *1:* 92 (ill.)
Atherosclerotic plaque *2:* 357 (ill.)
Athlete's foot *1:* 94-97, 95 (ill.)
Atopy *1:* 78
**Attention-deficit/hyperactivity disorder *1:*
   97-103**, 171
Audiometer *2:* 351
Auditory canal *2:* 351
Auditory nerve *2:* 351
Aura *2:* 288
Auricle *2:* 272
Autism *1:* 103-10
**Autoimmune disorders *1:* 55, 69, 73,
   110-15**, 223, *3:* 447, 487, 520, *4:* 623
Autoimmune hemolytic anemia *1:* 55, 111
Autoimmune hepatitis *2:* 386
Autoimmune thrombocytopenic purpura
   1: 111
AZT *1:* 21 (ill.)

B

Babies, effect of shaking on *4:* 669 (ill.)
Bacillus Calmette-Guérin (BCG) *4:* 774
Bacterial sore throat *4:* 707
Barium enema *1:* 195, 197, 223
Basal cell cancer *4:* 678, 681 (ill.)
Becker muscular dystrophy *3:* 534
Behring, Emil Adolf von *4:* 754
The bends. *See* **Decompression sickness**
Benign *1:* 124, 148
Benzodiazepine *1:* 118, *3:* 596
Berylliosis *3:* 483
Best, Billy *2:* 404 (ill.)
Beta-blockers *2:* 360
Beta-receptor agonist *1:* 83
Billups, Chauncy *2:* 315 (ill.)
Binge *1:* 136
Biofeedback *2:* 345, *3:* 437 (ill.)

Biopsy *1:* 124, 148
Bipolar disorder *1:* 117-23
Blackheads. *See* **Acne**
Bladder, inflammation of. *See* **Cystitis**
Blind spot *2:* 324
Blood cells *4:* 671 (ill.)
Blood pressure, measurement of *2:* 410
Blood sugar, low. *See* **Hypoglycemia**
Blood-brain barrier *3:* 509, 575
Bone atrophy *3:* 562 (ill.)
Bone fracture *2:* 311 (ill.), 312
Bone marrow *1:* 148
Bone marrow transplantation *1:* 156, *3:* 475
Borrelia burgdorferi 3: 492
Bortadella pertussis 4: 809
Botulism *2:* 299
Bovet, Daniele *4:* 625
Brain, CAT scan of after stroke *4:* 732 (ill.)
Brain tissue, diseased *1:* 42 (ill.)
Branham, Sara Elizabeth *3:* 512
Breast cancer *1:* 123-28, 126 (ill.)
Bronchi *1:* 129, *2:* 277
Bronchial tubes *1:* 199
Bronchiole *2:* 277
Bronchitis *1:* 128-35
Bronchodilator *1:* 37, 38, *2:* 277, *4:* 702
Bronchoscope *4:* 702
BSA *1:* 141
Bulimia nervosa *1:* 135-40
Bunyaviruses *2:* 381, 382
Burns and scalds *1:* 140-46
Burns, classification of *1:* 143 (ill.)
Butterfly rash *3:* 490 (ill.)
Bypass surgery *2:* 361

C

C. botulinum. See Clostridium botulinum
C. jejuni. See Campylobacter jejuni
Caisson disease *2:* 239
Calcitonin *3:* 558
Calcium channel blockers *2:* 349, 412
Campylobacter jejuni 2: 299, 302
Cancer *1:* 147-58. *See also* **Breast cancer,
   Colorectal cancer, Hodgkin's disease,
   Kaposi's syndrome, Leukemia, Lung
   cancer, Prostate cancer, Skin cancer**
Cancer, breast. *See* **Breast cancer**
Cancer cells *1:* 152 (ill.), *3:* 473
Cancer, colorectal. *See* **Colorectal cancer**
Cancer, lymphatic. *See* **Hodgkin's disease**
Carbamazepine *1:* 121
Carcinogen *1:* 148
Carcinomas *1:* 149
Cardiac muscle *4:* 626 (ill.)
Cardiopulmonary resuscitation (CPR)
   2: 359

Carditis *4:* 624, 625

Carpal tunnel syndrome *1:* 158-62, 160 (ill.)

Cartilage *1:* 69

CAT scan. *See* Computerized axial tomography (CAT) scan

Cataract surgery *1:* 164 (ill.)

Cataracts *1:* 162-65

Catatonic schizophrenia *4:* 643, 644

Catheter *1:* 88

Catheterization *1:* 234

Cavities, development of *4:* 762 (ill.)

CD4 *1:* 16

Cephalosporin *2:* 272

Cerebral aneurysm *1:* 165-70, 167 (ill.), 168 (ill.), *4:* 728

Cerebral edema *4:* 668

Cerebral embolism *4:* 728

Cerebral palsy *1:* 170-80

Cerebral thrombosis *4:* 728

Cerebrospinal fluid *1:* 166, *2:* 280

Cerumen *2:* 272

Cervical traction *4:* 808

CFTR *1:* 227

Chelation therapy *3:* 463

Chemotherapy *1:* 126, 148, 155

Chernobyl *4:* 618

Chickenpox *1:* 180-85, 182 (ill.)

Chlamydia *4:* 660

Chlamydia trachomatis *4:* 664 (ill.)

Chloroquine *3:* 500

Cholesterol *1:* 88

Chorea *4:* 624

Chronic bronchitis *1:* 130 (ill.), 133-34

Chronic fatigue syndrome *1:* 185-91

Circadian rhythm sleep disorders *4:* 691

Circumcision *1:* 234

Cirrhosis *2:* 385

Clark, James M. *2:* 243 (ill.)

Clostridium botulinum *2:* 299, 302, 303

Clostridium tetani *4:* 752

Clotting factor *2:* 372

Cognex *1:* 45

Cognitive-behavioral therapy *3:* 552

Cold, common *1:* 199

Cold sores *2:* 395, 397 (ill.)

Colitis *4:* 781

Collapsed lung. *See* **Pneumothorax**

Colon with ulcerative colitis *4:* 784 (ill.)

Colonoscope *1:* 223

Colonoscopy *1:* 195, 197, *4:* 782, 784

Color blindness *1:* 191-94

Colorectal cancer *1:* 194-99, 196 (ill.)

Colostomy *1:* 195

Comedo *1:* 2

Comedolytic *1:* 2

Common cold *1:* 199-206

Computed tomography (CT) scan *1:* 68, 148

Computerized axial tomography (CAT) scan *1:* 68, *2:* 342

Concussion *1:* 206-11

Conduct disorder *1:* 98

Conductive hearing loss *2:* 351

Cone cells *1:* 191

Congenital disorder *1:* 166

Congenital muscular dystrophy *3:* 535, 536

Congenital problem *1:* 234

Conjunctivitis *1:* 211-15

Consumption. *See* **Tuberculosis**

Contact dermatitis *1:* 32

Contrast hydrotherapy *2:* 317

Cornea *1:* 162, *2:* 324

Coronary angioplasty *2:* 361

Coronary artery *1:* 90 (ill.)

Coronary bypass surgery *2:* 361

Coronavirus *1:* 199

Cough drops *4:* 708

Counseling session *1:* 10 (ill.)

CPR *2:* 359

Crabs *3:* 478

Creutzfeldt-Jakob disease *1:* 215-22

Crib death. *See* **Sudden infant death syndrome**

Crimean-Congo hemorrhagic fever *2:* 381

Crohn, Burrill B. *1:* 224

Crohn's disease *1:* 222-26, *4:* 781

Cryosurgery *4:* 802, 804

CT scan. *See* Computed tomography (CT) scan

Cyanosis *3:* 583

Cystic fibrosis *1:* 226-33

Cystic fibrosis transmembrane conductance regulator (CFTR) *1:* 227

Cystitis *1:* 233-37

Cytoreduction *1:* 154

D

Dalton, John *1:* 193

Daltonism *1:* 193

Debridement *1:* 141

Decompression sickness *2:* 239-44

Decompression stops *2:* 239

Decongestants *1:* 36, 37

Deer mouse *2:* 332 (ill.)

Deer tick *3:* 494 (ill.)

Defibrillation *2:* 359

Dengue fever *2:* 380

Densitometry *3:* 558

Dental cavities, development of *4:* 762 (ill.)

Dental drills *4:* 763

Dental plaque *4:* 761 (ill.)

Depressive disorders *2:* 244-51

Dermatitis *4:* 683, 684, 685 (ill.), 686 (ill.)

Detoxification *1:* 8, 29

Diabetes mellitus *1:* 111, **2: 251-59**
Diagnostic and Statistical Manual of Mental Disorders 1: 98, 117
Diaphragm *1:* 234
Diastolic blood pressure *2:* 406
Digital rectal examination *1:* 195
Dimethylglycine (DMG) *1:* 108
Diplegia *1:* 171
Diphtheria/tetanus/pertussis (DPT) vaccine *4:* 754
Disease reservoir *2:* 378
Disorganized schizophrenia *4:* 643
Distal muscular dystrophy *3:* 535
DMG. *See* Dimethylglycine (DMG)
Dole, Bob *3:* 602 (ill.)
Domagk, Gerhard *4:* 625
Donepezil hydrochloride *1:* 45
Dopamine *3:* 571
Dopamine agonist *3:* 576
Down's syndrome 2: 259-66
DPT *4:* 754
Drinker, Philip *3:* 592
Duchene muscular dystrophy *3:* 534
Duodenum *4:* 786
Dyslexia 2: 266-70. *See also* **Learning disorders**
Dyssomnia *4:* 690
Dysthymic disorder *2:* 244-246
Dystonia *1:* 171

E

E. coli. See Escherichia coli
Ear *2:* 274 (ill.)
Ear, hearing loss in. *See* **Hearing loss**
Earache 2: 271-76
Eating disorders *1:* 61
Ebola *2:* 379, 380 (ill.)
Echocardiogram *1:* 88
ECT. *See* Electroconvulsive therapy
EEG. *See* Electroencephalogram (EEG)
Ehrlich, Paul *4:* 661, 754
Eldepryl *3:* 574
Electrocardiogram *1:* 88, *2:* 277
Electroconvulsive therapy *1:* 118, 121, *2:* 249
Electroencephalogram (EEG) *2:* 280, 291
Electrolytes *2:* 299, 367
Electromagnetic waves *4:* 613
Electromyography *1:* 158
Emergence: Labeled Autistic 1: 106
Emery-Dreifuss muscular dystrophy *3:* 534
Emphysema *1:* 129, **2: 276-83**
Encephalitis *1:* 104, **2: 283-87,** *3:* 506
Encephalopathy *1:* 215
Enders, John F. *3:* 532
Endoscope *4:* 786
Enema *1:* 195, 197, 223

Epilepsy 2: 287-94
Epithelium *1:* 148
Epstein-Barr disease *1:* 186
Epstein-Barr virus *3:* 423
Escherichia coli 2: 299, 300 (ill.), 302
Ethambutol *4:* 779
Eustachian tube *1:* 199
Evoked potential test *3:* 521, 525
Extrapulmonary tuberculosis *4:* 776, 777
Eye *1:* 212 (ill.)
Eye, internal view of (ill.) *2:* 327
Eye, rods and cones of (ill.) *1:* 192
Eyesight, problems with. *See* **Vision disorders**

F

Facioscapulohumeral muscular dystrophy *3:* 535
Fasting hypoglycemia *2:* 414, 415
Fecal occult blood test *1:* 195
Fetal alcohol syndrome *3:* 516
Fever blisters *2:* 395
Fibrin *2:* 371, 372
Fibromyalgia *1:* 186
Filoviruses *2:* 379
Finsen, Niels Tyberg *4:* 656
Fire sprinkler systems *4:* 703
Fistula *1:* 223
Flaviviruses *2:* 380, 381
Flesh-eating disease 2: 295-98, 296 (ill.)
Flu. *See* **Influenza**
Flumandine *3:* 430
Fluoxetine *3:* 599
Fluroxamine *1:* 108
Folic acid deficiency anemia *1:* 54
Food irradiation *2:* 301
Food poisoning 2: 298-309
Fractures *2:* 311 (ill.), 312 (ill.)
Fractures, sprains, and strains 2: 309-17
Fragile X syndrome *1:* 104
Frostbite 2: 317-22, 419

G

Gangliosides *4:* 741, 743 (ill.)
Gangrene *1:* 88, *2:* 295
Gastric ulcer *4:* 786
Gastrointestinal system *1:* 223, 228
Gehrig, Lou *1:* 49 (ill.)
Gel electrophoresis *4:* 670
Gene therapy *1:* 232
Genetic testing *4:* 713
Genital herpes *2:* 396
Genital warts *4:* 660. *See also* **Sexually transmitted diseases**
German measles. *See* **Rubella**

Gilles de la Tourette, George *4:* 765
Gingivitis *3:* 579
Glaucoma 2: 323-28
Glaucoma test *2:* 326 (ill.)
Gliomas *1:* 149
Glucose *2:* 251
Gonorrhea *4:* 660
Goodpasture's syndrome *1:* 110
Gout *1:* 68, 73
Grand mal *2:* 288
Grandin, Temple *1:* 106
Granules *2:* 334
Grave's disease *1:* 111
Green, George F. *4:* 763
Greenwood, John *4:* 763
Group A streptococcus *4:* 623, 726 (ill.)

H

Hairy leukoplakia of the tongue *1:* 16
Hales, Stephen *2:* 410
Hantavirus infections 2: 329-33, 331 (ill.)
Hantavirus Pulmonary Syndrome (HPS) *2:* 330, 331
Harrington, George F. *4:* 763
Harvey, William *2:* 410
Hashimoto's thyroiditis *1:* 111
Hawking, Stephen *1:* 51 (ill.)
Hay fever 2: 333-39. *See also* **Allergies**
Head injury 2: 340-45. *See also* **Concussion**
Headache 2: 346-51
Hearing loss 2: 351-55
Heart attack 2: 355-63
Heart murmur 2: 363-66
Heat cramps *2:* 367
Heat disorders 2: 367-71
Heat exhaustion *2:* 368
Heat stroke *2:* 368
Helicobacter pylori 4: 786
Hemiplegia *1:* 171
Hemodialysis *2:* 330
Hemoglobin *4:* 670
Hemolytic anemia *1:* 55
Hemophilia *1:* 16, **2: 371-77**
Hemophilia, genetic transmission of *2:* 374 (ill.)
Hemorrhage *2:* 372
Hemorrhagic fever with renal syndrome (HFRS) *2:* 329, 330
Hemorrhagic fevers 2: 378-84. *See also* **Hantavirus infections**
Hepatitis 2: 384-91
Hepatitis A virus *2:* 388 (ill.)
Hepatitis B virus *2:* 390 (ill.)
Hernia 2: 391-95
Hernia, abdominal *2:* 393 (ill.)

Herpes infections 2: 395-400
Herpes virus *1:* 211, *3:* 423
High blood pressure. *See* **Hypertension**
Histamine *1:* 32, *2:* 334
HIV *1:* 14-16, *3:* 583, *4:* 660
Hodgkin's disease 2: 401-06, 403 (ill.). *See also* **Cancer**
Hormone therapy *1:* 148, 155, *3:* 558
Hug box *1:* 106
Human immunodeficiency virus. *See* HIV
Human papilloma virus *4:* 801
Hydrocephalus *3:* 516, *4:* 711
Hydrophobia. *See* **Rabies**
Hydroxyurea *4:* 670
Hyperbaric chamber *2:* 239
Hypermobility *4:* 746
Hyperopia *4:* 794, 796 (ill.)
Hypersomnia *2:* 244, *4:* 690
Hypertension 2: 406-13
Hypertension, effects of *2:* 411 (ill.)
Hyperthermia *2:* 367
Hyperthyroidism *3:* 516
Hypoglycemia 2: 413-18
Hypothermia 2: 419-22
Hypotonia *1:* 171

I

Iatrogenic *1:* 215
Idiopathic epilepsy *2:* 288
Idiopathic hypoglycemia *2:* 414
Immune system *1:* 69, 111
Immunotherapy *1:* 148, 155, *2:* 337
Infectious mononucleosis 3: 423-27
Inflammatory bowel disease *1:* 222, *4:* 781
Influenza 3: 427-33
Influenza virus *3:* 428 (ill.)
INH *4:* 779
Insomnia 3: 434-39, *4:* 690
Insulin *2:* 256, 257
Interferon *3:* 454
Internal derangement *4:* 746
Intestinal perforation *4:* 781
Intracerebral hemorrhage *4:* 728
Intracranial hemorrhage *2:* 342
Intraocular pressure *2:* 324
Iron deficiency anemia *1:* 54
Iron lung *3:* 592
Irritable bowel syndrome 3: 439-43
Isaacs, Alick *3:* 454
Isoniazid *4:* 779
Isotretinoin *1:* 2, 5

J

Jaundice *2:* 385
Jock itch *4:* 629

Julian, Percy *2:* 325
Juvenile arthritis *3:* **445-50.** *See also*
   Arthritis
Juvenile diabetes *2:* 252

K

Kaposi's sarcoma *1:* 17, *3:* **451-55.** *See*
   also **Cancer**
Karyotype *2:* 260
Ketoacidosis *2:* 251
Kitasato, Shibasaburo *4:* 754
Koch, Robert *4:* 754, 776
Koplik's spots *3:* 506
Kuru *1:* 218

L

Lactobacillus acidophilus 4: 723
Laniazid *4:* 779
Laparascopy *1:* 68
Laparotomy *1:* 68
Large intestine with irritable bowel syn-
   drome *3:* 441 (ill.)
Laryngitis *3:* **457-59**
Larynx *3:* 457
Late-stage AIDS *1:* 19, 20
Latency period of AIDS *1:* 18, 19
Lead poisoning *3:* **460-67**
Lead poisoning, sources of *3:* 465 (ill.)
Learning disorders *3:* **467-71.** *See also*
   Dyslexia
Legionnaire's disease *3:* 584
Leukemia *1:* 149, *3:* **471-78.** *See also*
   Cancer
Leukemia cells *3:* 474 (ill.)
Leukotriene modifiers *1:* 83
Lice *3:* **478-81,** 479 (ill.)
Ligament *2:* 310
Limb-girdle muscular dystrophy *3:* 534
Lindane *3:* 478
Lindenmann, Jean *3:* 454
Lock jaw. *See* **Tetanus**
Lou Gehrig's disease. *See* **Amyotrophic lat-**
   eral sclerosis
Low blood sugar. *See* **Hypoglycemia**
Lower urinary tract infections *1:* 233
Lumbar puncture *1:* 166
Lumpectomy *1:* 124, 125 (ill.), 126
Lung cancer *3:* **482-87,** 486 (ill.). *See also*
   Cancer
Lung, collapsed. *See* **Pneumothorax**
Lung tissue *2:* 278 (ill.), 279
Lung transplantation *1:* 231 (ill.)
Lupus *1:* 110, 113 (ill.), *3:* **487-92**
Luvox *1:* 108
Lyme disease *3:* **492-97**

Lymph nodes *1:* 186
Lymphatic system *2:* 401
Lymphocyte *1:* 17
Lymphomas *1:* 17, 149

M

Macrophage *1:* 17
Mad cow disease. *See* **Creutzfeldt-Jakob**
   disease
Magnetic resonance imaging (MRI) *2:* 280,
   3: 522 (ill.)
Malaria *3:* **499-505**
Malaria, transmission of *3:* 501 (ill.)
Malathion *3:* 478
Malignant melanoma *4:* 678, 679 (ill.)
Malnutrition *2:* 419
Mammogram *1:* 124
Mania *1:* 118
Manic depression. *See* **Bipolar disorder**
Mantoux text *4:* 774
Mast cells *1:* 32, *2:* 334
Mastectomy *1:* 124, 126
MD. *See* **Muscular dystrophy**
Measles *3:* **505-09**
Meconium ileus *1:* 227
Median nerve *1:* 158
Mefloquine *3:* 500
Melanomas *1:* 149
Melatonin *4:* 655
Meninges *3:* 509
Meningitis *3:* **509-15**
Menopause *1:* 124, *3:* 558
Mental retardation *2:* 260, *3:* **515-20**
Metastasis *1:* 124, 148
Methadone *1:* 8
Methylphenidate *1:* 100, 108
Methylxanthines *1:* 83
Migraine headache, phases of *2:* 349 (ill.)
Miliary tuberculosis *4:* 774
Miller, Reggie *1:* 209 (ill.)
MMR vaccine *4:* 634
Mononucleosis *3:* 423. *See also* **Infectious**
   mononucleosis
Moore, Matt *4:* 718 (ill.)
Morgagni, Giovanni Battista *1:* 224
Mosaic *2:* 260
Motor tics *4:* 765
MRI. *See* Magnetic resonance imaging
   (MRI)
MS. *See* **Multiple sclerosis**
Mucolytic *1:* 227
Mucus *1:* 227
Mucus production *2:* 336 (ill.)
Multiple sclerosis *3:* **520-29**
Mumps *3:* **529-34**
Muscular dystrophy *3:* **534-42**

Myalgia *1:* 186
Myalgic encephalomyelitis. *See* **Chronic fatigue syndrome**
Myasthenia gravis *1:* 111
Mycobacteria *4:* 774
Mycobacterium tuberculosis 4: 775 (ill.)
Myelin *3:* 521
Myelograph *4:* 711
Myocardial infarction. *See* **Heart attack**
Myopia *4:* 794 (ill.)
Myotonic dystrophy *3:* 535

N

Naltrexone *1:* 108
Narcolepsy *4:* 690
National Bone Marrow Donor Registry *3:* 475
Natural killer cell disease *1:* 186
Necrosis *2:* 295
Neisseria gonorrhoea 4: 662 (ill.)
Neonatal herpes *2:* 396
Nervous tic *1:* 98
Neural tube defect *3:* 516
Neurasthenia *1:* 186
Neurodegenerative disease *1:* 48
Neurotransmitter *1:* 118, *2:* 244
Nits *3:* 478
Noninfectious sore throat *4:* 707, 708
Nucleoside analogues *1:* 17
Nydrazid *4:* 779

O

Obesity 3: 543-51
Obsessive-compulsive disorder 3: 551-57
Oculopharyngeal muscular dystrophy *3:* 535
Opiate blockers *1:* 103, 104, 108
Opportunistic infection *1:* 17
Optic nerve *2:* 324
Oral herpes *2:* 395
Organ transplantation *1:* 112
Ossicles *2:* 272, 351
Osteoarthritis *1:* 68, 69, 73
Osteoporosis *2:* 310, **3: 558-64**, 560 (ill.)
Otitis externa *2:* 273
Otitis media *2:* 272, 273
Otosclerosis *2:* 351

P

Palliation *1:* 154
Palsy. *See* **Parkinson's disease**
Pancreas *1:* 227, *2:* 251

Panic disorder 3: 565-70
Paranoid schizophrenia *4:* 643
Parasomnias *4:* 692
Parkinson, James *3:* 572
Parkinson's disease *1:* 207, **3: 571-78,** 576 (ill.)
Particulate radiation *4:* 613, 614
Pauciarticular juvenile arthritis *3:* 447, 448
Pemphigus vulgaris *1:* 111
Penicillin *2:* 272
Peptic ulcer *4:* 786
Periodontal disease 3: 579-82
Periodontitis *3:* 579, 581 (ill.)
Peristalsis *3:* 440
Peritonitis *1:* 68, *4:* 783
Permethrin *3:* 478
Pernicious anemia *1:* 111
Pertussis. *See* **Whooping cough**
Pertussis toxin crystal *4:* 811 (ill.)
Petit mal *2:* 288
Pharynx *2:* 272
Phenylketonuria (PKU) *1:* 104
Physiological dependence *1:* 8
Physostigmine *2:* 325
Pink eye. *See* **Conjunctivitis**
PKU. *See* Phenylketonuria (PKU)
Plaque, arterial *1:* 88
Platelets *2:* 299
Pneumonia 3: 582-87, 584 (ill.)
Pneumothorax 3: 587-91, 589 (ill.)
Polio 3: 591-96
Poliomyelitis. *See* **Polio**
Polyarticular juvenile arthritis *3:* 448
Polysomnograph *4:* 694 (ill.)
Polysomnography *4:* 691
Positron emission tomography (PET) *2:* 340
Posttraumatic stress disorder 3: 596-600
Post-viral syndrome *1:* 186
Prion *1:* 215
Process addiction *1:* 8
Prodrome *2:* 395
Prophylactic *2:* 346
Prostate cancer 3: 601-06
Protease inhibitors *1:* 17
Proteins *1:* 162
Prozac *3:* 599
Psoriasis *4:* 684
Psoriatic juvenile arthritis *3:* 448
Psychological addiction *1:* 10, 11
Psychological dependence *1:* 8
Psychosocial therapy *2:* 244, 249
Pulmonary function test *2:* 277
Pulmonary hypertension *2:* 277
Purge *1:* 136
Pyrazinamide *4:* 779
Pyrimethamine *3:* 500

Q

Quadriplegia *1:* 171
Queen Victoria *2:* 376
Quinine *3:* 500

R

Rabies *4:* 607-12
Rabies virus *4:* 609 (ill.)
Radial keratotomy *4:* 794
Radiation injuries *4:* 612-19
Radiation therapy *1:* 148, 155
Radical mastectomy *1:* 124
Radioactive isotope *1:* 88
Reactive hypoglycemia *2:* 414
Recommended Dietary Allowances (RDA)
   1: 58
Reconstructive surgery *1:* 124, 126
Red blood cells *1:* 56 (ill.)
Residual schizophrenia *4:* 644
Respiratory tract *1:* 228
Restless leg syndrome *4:* 691
Retina *1:* 162, 191, *2:* 324
ReVia *1:* 108
Reye's syndrome *1:* 181, *3:* 423, **4:** 620-23
Rhabdovirus *4:* 608
Rheumatic fever *4:* 623-28
Rheumatoid arthritis *1:* 68, 69, 73, 110
Rhinovirus *1:* 199, 201 (ill.)
Riadin *4:* 779
Ribavirin *2:* 378
Rickets *2:* 310
Rifampin *4:* 779
Rift Valley fever *2:* 381
Rimactrane *4:* 779
Rimantadine hydrochloride *3:* 429
Ringworm *4:* 628-33, 630 (ill.), 631 (ill.)
Ritalin *1:* 100, 108
Rubella *4:* 633-37, 635 (ill.), 636 (ill.)
Rubeola. *See* **Measles**
Rubivirus *4:* 634

S

SAD. *See* **Seasonal affective disorder**
Salicylic acid *2:* 348
Salk, Jonas *3:* 594
Salmonella *2:* 299, 301
Salvarsan *4:* 661
Sarcomas *1:* 149
Scalds. *See* **Burns and scalds**
Scarlet fever *4:* 639-42, 640 (ill.)
Schizophrenia *4:* 642-48
Scleroderma *1:* 111
Scoliosis 1,:176, *4:* 649-54, 653 (ill.)

Seasonal affective disorder *4:* 654-58
Sebum *1:* 1, 2
Seizure, absence *2:* 289
Seizures *1:* 176, *2:* 288
Seizures, tonic-clonic *2:* 289
Selective serotonin reuptake inhibitors *3:* 596
Selegiline *3:* 574
Seminal vesicles *3:* 601
Sensory hearing loss *2:* 351
Sexually transmitted diseases *4:* 659-66
Shaken baby syndrome *4:* 667-70
Shigella *2:* 299, 302
Shingles *1:* 181
Shock *1:* 141
Sickle cell anemia *1:* 55, 56, **4:** 670-77
SIDS. *See* **Sudden infant death syndrome**
Sigmoidoscopy *1:* 195, 197
Silicosis *3:* 483
Sjögren's syndrome *1:* 111
Skin cancer *4:* 677-83. *See also* **Cancer**
Skin disorders *4:* 683-89
Skin graft *1:* 141
Skull fracture *2:* 342, 344 (ill.)
Sleep apnea *4:* 691
Sleep disorders *4:* 690-97
Sleep terror disorder *4:* 692
Sleeplessness. *See* **Insomnia**
Sleepwalking disorder *4:* 692
Smallpox *4:* 697-701
Smallpox rash *4:* 700 (ill.)
Smith, James *4:* 708
Smoke inhalation *4:* 701-06
Somnambulism *4:* 691
Sore throat *4:* 706-11
Spastic *1:* 171
Spasticity *1:* 176
Sphygmomanometer *2:* 406, 410
Spina bifida *4:* **711-16**, 714 (ill.)
Spinal cord injury *4:* 716-22
Spinal tap *1:* 166
Spine, curvature of. *See* **Scoliosis**
Spirometer *1:* 78
Spondyloarthropathy *3:* 448
Spondylosis *4:* 649
Spongiform encephalopathies *1:* 215
Sprains. *See* **Fractures, sprains and
   strains**
Squamous cell cancer *4:* 678
Staphylococcus aureus *2:* 299, 301, 302
Staphylococcus *4:* 769
STDs. *See* **Sexually transmitted diseases**
Stenkert, Zack *3:* 548 (ill.)
Steroids *1:* 83, 111
Stimulants *1:* 104
Stomach with peptic ulcer *4:* 789 (ill.)
Strabismus *1:* 177
Strains. *See* **Fractures, sprains, and
   strains**

Strep throat 4: 723-27
Streptococcal infections 4: 623, 639, 723
Streptococcal toxic shock syndrome 4: 769
Streptomycin 4: 779
Stress test 1: 88
Stroke 2: 419, 4: 727-34
Strokes, comparison of 4: 730 (ill.)
Subarachnoid hemorrhage 1: 166, 4: 728
Subdural hematoma 4: 668
Substance addiction 1: 8
Substantia nigra 3: 571
Sudden infant death syndrome 4: 734-39
Sulfadoxine 3: 500
Sulfasalazine 4: 781
Sulfonylurea 2: 255
Symadine 3: 429
Symmetrel 3: 429
Symptomatic epilepsy 2: 288
Synovial fluid 1: 69
Synovial membrane 1: 69, 3: 445
Syphilis 4: 660
Systemic lupus erythematosus. See Lupus
Systemic onset juvenile arthritis 3: 448
Systolic blood pressure 2: 406

T

Tacrine 1: 45
Tamoxifen 1: 124
Tampons, use of 4: 769
Tay-Sachs disease 4: 741-44
TB. See Tuberculosis
T-cells 1: 17
Temporomandibular joint disorders 4: 745-48
Tendinitis 4: 748-52
Tendons, inflammation of. See Tendinitis
Tennis elbow 4: 749
Testosterone 3: 601
Tetanus 4: 752-56
Thalassemia 1: 55
Thermal burns 1: 141-43
Thinking in Pictures 1: 106
Thoracentesis 3: 587
Thrombolytics 2: 359
Thrombosis 1: 88
Thyroid 2: 419
Ticks 3: 492
Tinea capitis 4: 629
Tinea corporis 4: 628
Tinea cruris 4: 629
Tinea unguium 4: 629
Tonic-clonic seizures 2: 289
Tonometer 2: 324
Tonsillectomy 4: 756, 758 (ill.)
Tonsillitis 4: 723, 756-60, 757 (ill.)
Tonsils 4: 756

Tooth decay 4: 760-64
Tourette syndrome 4: 765-69
Toxic dilation of the colon 4: 781, 783
Toxic shock syndrome 4: 769-72
Trachea 1: 129, 2: 277
Traction 2: 310
Tranquilizers 1: 104, 2: 360
Transcutaneous electrical nerve stimulation 2: 346
Translocation 2: 260
Tretinoin 1: 2
Triglyceride 1: 88
Trisomy 2: 260
Tuberculosis 4: 773-80
Twelve-step program 1: 8, 12
Tympanic membrane 2: 351
Type I diabetes 2: 252
Type II diabetes 2: 252

U

Ulcer 2: 395
Ulcerative colitis 4: 781-85, 782 (ill.), 784 (ill.)
Ulcers 4: 786-91
Ultrasound 1: 175
Undifferentiated schizophrenia 4: 644
Urethra 1: 234
Urethritis 1: 233
Uric acid crystals 1: 74 (ill.)

V

Vaccine 2: 280
Valproate 1: 121
Varavix 1: 181
Varicella. See Chickenpox
Varicella-zoster immune globulin (VZIG) 1: 181
Varicella-zoster virus 1: 181
Variola 4: 697
Vasculitis 1: 111
Vasodilator 2: 361, 406
Vector 2: 378
Viral sore throat 4: 706, 707
Virus 2: 280
Vision disorders 4: 793-99
Vitamin B$_{12}$ deficiency anemia 1: 55
Vitamin D 4: 656
Vitiligo 4: 684, 688 (ill.)
Vocal cords with laryngitis 3: 458 (ill.)
Vocal tics 4: 765
Voice, loss of. See Laryngitis
Volume reduction surgery 2: 277
Von Basch, Samuel Siegried 2: 410

W

Warts *4:* **801-06,** 803 (ill.), 804 (ill.)
Weathers, Beck *2:* 320 (ill.)
Whiplash *4:* **807-09**
Whiteheads. *See* **Acne**
Whooping cough *4:* **809-14**
Withdrawal *1:* 8
Withdrawal symptoms *1:* 29, 30
Withdrawal therapy *1:* 12
Wrist *1:* 160 (ill.)

X

X rays *1:* 148

Y

Yellow fever *2:* 380
Yuppie flu *1:* 186